Hellenic Studies 81

ACHILLES UNBOUND

Recent Titles in the Hellenic Studies Series

ACHILLES UNBOUND

MULTIFORMITY AND TRADITION
IN THE HOMERIC EPICS

by
Casey Dué

CENTER FOR HELLENIC STUDIES
Trustees for Harvard University
Washington, DC
Distributed by Harvard University Press
Cambridge, Massachusetts, and London, England
2019

This book is dedicated to
my friend and collaborator in all things,

MARY EBBOTT

σύν τε δύ᾽ ἐρχομένω καί τε πρὸ ὃ τοῦ ἐνόησεν
ὅππως κέρδος ἔῃ

Contents

Color plates follow page 18.

Preface

THE OCCASION OF THE WRITING OF THIS BOOK is the completion of the Homer Multitext project's digital edition of the Venetus A manuscript of the *Iliad* (http://www.homermultitext.org), the culmination of eighteen years of collaborative, intergenerational theorizing, experimentation, and editing.[1]

The Homer Multitext is an interdisciplinary project that has brought together researchers from a variety of fields in the humanities and computer science and from institutions across the United States and Europe. Mary Ebbott and I are the project's coeditors, but we are partners in all aspects of the project with its information architects, Christopher Blackwell and Neel Smith. Douglas Frame, Leonard Muellner, and Gregory Nagy are associate editors and have been integral to the project since its inception. The Homer Multitext seeks to present the textual transmission of the Homeric *Iliad* and *Odyssey* in a historical framework, one that takes into account that these poems were composed orally over the course of hundreds if not thousands of years by countless singers who composed in performance. When the tradition in which these songs were composed was flourishing, no two performances were ever exactly the same. Our historical sources still reflect such multiformity, which is natural and expected in an oral tradition, but scholarly editions in print typically obscure rather than highlight these natural variations. Using technology that takes advantage of the best available practices and open source standards that have been developed for digital publications, the web-based Homer Multitext offers free access to a library of texts and images and tools that allow readers to discover and engage with the dynamic nature of the Homeric tradition. The project publishes high-resolution images of the most ancient documents that transmit the *Iliad*

---

[1] For more on the significance of the Venetus A manuscript (Marciana 454 = 822), see Dué 2009a and the introduction to the edition online at http://www.homermultitext.org/manuscripts-papyri/venetusA.html.

(including five of the oldest medieval manuscripts that preserve the *Iliad*) together with edited transcriptions of their texts, including their accompanying scholia (marginal commentary derived from ancient scholarship on the poems). The project is generously supported by the University of Houston's Research Computing Center and Harvard University's Center for Hellenic Studies, but we have also received crucial funding from a variety of sources, including the National Endowment for the Humanities, the Mellon Foundation, the National Science Foundation, and the Gladys Krieble Delmas Foundation.

It has been fairly customary practice in the long history of textual criticism of ancient works for editors to publish a book, or at the very least a lengthy introduction (in Latin), to set forth what the editor has accomplished and to defend his (until very recently, in almost every case, his) choices. That is not the purpose of this volume. These chapters represent a good deal of what I have learned in the course of thinking about why and how to make a Multitext edition of Homer and in editing the Venetus A with various teams of students and faculty, all of which took place, primarily in the summers, at the Center for Hellenic Studies in Washington, DC. But rather than a congratulatory setting forth of what we have accomplished, I see this volume as being merely preliminary to the very necessary work that has only now become possible. As Matthew Jockers has written, "The literary scholar of the twenty-first century can no longer be content with anecdotal evidence, with random 'things' gathered from a few, even 'representative,' texts. We must strive to understand these things we find interesting in the context of everything else, including a mass of possibly 'uninteresting' texts" (Jockers 2013:8). The editors of the Homeric texts and scholia of past eras have made enormous contributions to our understanding of the *Iliad* and *Odyssey* and the ancient scholarship on those poems, but they were limited by the technologies of their day (primarily paper, ink, the printing press, and human learning, memory, and intellect). They could not test and verify their data sets or replicate their results. Their editions were selective, and their conclusions were necessarily speculative—as are mine in this book. The chapters I have written here provide the hypothesis—the "proposed explanation made on the basis of limited evidence as a starting point for further investigation" (*Oxford English Dictionary*)—that explains why my colleagues and I wanted to make a Homer Multitext. But the work of interpreting the Homeric epics multitextually has only just begun.

Our editorial work thus far has been accomplished by teams of undergraduates working with professors, who are trained at an annual two-week summer seminar hosted by the Center for Hellenic Studies. Students at the seminar are introduced by myself and Mary Ebbott to the theoretical background of the project and its implications for our understanding of Homeric poetry, and they are trained by project architects Neel Smith and Christopher Blackwell and project managers Stephanie Lindeborg and Brian Clark in our editing procedures. (For examples of the kind of topics discussed, see our research blog at http://homermultitext.blogspot.com.) The students then work with faculty in teams to create an edition of the text and scholia of a book of the *Iliad* during the seminar. After the seminar, students return to their home institutions and continue to edit assigned manuscript folios together with their faculty mentors. The editions they create are then subjected to a number of automated tests, which are reviewed by the project editors. It is safe to say that the vast majority of new discovery in connection with the Homer Multitext is made by undergraduate researchers, who regularly present at national and international conferences. Between 2014 and the writing of this book in 2017, seven Homer Multitext undergraduate researchers have been awarded Fulbright fellowships to continue their research after graduation.

The Homer Multitext project officially began in the summer of 2000, when a group of us initially conceived of creating a multitextual edition of the *Iliad*, and, upon paging through Domenico Comparetti's 1901 facsimile edition of the Venetus A, thought that that particular manuscript would make a good starting place. We received early encouragement and support from two people who profoundly influenced the project in very different ways: Greg Nagy, whose lifetime of work on Homer and whose initial call for a multitext edition of the Homeric texts have inspired us throughout, and Ross Scaife, a pioneer in digital humanism (long before the term "Digital Humanities" was coined), who died, far too young, in 2008. Little did we know how much trial and error and international travel would be involved in actually accomplishing our edition of the Venetus A.

After successfully capturing high-resolution images of three manuscripts with scholia in Venice's Marciana Library in 2007, an NEH collaborative research grant ("The Oral Poetics of the Homeric Doloneia," 2007–2008) gave my coeditor Mary Ebbott and me the opportunity to write a sustained demonstration of the need for a multitextual approach to the *Iliad*. The research leave afforded by that funding enabled us write a series of essays and a commentary on book 10 of the *Iliad* (*Iliad 10 and the Poetics of Ambush: A Multitext Edition with Essays and Commentary*, Washington, DC, 2010) as a kind of test case. Our printed edition was multitextual in that we included an edited transcription of the Venetus A manuscript's text of book 10 together with three fragmentary papyrus texts. Along with these texts we provided commentary on the multiforms presented by them. In our essays we articulated how an awareness of multiformity changes and in fact deepens our understanding of the poetics of the *Iliad*.

Building on that rationale, we have directed our efforts since 2010 toward the creation of a complete digital edition of the Venetus A manuscript of the

Iliad. The Venetus A is a tenth-century CE manuscript (now housed in Venice) that contains a wealth of scholia deriving from the scholarship of Alexandrian editors such as Aristarchus and Zenodotus. The debates preserved in the margins of this particular manuscript more than any other show us that the *Iliad* was not fixed and monolithic in antiquity, it was multiform—and the wider epic tradition from which the *Iliad* emerged was more multiform still. The Venetus A is an inherently multitextual document, because it contains material from a variety of different scholarly traditions in its front matter and in its margins, including discussions of alternative versions of the text that were known in antiquity. Access to the full contents of the Venetus A will enable scholars who are open to a multitextual approach to gain a much greater understanding of the history of a poem that evolved over many centuries and the multiformity of the tradition of composition in performance in which the *Iliad* and *Odyssey* were created.

Our edition of the Venetus A was funded by an NEH Scholarly Editions and Translations grant ("Editing as a Discovery Process: Accessing centuries of scholarship in one 10th-century manuscript of the *Iliad*"). Work (and funding) began in 2013 and was completed in 2017 with total funding of $276,115. The project we undertook is a complete scholarly edition of the oldest surviving and richly annotated manuscript of the Homeric *Iliad*: its text, scholia, and all other elements on its 654 pages. Our edition is based on the high-resolution digital photographs of the manuscript that we obtained (and have already published under a Creative Commons license for other scholars' use) in 2007. The text and scholia were transcribed (as a diplomatic edition, representing faithfully the text of the manuscript, including accents and spelling that are not "standard" from our point of view), and marked up with TEI-XML encoding for several key features. Each portion of the digital text, that is, each individual scholion, is linked precisely to the location on the digital image of the folio that contains it. Any user can easily move from the transcription to the image of the primary source and see for herself what the manuscript says.

This NEH funding, combined with Gladys Krieble Delmas Foundation and National Science Foundation funding for our photography of the manuscripts and Mellon Foundation funding for undergraduate research, has been transformational for the Homer Multitext. Our Scholarly Editions and Translations grant has in recent years encouraged us to focus our energies on a particularly valuable and complex historical artifact, the Venetus A, which will now become the cornerstone of the much larger project. In creating this edition we have experimented with editorial processes and computational approaches and have done the hard work of trying and failing and trying again necessary for producing something that will last. The Homer Multitext is a digital project: the scholarship that results will be undertaken using computational methods and will be published digitally. We are grateful for the opportunity this funding has given us to create a new kind of edition of the *Iliad*, one that we feel will allow for new perspectives and new questions and offer a new means for evaluating the evidence for the oral tradition preserved in the textual record of these poems.

This book will be published in both analogue and digital forms as part of the HMT. It gathers together much of my writings over the time period I have outlined here, writings which I have extensively revised and rewritten for their present place. The process of coming to understand why Homeric poetry is best understood multitextually has been a long one, beginning with my earliest days as a student of Greg Nagy, and I hope this book will provide a coherent rationale for our project as whole. Over the course of these nearly twenty years I have benefitted tremendously from discussions with my fellow editors and the faculty and students of our annual summer seminars at the Center for Hellenic Studies. My favorite moments of the project have come from these seminars, when in varying combinations Chris Blackwell, Mary Ebbott, Doug Frame, Lenny Muellner, Greg Nagy, Neel Smith, and I learned to read Homer differently by sharing our evolving multitext with teams of undergraduate researchers and subjecting it to their scrutiny. We were joined over the years by Tazuko van Berkel, Eric Dugdale, Madeleine Goh, Olga Levaniouk, Corinne Pache, and Ineke Sluiter, all of whom brought their particular expertise and their own students into the fold as contributing editors. I will not list the more than one hundred student editors who have contributed to the Homer Multitext, but their names can be found on the project website, and I am deeply grateful to them for their time, energy, enthusiasm, and brilliant presentations at the CHS and at national and international conferences. Special *kudos* must be conferred upon Stephanie Lindeborg and Brian Clark (both of whom began as undergraduates and are now our project managers) and Melissa Browne, who likewise began as an undergraduate (in fact she was our first undergraduate contributor) and who has contributed much to our project and to our summer seminars while pursuing her PhD.

Of course the best part about these past twenty years has been the collaboration. Working closely with Mary Ebbott, Chris Blackwell, and Neel Smith has been the joy of my professional life, matched only by the mentorship and inspiration I have received along the way from Doug Frame, Lenny Muellner, and Greg Nagy. A thrill of working on a large digital project is the opportunity it offers to contribute to something much bigger than ourselves, and the Homer Multitext has been that opportunity for me. I cherish the friendship that our collaboration has forged.

Introduction

HOW MANY WAYS ARE THERE TO TELL THE STORY OF TROY? A passage from *Iliad* 20 makes me wonder just how flexible the Homeric tradition might be. At the beginning of book 20, Zeus calls the gods to an assembly. He tells them that they may now join the battle taking place before the walls of Troy on whichever side they wish, something that he had expressly forbidden them to do at the beginning of book 8. The reason he has changed his mind, he explains, is that Achilles is now preparing to return to battle for the first time since his withdrawal in book 1, and Zeus is afraid that the Trojans will not be able to withstand him for even a little while:

> καὶ δέ τέ μιν καὶ πρόσθεν ὑποτρομέεσκον ὁρῶντες·
> νῦν δ' ὅτε δὴ καὶ θυμὸν ἑταίρου χώεται αἰνῶς
> δείδω μὴ καὶ τεῖχος ὑπερ μόρον ἐξαλαπάξῃ.

Iliad 20.28–30[1]

Even before now they would tremble before him when they
saw him.

---

[1] Throughout this book the Greek text of the *Iliad* I cite is from the Venetus A manuscript (with only superficial editorial intervention, such as the addition of quotation marks for quoted text or punctuation, which the scholia of the Venetus A frequently omit). Discrepancies from printed editions often point to interesting examples of multiformity in the textual transmission of the *Iliad*, as here. For example, there was debate in antiquity about the reading of τέ in line 20.28 (the Venetus A scholia tell us that Aristarchus read τί, whereas most manuscripts and papyri, including the Venetus A, read τέ). Likewise ancient scholars were divided as to whether ὑπερ μόρον should be read as one word or two. In the Venetus A (folio 260v) there appears to be a space here between ὑπερ and μόρον (no accent on ὑπερ), even though the scribe has clearly used a hyphen to join ὑπέρμορα at *Iliad* 2.155. (The correct reading is also debated in the main scholia at 20.30 and in both the interlinear and main scholia surrounding 2.155 [folio 27r in the Venetus A].) Boreel and Yi (2017) have argued that the scholion at 20.30 in the Venetus A is a first-person extract from the *On Prosody* of Herodian.

> And now when he is terribly angry in his heart because of [the death
> of] his companion
> I fear lest the wall [of Troy] will be sacked beyond [i.e., contrary to]
> fate.

Apollo, the god of prophesy and the one besides Zeus most often associated with seeing into the future, likewise fears that the Trojan walls will come down too soon at Achilles' hands: μέμβλετο γάρ οἱ τεῖχος ἐϋδμήτοιο πόληος/μὴ Δαναοὶ πέρσειαν ὑπὲρ μόρον ἤματι κείνῳ ("For he was concerned about the wall of the well-built city, lest the Danaans destroy it on that day beyond fate," *Iliad* 21.516–517). Zeus' and Apollo's fear in these passages is remarkable, and begs questions that anyone who has read the *Iliad* with undergraduates will be familiar with. If the walls of Troy are destined to fall at a particular moment, how could they fall before that? Is fate something that can be changed? Is Zeus subject to fate or can Zeus alter it?

The question of whether an individual's fate can be changed creates a tension that runs throughout the *Iliad*. In *Iliad* 16 and 22 Zeus contemplates saving Sarpedon and then Hektor from death. Both times he is met with outrage (on the part of Hera and Athena respectively) and is rebuked via the formula ἔρδ'· ἀτὰρ οὔ τοι πάντες ἐπαινέομεν θεοὶ ἄλλοι at 16.443 and 22.181 ("Do it, but not all the rest of us gods will approve"; see also 4.29), and he does not follow through on the threat. Despite what the formula implies (i.e., that Zeus can change the fate of these mortal men), the fact that he never acts on this suggests either that he cannot or that the consequences would be so grave that he will not risk it.

In *Iliad* 2.155 we are told that the Argives would have returned home "contrary to fate" (ὑπέρμορα) if Hera had not intervened. At the beginning of *Iliad* 4, Zeus contemplates ending the war with Menelaus' apparent victory over Paris (thus saving Troy), but he meets with strong resistance from Hera and agrees to accept a deal whereby he has the right to destroy Argos, Sparta, and Mycenae in the future. Athena then restarts the Trojan War by provoking Pandaros to shoot Menelaus with his bow. In *Iliad* 20.290ff. Poseidon saves Aeneas from death at the hands of Achilles, because it is his destiny (μόριμον 302) to survive. In none of these cases, however, is fate actually changed, and we are left to wonder what would have happened if the gods had not intervened.[2]

---

[2] Conceptually, such incidents seem related to the frequent appearance of contrafactual statements in Homeric epic (if x had not happened, then y would have), on which see De Jong 2004:68–81, with further bibliography *ad loc.* On the phrase ὑπερ μόρον (or ὑπὲρ μοῖραν or κατὰ μοῖραν) see, in addition to De Jong, Pestalozzi 1945: 40; Kullmann 1956; Fränkel 1962: 62–64; Matthews 1976, and note 23 below.

We could also reframe these questions in terms of narrative. If the *Iliad* tells a traditional story, shouldn't Zeus and Apollo know how the story ends?[3] Would it really be possible to change the story now and have Troy fall while Achilles is still alive, and indeed at his hands? In fact all of book 20 seems preoccupied with the possibility that the story could unfold in the wrong way. Hera says that the gods have come down to fight in order to make sure that Achilles does not suffer anything before what is fated (20.125–128). As I have already noted, Poseidon saves Aeneas from his encounter with Achilles (20.288–339), lest he not go on to continue the family line of Dardanos, as fated (μόριμον), and Apollo (with no stated explanation) protects Hektor from dying at the hands of Achilles two books too soon (20.419–454).

In his 1979 book *The Best of the Achaeans*, Gregory Nagy argued that the first song of Demodokos in *Odyssey* 8, in which the Phaeacian bard narrates a quarrel between Odysseus and Achilles, is in fact a compressed reference to an epic tradition in which Achilles and Odysseus quarreled over whether Troy would be taken by cunning (*mētis*) or by force (*biē*).[4] Nagy reads the scholia preserved in the manuscripts at *Odyssey* 8.75 and 77 as likewise pointing to such a tradition, which is otherwise not attested in our surviving sources (Nagy 1979:46). Might we find here in the fears of Zeus and Apollo another glimpse of these two rival possibilities for the fall of Troy? If so, we have to wonder if the Iliadic tradition is indeed so multiform, so flexible, that such a radically different ending could be possible. Is there (or was there) an alternative epic universe, in which Achilles really did take Troy by force? And if not, why does Zeus entertain the idea?

As it turns out, ancient commentators on the *Iliad* were concerned about these same questions. And so the scholia in the margins of the so-called Townley manuscript (Burney 86, folio 220v) record for us a fascinating variation on these verses from book 20:

τινὲς γράφουσιν ἀντὶ τοῦ <δείδω, μὴ καὶ τεῖχος>
οὐ μέντοι μοῖρ' ἐστὶν ἔτι ζωοῦ Ἀχιλῆος
Ἰλίου ἐκπέρσαι εὖ ναιόμενον πτολίεθρον.

---

[3] Cf. Slatkin 1991:111 on Hera's seduction of Zeus as an unraveling of the plot of the *Iliad*, over which Zeus must reassert control at the start of *Iliad* 15: "Zeus' omniscience fails in the face of his own desire. Invincible and all-knowing, he is nevertheless baffled by *eros*. In the [deception of Zeus] he is unable to see beyond his desire for Hera ... and the consequence is that the plot of the *Iliad* is temporarily out of his control. Thus when he awakes to find what has happened, his response has less to do with punishing Hera than with reclaiming control over the narrative: he declares what the plot of the rest of the poem will be, and goes beyond." On *moira* ("destiny") as a function of tradition, see also Nagy 1979:40–41 and 268 (§3n9) and Scodel 2002:68–69.
[4] Nagy 1979:45–48 and *passim*; see also Wilson 2005.

πέρσει δουράτεός [θ’][5] ἵππος καὶ μῆτις Ἐπειοῦ.
πῶς γὰρ ὁ εἰδὼς "μοῖράν τ' ἀμμορίην τε" [= *Odyssey* 20.76] νῦν διστάζει;

Some write instead of "I fear lest the wall"
>   It is not fated, however, with Achilles still alive
>   to sack the well-inhabited citadel of Ilium.
>   A wooden horse will destroy it and the craftiness [*mētis*] of Epeios.
>   For how is he [= Zeus], the one who knows "what is fated and not fated"
>   [= *Odyssey* 20.76], now in doubt?

These alternative verses make clear that Troy is not going to fall at the hands of Achilles, but rather as a result of the *mētis* of the wooden horse. Problem solved. But the commentator, in seeking to solve a narratological, mythological, and indeed existential problem, now presents us with a textual one. What is the source of these verses that "some write," and how do we reconcile them with our received text?

A similar interpretive crisis can be found in the scholia on *Iliad* 19.108.[6] Here Agamemnon tells the story of how Hera made Zeus swear an oath that the descendent of his born on that day would be king of all those around him. It is in this way, through Hera's machinations, that Eurystheus becomes king of Argos instead of Herakles. A comment preserved in the Venetus A manuscript asks:

εἰ δ' ἄγε νῦν μοι ὄμοσσον: διὰ τί ἡ Ἥρα ὀμόσαι πρὸς τὸν Δία; ἢ δῆλον ὡς οὐ ποιοῦντα, ἃ ἂν φῇ. εἰ δὲ τοῦτο διὰ τί οὐ κατανεῦσαι ἀλλὰ καὶ ὀμόσαι ἠξίωσεν ὡς καὶ ψευδομένου ἂν μὴ ὀμόσῃ; ὁ δὲ ποιητής φασιν ἀληθεύειν "ὅ τί κεν κεφαλῇ κατανεύσῃ" [~ *Iliad* 1.527]. τὸ μὲν οὖν ὅλον μυθῶδες· καὶ γὰρ οὐδ' ἀφ' ἑαυτοῦ ταῦτά φησιν Ὅμηρος οὐδὲ γινόμενα εἰσάγει, ἀλλ' ὡς διαδεδομένων περὶ τὴν Ἡρακλέους γένεσιν μέμνηται ... οὕτως Ἀριστοτέλης.

"Come now and swear to me": Why does Hera make Zeus swear an oath? Certainly it is clear that he is not doing what she says. But if this is the case, why does she want him not only to nod in assent, but also to swear, as if he would be lying if he did not swear? But the poet says that he tells the truth with respect to "whatever he nods in assent to." Therefore the story is mythological. For Homer doesn't invent things nor does he introduce the things that happen, but he recalls the birth of Herakles as these things have been handed down.... This was the view of Aristotle.

This particular comment derives from the ancient tradition of scholarship known as the "Homeric Questions," best known from the surviving writings of Porphyry but which, as we can see here, goes back at least as far as Aristotle.[7] The commentator wonders why Hera required Zeus to swear an oath, when elsewhere in the *Iliad* (notably in *Iliad* 1.527) Zeus asserts that whatever he assents to will come true. Underlying the question seems to be anxiety similar to that which we find in the *Iliad* 20 scholion. Is it possible that what Zeus agrees to won't come true? Could the story of Herakles have turned out another way if Hera hadn't made him swear the oath? But the commentator has a solution and goes on to excuse Homer here. He is working with a traditional story, a myth (τὸ μὲν οὖν ὅλον μυθῶδες): "Homer doesn't invent things nor does he introduce the things that happen, but he recalls the birth of Herakles as these things have been handed down."

I submit that this comment has deep implications not just for an understanding of the relationship between myth and poetry in the Homeric epics but also for our understanding of the textual tradition that transmitted these poems over two and a half millennia. In my earlier work (especially Dué 2002 and Dué and Ebbott 2010) I have argued that the multiformity of the mythological tradition from which epic singers wove their tales and the textual tradition of Homeric epic go hand in hand. The *Iliad* and the *Odyssey* are synoptic representatives of an entire system of traditional songs that developed over many hundreds of years. In its earliest phases, this system included the song traditions of the Epic Cycle and still further epic traditions to which the *Iliad* and the *Odyssey* sometimes allude, such as the voyage of the Argo, together with the mythological traditions on which those songs were based.[8] As we will see, these song traditions were multiform. They did not exist in a fixed form until very late

---

[7] For more on the scholia derived from the Homeric Questions, see the Homer Multitext research blog: http://homermultitext.blogspot.com/2012/03/homeric-questions.html.

[8] On the wide-range ancient hexameter poetry that was being composed and performed contemporaneously with the *Iliad* and the *Odyssey* see Marks (forthcoming). Burgess (2001) demonstrates the antiquity of Cyclic epic traditions, even though they likely reached the textual form summarized by Proklos later than the *Iliad* and the *Odyssey* did. Burgess makes careful distinction between Homeric epic, Cyclic epic, and Cyclic myth. I too wish to observe this distinction, but my emphasis in this book is on how the multiformity of the mythological tradition comes to be reflected in the multiformity of the poetic tradition. Where there is multiformity in our attested sources for the text of the *Iliad* and the *Odyssey*, often, though not always, we can uncover an underlying multiformity in the mythological tradition.

in their evolution. But at the same time they were traditional, in that they told the story *as it had been handed down.*

As Milman Parry showed in his analysis of Homeric diction in the 1920s and 30s, any innovations that are present in the text as we now have it were introduced by means of a complex process over time and in the context of performance, and cannot be attributed to any one poet.[9] The same is true for the content expressed by that diction. Myth is by nature multiform, as were the epic song traditions that narrated such myths as the story of the Trojan War and the exploits of the hero Achilles, but it is simply not possible to call any one character or plot development the "invention" of a particular poet (Dué 2002:21–36). As the commentator remarks in connection with Zeus' oath, "Homer" does not invent the myth but rather recalls what has been handed down, using the formulaic diction that has evolved over centuries to relate these stories.

So too the textual variations that we find attested in the multitude of ancient sources—quotations from ancient authors, fragments on papyrus, and the scholia in the margins of medieval manuscripts (which derive ultimately from the work of Alexandrian and Roman scholars)—are just as likely to have been generated by the system of oral traditional poetry in which the *Iliad* and the *Odyssey* were composed, and therefore can be considered every bit as "Homeric" as those that we find in our modern printed editions. Modern editions are primarily based on the texts found in a handful of medieval manuscripts, which postdate the oral tradition by more than a millennium. In this book I propose to take these far more ancient sources seriously and to treat the variations, or multiforms, that they preserve as traditional variations generated in performance whose poetic implications are worthy of exploration.

It is this nexus of multiformity and tradition that I want to explore. As we will see, the mythological and narratological questions being grappled with by

---

[9]   See Parry 1932:7–8 (= Parry 1971:330): "A single man or even a group of men who set out in the most careful way could not make even a beginning at such an oral diction. It must be the work of many poets over many generations. When one singer...has hit upon a phrase which is pleasing and easily used, other singers will hear it, and then, when faced at the same point in the line with the need of expressing the same idea, they will recall it and use it. If the phrase is good poetically and so useful metrically that it becomes in time the one best way to express a certain idea in a given length of verse, and as such is passed on from one generation of poets to another, it has won a place for itself in the oral diction as a formula. But if it does not suit in every way, or if a better way of fitting the idea to the verse and the sentence is found, it is straightaway forgotten, or lives only for a short time, since with each new poet and with each new generation of poets it must undergo the two-fold test of being found pleasing and useful. In time the needed number of such phrases is made up: each idea to be expressed in the poetry has its formula for each metrical need, and the poet, who would not think of trying to express ideas outside the traditional field of thought of the poetry, can make his verses easily by means of a diction which time has proved to be the best."

the scholars of Alexandria and the later authors whose comments survive in the scholia of our medieval manuscripts can sometimes have profound implications for the textual transmission of the *Iliad* and the *Odyssey*. The scholion on *Iliad* 20.30 with which I began is a perfect example of the interdependence of the two. In this one comment not only can we possibly catch a glimpse of a now-lost epic tradition in which Achilles and Odysseus contend to be the sacker of Troy and the "best of the Achaeans," but we also learn about three verses that do not survive in our medieval manuscripts of the poem. All we are told, in the typically compressed way of the scholia, is that "some" (presumably editors) write these verses (presumably in their editions). They are not a seamless replacement for *Iliad* 20.30, however. If we replaced 20.30 with the verses that "some write," we would get this:

[20.28] καὶ δέ τέ μιν καὶ πρόσθεν ὑποτρομέεσκον ὁρῶντες·
[20.29] νῦν δ᾽ ὅτε δὴ καὶ θυμὸν ἑταίρου χώεται αἰνῶς
[20.30a] οὐ μέντοι μοῖρ᾽ ἐστὶν ἔτι ζωοῦ Ἀχιλῆος
[20.30b] Ἰλίου ἐκπέρσαι εὖ ναιόμενον πτολίεθρον.
[20.30c] πέρσει δουράτεός <θ᾽> ἵππος καὶ μῆτις Ἐπειοῦ.

[20.28] Even before now they would tremble before him when they saw him.
[20.29] And now when he is terribly angry in his heart because of [the death of] his companion...
[20.30a] It is not fated, however, with Achilles still alive
[20.30b] to sack the well-inhabited citadel of Ilium.
[20.30c] A wooden horse will destroy it and the craftiness [*mētis*] of Epeios.

If we assume an ellipsis here (as sometimes occurs, as at *Iliad* 1.135–136), we can make it work, but it is more likely that the scholia are quoting from an edition in which the entire passage was substantially different from what we find in the medieval manuscripts of the *Iliad*.[10] But these verses are in no way objectionable beyond the fact that they do not survive elsewhere (Edwards 1991 *ad loc.*).[11]

---

10 West (2001:254) argues similarly: "The three lines quoted in sch^T [= the scholia in the Townley manuscript, Burney 86] are a gloss on 30 ὑπὲρ μόρον. The scholiast says that they were read by some in place of line 30, but this cannot be right: they must either have been substituted for 28–30 or (more likely) appended after 30."

11 Bolling (1925:187) argues that the verses derive from a Cyclic epic. Implicit in his argument is a conception of the *Iliad* as a fixed text that can be "interpolated" with verses from another poem. Such a view is incompatible with my own understanding of not only the oral tradition in which the *Iliad* was composed but also the methodology of ancient editors, on which see further below.

There is nothing "un-Homeric" about them—they are simply an attested multiform of the verses transmitted by our medieval manuscripts.

I hope to show that variations like the one discussed here are not aberrations but are in fact attested in many different ancient historical sources. In other words, I will highlight and call attention to the surviving examples of the multiformity of the epic tradition, rather than try to explain them away, dismiss them, or hide them in the dark recesses of an *apparatus criticus*, as is usually done.[12] Building on my previous work on this subject (especially Dué 2001a and 2002 and Dué and Ebbott 2010), I will explore these examples of multiformity as a necessary reflex of an oral tradition in which epic tales are composed in performance, and I will show how awareness of multiforms leads to a greater understanding of the poetics of the tradition in which the *Iliad* and the *Odyssey* were composed. By treating attested multiforms as manifestations of a traditional system, I am able to explore what kinds of multiformity were natural to this system in different historical eras and how ancient audiences may have understood them.

In so doing I will be drawing on nearly two decades as coeditor with Mary Ebbott of the Homer Multitext, a digital project that seeks to make the full complexity of the textual transmission of the *Iliad* accessible by means of high-resolution images of the historical documents that transmit the poem together with digital, diplomatic editions of their contents. I and my principal collaborators on this project (which include, in addition to Mary Ebbott, the project architects, Christopher Blackwell and Neel Smith, and the associate editors, Douglas Frame, Leonard Muellner, and Gregory Nagy) assert that a multitext edition is a methodologically superior way of representing the transmission of an oral tradition, in that it does not seek to establish a single original from which all other surviving texts derive but rather endeavors to make accessible as many historical instantiations of the text as possible together with their historical contexts.[13] In this belief we have been profoundly influenced by the fieldwork and scholarship of Albert Lord, who wrote that "the word *multiform* is

---

[12] On the scholarly contempt with which variation, including and especially additional verses, is typically greeted by scholars, see Dué 2001a and chapters 2 and 3 below. An exception is Bird 2010.

[13] Cf. Nagy 1996a:113. Nagy was in fact the first to assert the need for a multitext edition of Homer, for which his evolutionary model, discussed below and in chapter 1, forms a basis: "The ultimate purpose in drawing up this scheme is to lay the groundwork for an eventual multitext edition of Homer, one that would be expected not only to report variant readings but also relate them wherever possible to different periods in the history of textual transmission." For more on the goals and theoretical underpinnings of the Homer Multitext see the project website (http://www.homermultitext.org) as well as Dué and Ebbott 2010: 153–165, Bierl 2015:193–194, and Dué and Ebbott 2017.

more accurate than 'variant,' because it does not give preference or precedence to any one word or set of words to express an idea; instead it acknowledges that the idea may exist in several forms" (Lord 1995:23; see also Lord 1960:100).

Albert Lord's 1960 book *The Singer of Tales* was the culmination of decades of close observation of a living oral epic tradition in Yugoslavia and careful application of that work by analogy to the Homeric epics. Lord went to Yugoslavia initially in the early 1930s, as the undergraduate assistant of Milman Parry. Parry's 1928 doctoral dissertation on the traditional epithet in Homer had been a brilliant demonstration of the economy and traditionality of Homeric diction, but even Parry himself did not fully grasp the implications of this work until Parry and Lord went to Yugoslavia to observe the still-flourishing South Slavic oral epic song tradition (Parry 1971:439). It was in the context of this fieldwork that Parry came to understand that Homeric poetry was not only traditional but oral—that is, composed anew every time in performance, by means of a sophisticated system of traditional phraseology and diction. For Parry, witnessing the workings of a living oral epic song tradition was a paradigm shift. Through the analogy with the South Slavic tradition, the workings of the Homeric system of composition became clear to him.

In two expeditions to the former Yugoslavia, in 1933–1935, Parry and Lord together collected songs, stories, and conversations from singers of the South Slavic epic song tradition. Albert Lord took additional trips in the 1950s and 1960s, and in many cases was able to rerecord the singers he and Parry had captured decades earlier. No two of the songs collected were exactly alike, nor did any two of the singers have exactly the same repertoire. These singers composed extremely long epic poems in performance. In order to do this they drew on a vast storehouse of traditional themes and phrases that worked within the metrical rules that give the poetry its rhythm. That is to say, they created and used what we call formulas to build each verse as they went along, instead of employing static, individual words or words memorized in a fixed order. Just as formulas are the building blocks of a line in performance, themes are the larger components that make up songs. The poets observed by Parry and Lord moved from one theme to another as they sang; themes were connected in the oral poet's mind and his plan for the song followed from their habitual association in the tradition. This performance method resulted in each song being a new composition, which is why no two songs that Parry and Lord recorded were exactly the same. Each song was a multiform of a notional song that never existed in a single "original" form.

Parry and Lord applied the findings of this fieldwork to the Homeric poems by analogy, and they were able to show that the workings of the South Slavic system reveal a great deal about how the *Iliad* and the *Odyssey* were composed.

Parry planned a series of publications based on his observations and subsequent analysis of Homeric poetry, but it was never completed. His surviving writings have been incredibly influential, but he died at the age of 33, long before he had a chance to pursue the many implications of his fieldwork. It became the work of his young undergraduate assistant, Albert Lord, to brings these ideas to the world. Of course, scholars before Parry and Lord had proposed that the *Iliad* and the *Odyssey* were composed orally, but never before had the system by which such poetry could be composed been demonstrated, nor were the implications of the creative process truly explored. *The Singer of Tales* does just that.

Lord asserts in *The Singer of Tales* that in an oral tradition like that in which the *Iliad* and the *Odyssey* were composed, "singing, performing, composing are facets of the same act" and that the implications of this process are "both broad and deep" (1960:13). Indeed they are. The work of Parry and Lord and the scholars who have built on their efforts suggests that, rather than there being a single master version of each poem from which all others descend, in its earliest stages of development there was a great deal of fluidity in the Greek oral epic tradition. Countless variations on the story of the Trojan War and the episodes within it— the anger of Achilles, the returns of the heroes, and any number of traditional tales—are known to have been current in different times and different places in antiquity, and were likely composed in performance by countless poets whose names are now lost to us. At the same time, because Greek oral epic poetry was already traditional in content in ancient times, any audience on any given occasion of performance would already have known the story and the characters. There would have been nothing about the story, the language, the rhythm of the song, or the characters that was new for that audience. A poet in a traditional song culture like that of the ancient Greeks could compose poetry in performance using techniques, plots, characters, and an ever-evolving corpus of formulaic language that he had inherited from many previous generations of singers. The material and techniques were traditional, but each performance was a new composition—a recomposition, in and for performance.

This dynamic necessarily affects how ancient epic poetry is understood and appreciated. To make an even more modern analogy than Parry and Lord's South Slavic one, for an audience that knows Anakin Skywalker will become Darth Vader, *Star Wars* is no less full of drama and tension as he proceeds down that path. Many a *Star Wars* fan has been content to watch that story replay itself again and again upon subsequent viewings. But for the Homeric epics there was an additional layer of tension. Certainly Achilles was always going to choose to return to battle and die at Troy, but the song that narrated that choice was always being composed anew. Not only might different singers arrange the song differently, and not only might there be variations on what episodes were included in any given performance, but there was always the lurking possibility, however unlikely, that the current performance would turn out differently.

Once we understand the *Iliad* and the *Odyssey* to have been composed this way, we can no longer attempt to stake rigid claims upon any one version of the text, as if the poem were fixed and unchanging. We have no reason to necessarily privilege one formulaic variation over another, even if one is well attested in our medieval manuscripts and one is known only from another source. Both are at least potentially authentically generated performance multiforms, and both have something to teach us about the compositional process and the poetics of the system in which they were generated.[14] Not all surviving multiforms would have been known to all singers at all times and in all places, yet each has the potential to reveal something about the poetics of the tradition in the time and place in which that multiform is attested.

But just how fluid, how multiform, was the Greek epic tradition? If the tradition was, as I have claimed, quite fluid in its early phases, why do our medieval manuscripts present us with a relatively uniform text? How do we get from the creative and vibrant oral epic song tradition that Albert Lord describes to the seemingly fixed text of the roughly two hundred manuscripts of the *Iliad* that survive from medieval times? Can't we simply regard the examples of multiformity such as we find in the scholia at *Iliad* 20.30 as anomalies or interpolations, perhaps the work of rogue singers, scholars, and scribes, and conceive of the "true" *Iliad* as having existed in a primarily static form for two and a half millennia or more?

This will be the subject of chapter 1, and indeed it is a central question for this book as a whole. The short answer is that we *could* imagine the *Iliad* to have become fixed in the eighth, seventh, or even sixth century BCE, and that certainly seems to be the prevailing approach taken by editors of the twentieth century,[15] but I will argue that our surviving evidence supports a different model, namely an evolutionary model for the Homeric text, like the one developed by Nagy. Nagy identifies five stages of evolution of the Homeric poems, which move from relatively most fluid (and most multiform) to relatively most rigid (and far less multiform) over a span of more than fifteen hundred years. Such a model accounts for a great deal of multiformity in the epic tradition as it

---

[14] Cf. Nagy 1996a:33 on the multiform πολυδευκέα at *Odyssey* 19.521 (attested in Aelian *De natura animalium* 5.38): "In considering these two variants...I am ready to argue that both are legitimate, both ultimately generated from the multiform performance tradition of Homer."

[15] On the twentieth-century desire to attribute the text fixation of the *Iliad* and the *Odyssey* to a single Archaic master poet see Dué 2006b and the conclusion. Martin West's 2017 edition of the *Odyssey* is the most recent example of this approach to editing the Homeric epics.

developed over the course of many centuries.[16] Nagy's basic assumption, based on both internal and external evidence, is that the Greek epic tradition evolved over time, and therefore we are required to take a diachronic perspective.

As Mary Ebbott and I note in our 2010 book (Dué and Ebbott 2010:19–20), and as I will explore in more depth in chapter 1, the implications of Nagy's model are many and significant. He fundamentally rejects the model which posits that an oral tradition came to an abrupt halt sometime in the eighth century BCE, when the new technology of writing was used to record the monumental epics of a single singer, who was able to transcend the limits of said tradition, which he effectively ended, and whose works we (for the most part) have in our textual sources dating only from the tenth century CE onward. Replacing that outdated and untenable paradigm,[17] Nagy's evolutionary model offers a framework for an understanding of how an oral tradition and the technology of writing coexist and influence one another for a long time before writing becomes the dominant means of transmission.

Nagy's model has many points of contact with that offered by E. S. Sherratt (1990). Sherratt analyzes various passages of the *Iliad* as examples of the difficulties of relating material culture to the poem for the purposes of "solving" questions of when and how it was composed, noting that many passages of the *Iliad* seem to present "the juxtaposition or super-imposition of more than one chronological reflection" (1990:810). She proposes to explain these archaeological layers as reflexes of the oral tradition in which the *Iliad* was composed, arguing that over a long period of evolution some historical periods would have been more generative than others, with corresponding changes in the formulaic diction and its representation of material culture.

While there are differences between the two models (Sherratt's arguments are primarily centered on eras that fall into period 1 in Nagy's model), both Nagy and Sherratt conceive of the *Iliad* as a work that evolved (with no teleology implied) over many centuries in a song tradition that dates at least as far back as the early palatial period of the Mycenaean Bronze Age, if not earlier. The work of both scholars makes clear that the process by which earlier and later material became incorporated into and integral to the oral formulaic diction resulted in a system from which it would be impossible to separate out and isolate the poetic contributions of different eras. Sherratt vividly illustrates that even within a single passage of the *Iliad* (for example the encounter on the battlefield between

---

[16] For an early formulation, see Nagy 1996a:107–110 and chapter 1 below. For a more recent and further-refined formulation see Nagy (forthcoming).

[17] For the recent demonstrations of the untenability of this model (and a survey of various dictation theories for the creation of the Homeric texts), see González 2013:15–70 and Ready 2015. See also chapter 1, pp. 42–44.

Achilles and Aeneas in *Iliad* 20) different eras of material culture are inextricably intertwined. Likewise the diction of Homeric poetry cannot be separated into distinct layers, even though it is clear to linguists that some formulas are earlier than others and were composed in different dialects in different eras.[18] And finally both scholars allow for a great deal of multiformity within the system up until the point that the *Iliad* and the *Odyssey* come to be prized Panhellenic possessions, at which point multiformity comes to be screened out.

***

Building on the work of earlier scholars who have demonstrated why we should expect the *Iliad* to be multiform (especially Lord 1960 and Nagy 1996a), this book asks two basic questions: First, what kinds of multiformity are attested in our surviving sources? And second, what are the implications of multiformity for our interpretation of the reception and transmission of Homeric poetry? The answers to these questions that I formulate in the following chapters have emerged from twenty years of collaborative work and discussion with numerous colleagues on the Homer Multitext.[19] I have often joked that the aim of the Homer Multitext is to "unedit" the *Iliad*, but indeed a central goal of the project is to present the historical witnesses of the *Iliad* unmediated by the interventions of editors seeking to reconstruct a hypothesized "original." Only in this way can we gain a clear picture of the multiformity with which the *Iliad* has been transmitted to us. In our experience, it can be incredibly difficult, sometimes impossible, to ascertain what the historical sources actually transmit if one relies solely on existing publications of the scholia in print or the cryptic reporting of an *apparatus criticus*.[20] The Homer Multitext allows each document to be viewed and considered on its own terms.

It is this desire to peel back centuries of editorial intervention that leads me to title this book *Achilles Unbound*. I want to remove the bindings, so to speak, from

---

[18] See especially the classic treatment by Milman Parry, "Studies in the Epic Technique of Oral Versemaking. II. The Homeric Language as the Language of Oral Poetry" (= Parry 1932; reprinted in A. Parry 1971:325–364).

[19] I wish to thank in particular those who have regularly participated in an annual seminar held since 2005 at the Center for Hellenic Studies: Tazuko van Berkel, Christopher Blackwell, Eric Dugdale, Mary Ebbott, Douglas Frame, Madeleine Goh, Olga Levaniouk, Leonard Muellner, Gregory Nagy, Corinne Pache, Ineke Sluiter, and Neel Smith.

[20] Before we had access to the images of the Venetus A manuscript that were taken in 2007, we attempted to reconstruct the texts of six of the oldest manuscripts of the *Iliad* using scholarly editions. The attempt was a failure because all scholarly editions report readings selectively and are prone to human error. One of the primary advantages of the Homer Multitext is that we provide not only diplomatic editions of the documents that transmit the *Iliad* but also links to high-resolution images of those documents, which allow for verification of our editions.

the medieval manuscripts and fully examine their contents,[21] I want to study the surviving papyrus fragments in all their multiform messiness, and I want us to try to visualize without judgment the *Iliad* known to Plato and Aeschines. But my title also, I hope, conveys a sense of possibility. The attested multiforms of the *Iliad* give us an opportunity to know and appreciate a wider range of performance traditions for this remarkable poem than most of us have been taught to do. Although our attested multiforms derive from the later stages of the evolution of the poem, even so I submit that they give us a glimpse of the very long history of the text, access to even earlier Iliads, and a greater awareness of the mechanisms by which such a poem could be composed in performance.

I do not plan to show that Iliads radically different from our own were known in antiquity. There is no *Iliad* in which Achilles goes home after quarreling with Agamemnon, and no *Iliad* in which Achilles himself sacks Troy. There is no *Odyssey* in which Odysseus decides to stay with Calypso after all. The *Iliad* and the *Odyssey* were traditional poems whose stories were deeply ingrained in the culture that produced them, and though the poems unquestionably evolved over time, they did so within a conservative and highly sophisticated system of composition in performance that claimed to be inspired by the Muses, who were believed to have witnessed the events recounted.[22]

Here again we can see that myth and narrative are inextricably intertwined, and that fate, at least as it is presented in epic, is in many ways a reflex of both. There are many places within the *Iliad* where fate is suggested to be at least potentially multiform. Most famous is Achilles' stated choice between fates in *Iliad* 9, where he implies that there are two possibilities for how his life will turn out: either he will die at Troy and have *kleos* ("glory in song") that is "unwilting" (*Iliad* 9.413) or he will return home and have a long but unremembered life. Could Achilles really have chosen to return home at this point? Certainly in terms of narrative, it cannot be a viable variation. There is no *Iliad* if Achilles goes home. Likewise in terms of myth Jonathan Burgess (2009:43–55) has convincingly argued that Achilles does not really have a choice of fates in the *Iliad* (though he may have traditionally had such a choice before the war). The *Iliad* consistently presents Achilles as fated to die at Troy at the hands of Apollo: "It is clear that no other passages in the *Iliad* support Achilles' assertion in book 9 that he

---

[21] Collaboration with the E-codices project of Switzerland and the Bibliothèque de Genève allowed for the unbinding and photography of the thirteenth-century manuscript of the *Iliad* known as the Genavensis 44. Likewise the extremely tight binding of the eleventh-century manuscript known as the Townley (Burney 86) made it largely inaccessible to scholars until recent high-resolution images of the manuscript were captured and made publicly available by the British Library (https://www.bl.uk/collection-items/the-townley-homer).

[22] See Nagy 1979:271–272.

can choose to live. Achilles is never unaware that he will die at Troy, nor does he ever really think that his fate is avoidable" (51–52). Indeed Thetis is said to have foretold his death repeatedly to Achilles (πολλάκι, *Iliad* 17.406–408). Instead the proclaimed "choice" is part of a larger struggle on the part of Achilles to accept his mortality, a major theme of the poem: "The dishonor of Achilles by Agamemnon and the death of Patroklos are major events that provoke Achilles to undergo contemplation and eventual (re)acceptance of his fate" (55). Here again then, as in *Iliad* 20, we find contemplation of a narrative alternative that probably was never a genuine multiform in myth, nor did it ever actually come into being in song. It is the contemplation of the alternative that is part of the tradition.[23] The alternative was never in fact chosen, nor could it be, because the poet and his audience already know the tradition; they know what Achilles "chose."

Indeed if any character is "bound" by fate it is Achilles, as Laura Slatkin has shown in *The Power of Thetis* (1991). Zeus, the third ruler of the universe, does not get overthrown. In every case, he thwarts the next generation from taking over. A perfect example is Achilles, who is the son Zeus never had, according to Pindar, *Isthmian* 8:

> ταῦτα καὶ μακάρων ἐμέμναντ' ἀγοραί,
> Ζεὺς ὅτ' ἀμφὶ Θέτιος ἀγλαός τ' ἔρισαν Ποσειδᾶν γάμῳ,
> ἄλοχον εὐειδέ' ἐθέλων ἑκάτερος
> ἐὰν ἔμμεν· ἔρως γὰρ ἔχεν.
> ἀλλ' οὔ σφιν ἄμβροτοι τέλεσαν εὐνὰν θεῶν πραπίδες,
> ἐπεὶ θεσφάτων ἐπάκουσαν· εἶπε δ'
> εὔβουλος ἐν μέσοισι Θέμις,
> οὕνεκεν πεπρωμένον ἦν φέρτερον γόνον ἄνακτα πατρὸς τεκεῖν
> ποντίαν θεόν, ὃς κεραυνοῦ τε κρέσσον ἄλλο βέλος
> διώξει χερὶ τριόδοντός τ' ἀμαιμακέτου, Δί τε μισγομέναν ἢ Διὸς παρ'
>   ἀδελφεοῖσιν.—'ἀλλὰ τὰ μὲν παύσατε· βροτέων δὲ λεχέων
>   τυχοῖσα
> υἱὸν εἰσιδέτω θανόντ' ἐν πολέμῳ,
> χεῖρας Ἄρεΐ τ' ἐναλίγκιον στεροπαῖσί τ' ἀκμὰν ποδῶν.

---

[23] Cf. Burgess 2009: 52: "Counterfactual musings are part of Homeric poetry." Cf. *Iliad* 21.275–278, in which Achilles (in his fight with the river) speculates that his mother lied to him about his fate: ἄλλος δ' οὔ τις μοι τόσον αἴτιος οὐρανιώνων / ἀλλὰ φίλη μήτηρ ἥ με ψεύδεσσιν ἔθελγεν / ἥ μ' ἔφατο Τρώων ὑπὸ τείχεϊ θωρηκτάων / λαιψηροῖς ὀλέεσθαι Ἀπόλλωνος βελέεσσιν ("No other of the Olympians is so responsible as my dear mother, who used to enchant me with lies, who claimed that I would be destroyed beneath the wall of the Trojans by Apollo's swift arrows"). For other examples, see Macleod 1982:151. See also De Jong 2004:68–81.

> This the assembly of the Blessed Ones remembered,
> When Zeus and glorious Poseidon
> Strove to marry Thetis,
> Each wishing that she
> Should be his beautiful bride.
> Love held them in his grip.
> But the Gods' undying wisdom
> Would not let the marriage be,
> When they gave ear to the oracles. In their midst wise-counseling
>   Themis said
> That it was fated for the sea-goddess
> To bear for son a prince
> Stronger than his father,
> Who shall wield in his hand a different weapon
> More powerful than the thunderbolt,
> Or the monstrous trident,
> If she wed Zeus or among the brothers of Zeus.
> "Put an end to this. Let her have a mortal wedlock
> And see dead in war her son
> With hands like the hands of Ares
> And feet like the lightning-flashes."   (trans. C. M. Bowra)

Zeus prevents his own overthrow by forcing Thetis to marry a mortal, Peleus, and their son of course turns out to be Achilles. Instead of becoming the supreme ruler of the universe, Achilles will be merely supreme among mortals, and doomed to die young, in battle. This same myth plays an important role in Aeschylus' tragedy *Prometheus Bound*. In that play there is a secret that is a crucial part of the plot: Prometheus knows the key to Zeus' downfall, and it is Thetis. As Slatkin has written (1991:101): "If Themis had not intervened, Thetis would have borne to Zeus or Poseidon the son greater than his father, and the entire chain of succession in heaven would have continued: Achilles would have been not the greatest of heroes, but the ruler of the universe. The price of Zeus' hegemony is Achilles' death."

Achilles is bound by fate and by narrative tradition, but Achilles' poem, the *Iliad*, was not fixed and monolithic in antiquity. It was multiform. And the wider epic tradition from which the *Iliad* emerged was more multiform still. It is my aim in this book to explore the traditionality and multiformity of the *Iliad* in a way that gives us a greater appreciation of what has been handed down to us.

Chapter 1

"Winged Words"

How We Came to Have Our *Iliad*

O UR *ILIAD* CONSISTS—TO QUOTE A WELL-KNOWN HOMERIC FORMULA— of "winged words" (ἔπεα πτερόεντα). An image in a Bronze Age fresco from Pylos suggests that as early as Mycenaean times, poetry in performance was conceived of as being in flight (Plate 1).[1] As we have seen, the nature of the *Iliad*—as a poem that is created only in performance—has profound implications for scholars seeking to establish an authoritative text. It has been suggested that, in Homeric epic, *epea pteroenta* are ones that, once uttered, cannot be taken back (Latacz 1968). And yet this is precisely what editors of Homer have throughout history hoped to do; we strive to recapture the authoritative performance and make it a text.

Building on the evolutionary model outlined in the introduction, I propose in this chapter to describe how a performance tradition that was already well underway in Mycenaean Greece eventually crystallized into what we know as the *Iliad*, and how that poem was transmitted in various media through more than three millennia so as to reach us in the textual form that we now have. The

---

[1] This chapter is a revised and expanded version of Dué 2009b. For an overview of the various meanings proposed for this famous phrase see Létoublon 1999. See also Martin 1989:30–37, Mackie 1996:56–58, and Beck 2005:41–43. A scholion to Euripides' *Orestes* 1176 explains "winged words" this way: "because in performance/reading they leave the mouth like birds" (πτηνοὺς ἐνταῦθα λέγει τοὺς λόγους διὰ τὸ δίκην πτηνῶν ἀπέρχεσθαι τῇ προφορᾷ). (For προφορά as both "reading out loud" and "performance," see Parsons 2012:19, whose translation I have adapted.) On the Pylos fresco see Lang 1969:79–80 (with additional bibliography *ad loc.*) and Immerwahr 1990:133–134. A Late Minoan IIIA ceramic pyxis from Aptera on Crete similarly depicts a lyre player surrounded by numerous large birds. (On the pyxis see also Betancourt 2007:190, who interprets the imagery differently than I do here, arguing that it is connected with cult ceremonies.)

processes of transmission that I will describe are certainly not without controversy, and in my notes I will point to important recent discussions of these complex issues. My overarching aim is to provide an overview of the research that forms the foundation of the Homer Multitext and to make plain the scholarly principles on which the discussions of the multiformity of the *Iliad* in the following chapters depend. I will explore above all two related questions. How did a poem that was repeatedly composed and recomposed in performance become a written text? If the *Iliad* is indeed ultimately derived from such performances, what are implications for the textual tradition of this poem?

Performance of the *Iliad* and the *Odyssey* in Ancient Times

Homeric poetry was known to the ancient world primarily in performance. Most scholars would agree that in their earliest incarnations the poems that came to be our *Iliad* and *Odyssey* were composed orally and in the context of performance, and that this process was occurring over hundreds of years and throughout a large geographical area. These basic facts about the creation of the *Iliad* and the *Odyssey* came to be known through two different kinds of investigation.

First, there is the evidence that can be gleaned from the poems themselves. The meter of the poetry is the dactylic hexameter, and the language of the poems is a poetic composite of several dialects that was never spoken in any one time or place (Parry 1932, Palmer 1962, Horrocks 1997 and 2010:44–49, Bakker, forthcoming). The predominant layer consists of Ionic Greek forms, with the result that a large portion of the poem might be surmised to have come into shape in archaic Ionia (Frame 2009:551–620, §4.20–4.71). But there are verses that are demonstrably much earlier, in Arcado-Cypriote and Aeolic dialects, and others much later, with a veneer of Attic Greek. Phrases, half-verses, whole verses, and even whole scenes are repeated with a regularity that indicates this poetic composite was formed within a traditional system—that is to say, it could not be the product of one person.[2] The work of Milman Parry and Albert Lord demonstrated that this traditional system of formulaic language evolved to serve the needs of poets composing in performance (Ebbott, forthcoming).

There are, moreover, several passages within the poems that depict the performance of epic poetry, such as the performances of Phemios for the suitors in the house of Odysseus and those of Demodokos for the Phaeacians in the

---

[2]   The traditionality of the language of the Homeric poems was established by Milman Parry in his 1928 doctoral thesis, *L'épithète traditionnelle dans Homère: Essai sur un problème de style homérique* (= "The Traditional Epithet in Homer" in Parry 1971). See the introduction, p. 6.

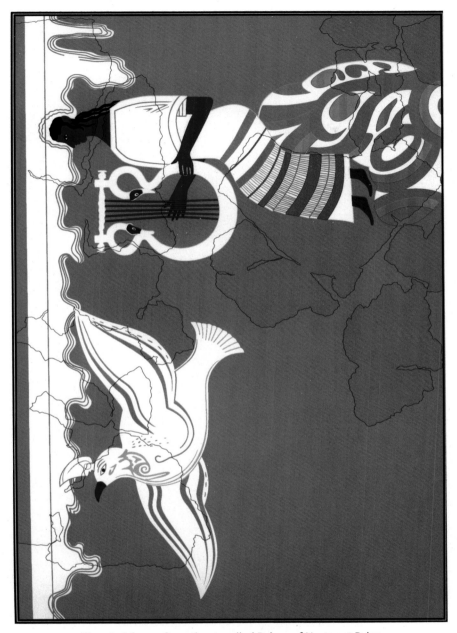

Plate 1. A fresco from the so-called Palace of Nestor at Pylos
suggests that as early as Mycenaean times, poetry in performance
has been conceived of as being in flight.
Drawing by Valerie Woelfel, after a reconstruction by Piet de Jong.

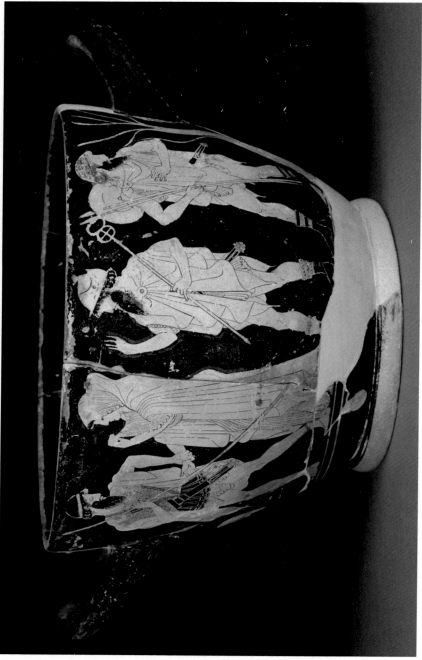

Plate 2. Red-figure skyphos attributed to Macron (Louvre G146),
depicting Agamemnon leading Briseis away (side A). Neither side A nor side
B (Plate 3) aligns with the scenes as narrated in our *Iliad*.
Photo © RMN-Grand Palais / Art Resource, NY.

Plate 3. Red-figure skyphos attributed to Macron (Louvre G146),
depicting the embassy to Achilles (side B). Achilles is veiled and grieving,
and does not address his comrades.
Photo © RMN-Grand Palais / Art Resource, NY.

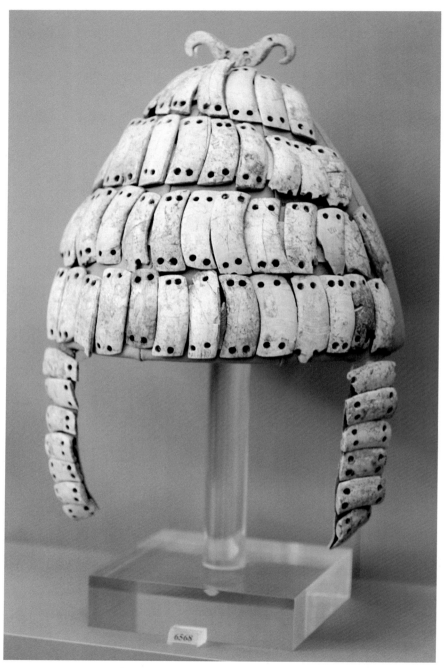

Plate 4. Boar's-tusk helmet from the National Archaeological
Museum, Athens.
Photo © Vanni Archive / Art Resource, NY.

Plate 5. The miniature fresco on the south wall of Room 5 (details shown here) in the West House on Thera might depict an epic tale of homecoming after a successful military expedition.
Photos © Erich Lessing / Art Resource, NY [*above*] and Nimatallah / Art Resource, NY [*below*].

Plate 6. Mycenaean warriors with oxhide shields and boar's tusk helmets attack a walled coastal city in the miniature fresco from the north wall of Room 5 in the West House on Thera.
Photo © De Agostini Picture Library / G. Dagli Orti / Bridgeman Images.

Plate 7a. Detail from the François Vase showing Dionysos carrying the golden amphora as a gift for Thetis at her wedding to Peleus.
Photo © Alinari / Art Resource, NY.

Plate 7b. White-ground lekythos, attributed to the Athena Painter (Louvre F366). Achilles crouches in ambush while Polyxena draws water from a fountain. Vase paintings depicting the ambush of Troilos regularly feature his sister Polyxena, as here.
Drawing by Joni Godlove.

Plate 8. Black-figure amphora signed by Exekias (British Museum B210),
depicting Achilles killing the Amazon Penthesileia. As their eyes meet, too
late, Achilles falls in love with her.

house of King Alkinoos. These passages show a bard performing at banquets, often taking requests for various episodes involving well-known heroes. Such passages in the Homeric texts that refer to occasions of performance are fascinating windows into how ancient audiences imagined the creation of epic poetry (Ebbott, forthcoming). Certainly the process is entirely oral. References to writing in the epics are famously few and mysterious.[3] The absence of writing in the composition of the poetry is also reflected in ancient biographical traditions about Homer that conceive of him as being blind (Graziosi 2002). In the *Homeric Hymn to Apollo*, the narrator proclaims that he is a blind man from Chios, and in *Odyssey* Book 8, the blind poet Demodokos who entertains the feasting Phaeacians (and whom many readers equate with "Homer") is said to be compensated for blindness by his talent: "Him the muse had dearly loved, but she had given to him both good and evil, for though she had endowed him with a divine gift of song, she had robbed him of his eyesight" (*Odyssey* 8.63–64).

From the perspective of the internal audience of these performances, such as the suitors who are entertained by Phemios in Odysseus' house on Ithaca in book 1 of the *Odyssey*, or the guests who listen in rapt silence to Demodokos in Alkinoos' house in Phaeacia in book 8, the events narrated are well known but at the same time come from the relatively recent past. The Trojan War has come to an end only ten years before the performances depicted. But for the external audience, such as Athenians at the Panathenaic festival in Athens in the Classical period, the songs of Phemios and Demodokos are the traditional material of poets working within the epic tradition. Phemios sings *nostoi*, songs about the homeward voyages of the various heroes from Troy; Demodokos sings about a quarrel between Odysseus and Achilles at Troy, and later, the sack of Troy. It is worth noting that despite the differences in occasion, for the external audience, the compositional process of these notionally "past" performances and that of the present, framing performance is imagined to be the same. In this way the very ancient performances represented within the poems are placed on a continuum that connects all the way to the audience's present.[4]

The second mode of inquiry into the creation of the *Iliad* and the *Odyssey* that I wish to highlight is the one I have already discussed in the introduction to this book. As we have seen, in the 1930s Milman Parry and his assistant Albert Lord went to Yugoslavia to study the oral epic tradition that at that time still flourished there, and soon came to understand that the Homeric poems were not only traditional in content, but were in fact oral poems—that is, products of sung performance rather than composition through the technology of writing.

---

[3] On the "baneful signs" (σήματα λυγρὰ) carried by Bellerophon to the king of Lycia (related in *Iliad* 6.168ff.), see Nagy 1996b:14 and Shear 1998 with additional bibliography *ad loc.*

[4] On this point see also Burgess 2005:127 and 2009:96.

Their fieldwork allowed Parry and Lord to discover in "Homer" the existence of a sophisticated, traditional, economical, and above all oral system that enabled great literature to be composed in performance. They showed how a singer, trained in techniques that were centuries if not millennia old, could draw upon a storehouse of traditional language, tales, and heroic figures to compose epic poetry on any given occasion.[5]

The work of Parry and Lord suggests that though both the techniques used to compose epic and the stories that were told in epic were highly traditional, in its earliest stages there would have been a great deal of multiformity in the Greek oral epic tradition, with different performance traditions competing against one another to be considered authoritative. We witness just such a dynamic in *Odyssey* 8, when Odysseus specifically requests that Demodokos sing the song of the sack of Troy by means of the wooden horse. Odysseus says to Demodokos:

> αἴ κεν δή μοι ταῦτα κατὰ μοῖραν καταλέξῃς,
> αὐτίκ᾽ ἐγὼ πᾶσιν μυθήσομαι ἀνθρώποισιν,
> ὡς ἄρα τοι πρόφρων θεὸς ὤπασε θέσπιν ἀοιδήν.

Odyssey 8.496–498

> If you relate these things to me in accordance with destiny
> Straightaway I will speak words before all men,
> saying how a god readily bestowed upon you a wondrous song.

Odysseus' words imply that there is a correct or authoritative way to perform this song, *but also that other singers might perform it differently.*

Here again, as we saw in connection with the passage from *Iliad* 20 with which I began my introduction, we find competing epic traditions evaluated in terms of fate or destiny (*moira*).[6] What is "fated" is the traditional and hence authoritative version of the story. For Odysseus, however, what is "tradition" for the external audience of the epic and even for the internal audience, the Phaeacians, is in fact his own life experiences, which took place only ten years prior to the current occasion of performance. He is therefore uniquely qualified to judge the authoritativeness of the current performance. His reaction,

---

[5] The collected works of Milman Parry are published in *The Making of Homeric Verse* (edited by his son Adam Parry, Oxford, 1971). After Parry's early death Lord went on to publish numerous articles and monographs over the course of six decades. See especially Lord 1948b, 1960/2000, and 1991 and the introduction by Mitchell and Nagy to the 2000 edition of Lord's *The Singer of Tales*.

[6] See also Nagy 1979:40–41 with further discussion of the semantic range of the word *moira*.

namely his tears, reveals to us that Demodokos has succeeded.[7] The passage as a whole suggests that what makes a song authoritative is not particulars of wording—that is, the "text" of the song—but a more deeply felt adherence to tradition that results in an emotional response from its listeners, who are themselves an integral part of the dynamic of tradition.[8] As Parry observed of the South Slavic epic song tradition, "The fame of a singer comes not from quitting the tradition but from putting it to the best use" (Parry 1971:335). So too will Demodokos become famous when Odysseus "speaks words before all" about what a gifted singer he is.

Such an understanding of tradition does not preclude multiformity. Lord observed for example that songs in the South Slavic tradition could be expanded or compressed as the occasion, time available, or the audience required, and that particular episodes could be included or not. He observed variations in different performances of the same singer and also when the notionally "same" song was performed by different singers.[9] In fact, the singers that Parry and Lord interviewed claimed to sing the song the same way every time, "word for word, and line for line," but their fieldwork shows that this was never actually the case. As Lord notes, "What is of importance here is not the fact of exactness or lack of exactness, but the constant emphasis by the singer on his role in the tradition ... the role of conserver of the tradition, the role of the defender of the historic truth of what is being sung; for if the singer changes what he has heard in its essence, he falsifies truth" (1960/2000:28).

In the ensuing chapters we will find many examples from the Greek epic tradition of a different kind of multiformity, in which competing and mutually incompatible alternatives present themselves. What is the cause of such multiformity? In my book *Homeric Variations on a Lament by Briseis* (2002:21–36 and 49–65), I argued that variations on the story of Achilles' captive prize woman Briseis are fundamentally connected with local as opposed to Panhellenic epic traditions. In so doing I was following Gregory Nagy, who has shown that Archaic Greek poetry refers to Panhellenic myth and poetry as "truth" while

---

[7] For Odysseus' reaction, cf. Penelope at *Odyssey* 1.328–344 and Telemakhos at *Odyssey* 4.113–116. In *Odyssey* 4.219–233, Helen drugs the drinks with *nēpenthes* so that they can tell tales about Odysseus at Troy without weeping.

[8] We may compare the words of the rhapsode Ion in Plato's *Ion* (535e): δεῖ γάρ με καὶ σφόδρ᾽ αὐτοῖς τὸν νοῦν προσέχειν· ὡς ἐὰν μὲν κλάοντας αὐτοὺς καθίσω, αὐτὸς γελάσομαι ἀργύριον λαμβάνων, ἐὰν δὲ γελῶντας, αὐτὸς κλαύσομαι ἀργύριον ἀπολλύς ("I have to give [the audience] very close attention, for if I set them weeping, I myself will laugh when I get my money, but if they laugh, it is I who will weep at losing it" [translation after that of Cooper 1938, as reprinted in Hamilton and Cairns 1961]). On the traditional audience see Dué and Ebbott 2010:27–28 and 99–100.

[9] See especially Lord 1960/2000:20–28 and 99–123, as well as Parry 1932:15 (= Parry 1971:336).

local versions of stories about gods and heroes are *pseudea,* or "lies."[10] Such a conception of truth and fiction is at work in the opening lines of the *Homeric Hymn to Dionysos*:

οἳ μὲν γὰρ Δρακάνῳ σ', οἳ δ' Ἰκάρῳ ἠνεμοέσσῃ
φάσ', οἳ δ' ἐν Νάξῳ, δῖον γένος, εἰραφιῶτα,
οἳ δέ σ' ἐπ' Ἀλφειῷ ποταμῷ βαθυδινήεντι
κυσαμένην Σεμέλην τεκέειν Διὶ τερπικεραύνῳ·
ἄλλοι δ' ἐν Θήβῃσιν, ἄναξ, σε λέγουσι γενέσθαι,
ψευδόμενοι· σὲ δ' ἔτικτε πατὴρ ἀνδρῶν τε θεῶν τε
πολλὸν ἀπ' ἀνθρώπων, κρύπτων λευκώλενον Ἥρην.

> For some say that you were born at Dracanum; others say on windy
>   Icarus;
> some say you were born in Naxos, divinely born, snatched from the
>   thigh,
> and others say that at the Alpheus River with deep eddies
> Semele conceived and bore you to Zeus who delights in thunder.
> Still others say, Lord, that you were born in Thebes,
> But they lie. The father of gods and men bore you
> far from men, hiding you from white-armed Hera.

As Nagy argues (1990b:43), "various legitimate local traditions are here being discounted as false in order to legitimize the one tradition that is acceptable to the poet's audience." The *Iliad* must likewise assert a version of the Achilles story that supersedes competing local variants. As I note with reference to Briseis, the *Iliad* does this in two ways. First, it leaves out or leaves obscure many local details about a romance between Achilles and the various girls from the many towns he captures. Second, the *Iliad* often includes within its own narrative allusions to other versions, thereby asserting the primacy of its own narrative at the expense of competing variations. A well-known example of this way of incorporating variation occurs at *Iliad* 5.634–647. In this battle exchange Tlepolemos taunts Sarpedon and claims that those who say that he is the son of Zeus are "liars"—*pseudomenoi*. As Miriam Carlisle has pointed out, in the *Iliad* Sarpedon is certainly the son of Zeus, but elsewhere there are traces of a competing versions of Sarpedon's lineage. Tlepolemos' use of *pseudomenoi*

---

[10] Nagy 1990a:60: "The *alētheia* of Greek poetry tends to contrast with the divergence of local poetic versions in the overarching process of achieving a convergent version acceptable to all Hellenes." On *pseudea* as variant versions and not necessarily "lies"—that is, deliberate falsehoods—see Carlisle 1999.

here is a way of referring to competing (and mutually exclusive) traditions, not objectively false tales.[11]

Another kind of evidence for the multiformity of Archaic Greek epic comes from Archaic and Classical Greek vase paintings, which sometimes depict "Homeric" scenes, but usually in ways that do not precisely correspond with how the story is told in the epics as they have come down to us (Snodgrass 1998). I argued in my 2002 book that while epic poets represent myth through verbal narrative, artists, drawing from the same storehouse of tradition, represent myth visually, each medium having its own rules and conventions (Dué 2002:32). The relationship between the vase paintings and poetry is therefore not linear but more like a triangle, with verbal and visual artists drawing on the same traditional narrative material and the two kinds of storytelling evolving alongside one another (and no doubt influencing one another). In this way I differ somewhat from other scholars, who have focused on the question of whether the Archaic vase painters knew "Homer" or "the *Iliad*." Rather, I argue that vase paintings can be used as evidence for different ways of telling the story of the Trojan War in a time when the *Iliad* and the *Odyssey* were themselves still to a certain degree fluid.[12]

When we take into account the evidence of vase paintings, we see that the narrative traditions about the Trojan War and even the events recounted in the *Iliad* were indeed multiform in the seventh and sixth centuries BCE. In my 2002 book, I looked at vases that depict the taking of Briseis from Achilles (Dué 2002:28–31). In some versions of the story, Agamemnon evidently came to take Briseis himself, while in other versions (including our *Iliad*) he sends two heralds. Both versions survive on vase paintings: see, for example, a red-figure skyphos attributed to Macron, which depicts Agamemnon leading Briseis away by the wrist (Plate 2). The *Iliad* too hints at the multiformity of the tradition here. In *Iliad* 1, Agamemnon threatens to come himself to take Briseis away:

> εἰ δέ κε μὴ δώωσιν ἐγὼ δέ κεν αὐτὸς ἕλωμαι
> ἢ τεὸν ἢ Αἴαντος ἰὼν γέρας, ἢ Ὀδυσῆος
> ἄξω ἑλών·

Iliad 1.137–139

---

[11] See Carlisle 1999:62–64 as well as Pratt 1993:29–30 (with n29).

[12] See Dué 2002:27–36 with references *ad loc.* On this point see also Lowenstam 2008:5 as well as González 2013:41–68. My approach differs from Lowenstam's slightly in that he still prefers to see the vase painters as being directly inspired by poetry (as opposed to mythological traditions independent of poetry and the inherited conventions of vase painting), but he acknowledges that the poetic tradition was still multiform at this time and that there was not yet a canonical *Iliad* or *Odyssey*. This is a subtle distinction, however, and for the most part my own take and that of Lowenstam are in agreement.

But if [the Achaeans] do not give me [a prize] I myself
>will take one,
your prize, or the one of Ajax or Odysseus
I'll go and take...

> ἐγὼ δέ κ' ἄγω Βρισηΐδα καλλιπάρῃον
> αὐτὸς ἰὼν κλισίηνδε τὸ σὸν γέρας

Iliad 1.184–185

>And I myself will go to the tent and take
>the fair-cheeked Briseis, your prize.

In actuality (as our text presents it) Agamemnon sends two heralds to take Briseis (1.318–325). Yet elsewhere characters refer to the incident as if Agamemnon had come in person (1.356; 1.507; 2.240; 9.107; 19.89). It seems as if two versions have become conflated in the received textual tradition. Agamemnon himself suggests the possibility of an alternative version of these events when he first orders the two heralds to take Briseis:

> οὐδ' Ἀγαμέμνων
> λῆγ' ἔριδος τὴν πρῶτον ἐπηπείλησ' Ἀχιλῆϊ,
> ἀλλ' ὅ γε Ταλθύβιόν τε καὶ Εὐρυβάτην προσέειπε,
> τώ οἱ ἔσαν κήρυκε καὶ ὀτρηρὼ θεράποντε·
> ἔρχεσθον κλισίην Πηληϊάδεω Ἀχιλῆος·
> χειρὸς ἑλόντ' ἀγέμεν Βρισηΐδα καλλιπάρῃον·
> εἰ δέ κε μὴ δώησιν ἐγὼ δέ κεν αὐτὸς ἕλωμαι
> ἐλθὼν σὺν πλεόνεσσι· τό οἱ καὶ ῥίγιον ἔσται.

Iliad 1.318–325

>Nor did Agamemnon
>let drop the contention with which he first threatened
>>Achilles,
>but he addressed Talthybius and Eurybates,
>who were his two heralds and quick attendants:
>"Go to the tent of Achilles the son of Peleus
>and taking beautiful-cheeked Briseis by the hand bring her
>>[to me].
>But if he won't give her I myself will take her,
>coming with many men. And it will be a very chilling
>>encounter."

The *Iliad*, through the voice of Agamemnon, directly alludes to an alternative sequence of events that was current, I suggest, in the song culture when these verses were composed.

A more fundamental and structural variation on the story of the *Iliad* has been explored by Leonard Muellner (2012), who argues that surviving vase paintings represent an alternative epic tradition in which Achilles' dominant emotion is *akhos* ('sorrow, grief'), not *mēnis* ('wrath'). In the *akhos* variation, Achilles covers his head and refuses to speak when his comrades beg him to return, which would be a substantial departure from *Iliad* 9 as we now know it. See for example Plate 3, showing the other side of the vase in Plate 2, where Achilles is veiled and looks down, not addressing his comrades. Muellner uncovers this variation in the vase paintings through the iconography of veiling, a visual way of representing *akhos* (cf. Penelope at *Odyssey* 1.334, Telemakhos in *Odyssey* 4.115, Odysseus in *Odyssey* 8.85). Achilles is no longer explicitly veiled in our texts, but at one time he may have been; Muellner argues that the *akhos* version has survived primarily in vase painting, while the *mēnis* version has survived in poetry. The *akhos* variation would seem to have very deep roots in the poetic tradition as well, however. As Muellner points out, the Catalogue of Ships in book 2 of the *Iliad* twice explains the reason for Achilles' absence from battle. In the first (2.686–694), the emphasis is on Achilles' grief for the taking of Briseis, while the second (2.768–773) emphasizes his wrath.[13] Even more fundamentally, the very name of Achilles contains the word *akhos* (Palmer 1963:79), and the *Iliad* shows "a pervasive nexus" between the word *akhos* and Ἀχιλ(λ)εύς, which is "integrated in the inherited formulaic system and hence deeply rooted in the epic tradition" (Nagy 1976:216).

Such glimpses of competing epic traditions point to an exceptionally creative and dynamic early performance history of the Homeric poems. Further below I will explore how such variation came to be largely screened out of the *Iliad* as we now have it. For now I simply want to observe that multiformity is a natural and expected phenomenon of Greek myth, and it should not surprise us that the artistic and poetic traditions that transmit these myths would likewise reflect this multiformity. The work of Parry and Lord and subsequent scholars shows that multiformity is a feature of oral epic traditions more generally, and helps us to understand by analogy the mechanisms by which the multiformity of myth entered the poetic system.

[13] Interestingly, Zenodotus athetized the first passage but not the second (Muellner 2012:213).

How Old Is the *Iliad*?

How far back does the performance tradition of the *Iliad* go? Possibly very far indeed. Greek is an Indo-European language, and Greek mythology and poetics are thought to have evolved out of an Indo-European tradition that predates the Greek language. The dactylic hexameter in which Homeric epic is composed is related to the lyric meters of Sanskrit poetry, and Gregory Nagy has argued that the Greek and Indic meters are cognate, stemming from Indo-European proto-types.[14] This relationship alone is suggestive of how very ancient the poetic traditions that produced our *Iliad* and *Odyssey* may be.

Linguists have shown, moreover, that it is possible, through examination of cognate formulas, to recover some of the poetics of the Indo-European tradition which Greek inherited. The first such formula ever discovered, and arguably the most telling, gave birth to the study of comparative Indo-European poetics.[15] The phrase κλέος ἄφθιτον 'imperishable glory' is attested both in Archaic Greek lyric poetry (Ibycus, *PMG* S151.47–48) and in epic (*Iliad* 9.413) and is cognate with the Indic *śrávas ... ákṣitam*, attested in the Sanskrit *Rig-Veda* (1.9.7; see also 1.40.4, 8.103.5, and 9.66.7). The passage in which the phrase appears in the *Iliad* is a crucial one, in which Achilles lays out his justification for continuing to sit out of the war:

> μήτηρ γάρ τέ μέ φησι θεὰ Θέτις ἀργυρόπεζα
> διχθαδίας κῆρας φερέμεν θανάτοιο τέλος δέ.
> εἰ μέν κ' αὖθι μένων Τρώων πόλιν ἀμφιμάχωμαι,
> ὤλετο μέν μοι νόστος, ἀτὰρ κλέος ἄφθιτον ἔσται·
> εἰ δέ κεν οἴκαδ' ἵκωμι φίλην ἐς πατρίδα γαῖαν,
> ὤλετό μοι κλέος ἐσθλόν, ἐπὶ δηρὸν δέ μοι αἰὼν
> ἔσσεται, οὐδέ κέ μ' ὦκα τέλος θανάτοιο κιχείη.

Iliad 9.410–416

My mother the goddess Thetis of the shining feet tells me
that there are two ways in which I may meet my end.
If I stay here and fight around the city of Troy,
my homecoming is lost, but my glory in song [*kleos*] will be unwilting
    [*aphthiton*]:
whereas if I reach home and my dear fatherland,

---

[14] See Nagy 1974 and 1990a:459–464 and Katz 2005:25.

[15] As Katz notes (2005:25), it was an observation by Adalbert Kuhn in 1853—that *śrávas ... ákṣitam* "fame ... unwithering" and *kléos áphthiton* are cognates—that led to the birth of comparative poetics as a scholarly discipline. On the subsequent scholarship see e.g. Haubold 2002, Volk 2002, and Katz 2010:361.

> my *kleos* is lost, but my life will be long,
> and the outcome of death will not soon take me.

As we will see further below, the theme of the hero as a plant that blossoms beautifully and dies quickly is an important thread in Greek lament traditions (Dué 2007), and it is also a metaphor that encapsulates what glory means in the *Iliad*. Here Achilles reveals not only the crux of this choice of fates around which the *Iliad* itself is built, but also the driving principle of Greek epic song. The unwilting flower of epic poetry is contrasted with the necessarily mortal hero, whose death comes all too quickly (Nagy 1979:174–184; Nagy 2013:408–410). κλέος ἄφθιτον is just one example among many, but it reveals that an essential theme of the *Iliad* long predates the *Iliad* itself and suggests that there may be many aspects of the Greek epic poem that are equally old.[16]

Moving forward in time, we can find tantalizing archaeological and linguistic evidence to suggest that something like our *Iliad* was already been being performed in the Greek Bronze Age. The fresco of the lyre player from Bronze Age Pylos cited at the beginning of this chapter would seem to illustrate for us a performance tradition in the Mycenaean palaces, but given that the Linear B texts from Mycenae, Pylos, and elsewhere preserve nothing like literature, do we have any way of linking the content of our *Iliad* to those Mycenaean performances? I believe that we can. Let me begin by outlining some of the points of contact between our *Iliad* and the Bronze Age more generally, before moving on to explore the antiquity of the poetry and the story as we now have it.

The Aegean Bronze Age is the context in which our *Iliad* appears to be set, and the Greeks themselves believed that the Trojan War took place at the end of the Bronze Age.[17] The major heroes, such as Agamemnon and Nestor, generally come from places that were Mycenaean palatial centers.[18] Conversely, Athens, while it certainly existed in Mycenaean times (Iakovidis 1983:73–90, Hurwit 1999:67–84), does not seem to have been the major center of power and

---

[16] Scholarship since 1853 has gone on to demonstrate many additional ways in which the *Iliad* exhibits parallels with Sanskrit epic and other Indo-European poetic traditions. Overviews of the Indo-European poetic context out of which Greek epic may have arisen include Katz 2005 and 2010, West 2007, Cook (forthcoming), and Levaniouk (forthcoming [a]). Important early studies are those of Schmitt (1967 and 1968) and Durante (1976). See also Watkins 1995 and the work of Nagy, especially Householder and Nagy 1972 and Nagy 1974, 1990b, 2004, 2008a, and 2008b, Frame 1978 and 2009, Jamison 1991, 1994, 1996, 1999, and 2001, and Muellner 1996.

[17] See, e.g., Herodotus 2.145 and 7.171, Thucydides 1.8–11, Eratosthenes (*FGrHist* 241 F 1d), with proposed dates ranging in ancient authors from 1334 (Douris, *FGrHist* 76 F 41) to 1135 BCE (Ephorus, *FGrHist* 70 F 223).

[18] The newly discovered Bronze Age palace at Sparta solves an old mystery as to why a place so integral to the narrative tradition of the Trojan War did not appear to be of significance in Mycenaean times.

influence that it came to be in later times, and Athenian heroes do not play a very important role in the *Iliad* either (Dué 2006a:91–95).[19]

Likewise, the Catalogue of Ships in book 2 of the *Iliad*, the roster of record for the Trojan War, would seem to have its origins in the Bronze Age, although it certainly evolved to contain information from later eras, and scholars differ widely in their approach to the Catalogue's relationship to history.[20] The Catalogue is controversial for many reasons, and we must proceed cautiously if we want to make any assertions about it all. It is by no means the only catalogue in surviving Homeric poetry, but at nearly four hundred verses in length it is by far the longest. Its placement in the narrative, at the start of a battle in the tenth year of the war, seems odd.[21] The list follows a circuitous geographical progression that begins in Boeotia, and the region of Boeotia and neighboring areas is disproportionately represented.[22] And although the Catalogue seems to reflect, for the most part, the political geography of Bronze Age Greece, there are many exceptions that are hard to explain. As Oliver Dickinson (2011: 154–155) has recently concluded:

> All in all, the Catalogue is a strange compilation, and it does not seem possible to devise any rational explanation for its peculiarities. Here, as with many Homeric problems, the lack of pre-Homeric or contemporary "heroic" poetry is a major obstacle to the creation of plausible hypotheses. The most that can be safely said is that the Catalogue is likely to have been compiled from materials of different origins and dates and that care has been taken to harmonize it to other Greek traditions; but, although in some parts it does show a degree of historical consistency, on the whole it is most unlikely to bear any resemblance to the probable political configuration of those parts of Greece that it covers at any time period.

[19] I do not mean to imply that Athens was completely insignificant in the Bronze Age or that it played no role in the song traditions then developing. Nagy (2015b) has argued that myths involving contact between Athens and the Minoans were already in circulation during the Mycenaean period on Crete.

[20] On the Catalogue's connections to the Bronze Age see Allen 1921, Page 1959, Simpson and Lazenby 1970, and Latacz 2004:219–249. Some scholars date the Catalogue considerably later, however; see Kirk 1985:129–170 with further references *ad loc.* and Sammons 2010:138–139. On the poetics of the catalogue and its relationship to the *Iliad* as a whole see Visser 1997, Sammons 2010:135–196, Tsagalis 2010b:329–330, and below, chapter 4. West (2007:70–71) includes catalogues of fighting groups and their leaders among the inherited elements of Indo-European poetic tradition in Greek epic.

[21] See also Sammons 2010:137 with additional citations *ad loc.*

[22] On the geographical progression, see Kirk 1985:183–186, Visser 1997, and Brügger, Stoevesandt, and Visser 2003:153–154.

In fact, as I will explore in more detail in chapter 4, many of the controversies associated with the Catalogue of Ships can be at least partially explained if we understand it to have been composed as part of a conservative system of oral composition in performance that evolved over many centuries. Names and places that seem obscure to us would have had a prominent place in the epic tradition at one time or another. Some places that flourished in the Bronze Age no doubt were obscure already even for ancient audiences of the Archaic period, but a brief record of their local heroes was preserved and eventually crystallized as part of the Catalogue. In chapter 4 I will argue that in many ways such a catalogue can function as an index to the full diachronic expanse of the epic tradition itself.

Similarly, the work by E. S. Sherratt on the archaeological layers in the *Iliad*, which I cited in the introduction, indicates that the poem reflects the material culture of more than one time period. Some aspects of material culture referenced in the *Iliad* undoubtedly reflect the understanding of a Bronze Age world, while others are demonstrably Iron Age or later in their worldview. Two of Sherratt's examples will demonstrate the complexities of the situation. In *Iliad* 23 Achilles offers a lump of iron as a prize in the funeral games for Patroklos:

αὐτὰρ Πηλεΐδης θῆκεν σόλον αὐτοχόωνον
ὃν πρὶν μὲν ῥίπτασκε μέγα σθένος Ἠετίωνος:
ἀλλ' ἤτοι τὸν ἔπεφνε ποδάρκης δῖος Ἀχιλλεύς,
τὸν δ' ἄγετ' ἐν νήεσσι σὺν ἄλλοισι κτεάτεσσι.
στῆ δ' ὀρθὸς καὶ μῦθον ἐν Ἀργείοισιν ἔειπεν:
'ὄρνυσθ' οἳ καὶ τούτου ἀέθλου πειρήσεσθε.
εἴ οἱ καὶ μάλα πολλὸν ἀπόπροθι πίονες ἀγροί,
ἕξει μιν καὶ πέντε περιπλομένους ἐνιαυτοὺς
χρεώμενος: οὐ μὲν γάρ οἱ ἀτεμβόμενός γε σιδήρου
ποιμὴν οὐδ' ἀροτὴρ εἶσ' ἐς πόλιν, ἀλλὰ παρέξει.

Iliad 23.826–835

Now the son of Peleus set in place a lump of pig-iron
which had once been the throwing-weight of Eetion in his great
     strength:
but now swift-footed brilliant Achilleus had slain him and taken
the weight away in the ships along with the other possessions.
He stood upright and spoke his word out among the Argives:
"Rise up, you who would endeavour to win this prize also.
For although the rich demesnes of him who wins it lie far off

> indeed, yet for the succession of five years he will have it
> to use; for his shepherd for want of iron will not have to go in
> to the city for it, nor his ploughman either. This will supply them."[23]

Sherratt assesses the passage as follows:

> We have here what seems to be a rather odd situation. A lump of
> unworked iron ... has been regarded as a prized possession for a long
> time, first as the favourite throwing-weight of a king and hero, then
> as something worth taking as a spoil of war, then as worth having as a
> prestigious prize. Yet it is suddenly—almost as an afterthought—recog-
> nized as having its prime desirability in a potential for utilitarian use,
> as a source of agricultural and pastoral tools.   (Sherratt 1990:810)

In the Bronze Age, iron was an exotic luxury, minimally worked, valuable simply
for being a precious metal. But after the Bronze Age, blades appear, and then
daggers and swords. Sherratt concludes:

> the first part of the passage in *Iliad* xxiii concerning the prize would
> seem to accord best with an attitude to iron which prevailed between
> the 16th and 12th centuries, while the second part belongs to a time
> from c. 1000 on when iron tools were regularly produced in Greece.
> (Sherratt 1990:811)

Shields are another item of material culture catalogued by Sherratt as
evidence for the long range of time in which the *Iliad* must have been being
composed. I quote Sherratt again:

> Aias' shield [is] an extraordinary affair which, as Aias enters the battle
> in *Iliad* vii.219, is described as tower-like (*eüte purgon*). It is made of seven
> layers of oxhide to which an eighth layer of bronze has been added,
> apparently as an afterthought (vii.223). As if this were not enough, this
> shield, a few lines further on in the thick of the fight, suddenly acquires
> a boss (*messon epomphalion*: vii.267) which has no part in the original
> description. Hector too has a very odd shield, at one point described
> as extending from his neck to his ankles (*Iliad* vi.117) and at another as
> completely circular (vii.250). That is a shield worth trying to imagine!
> (Sherratt 1990:810)

Sherratt points out that tower-like rectangular or figure-of-eight shields are
known from the early Mycenaean period, but they became redundant once

---

[23]   Translation is that of Lattimore (1951), as quoted by Sherratt (1990).

bronze body armor was introduced in the fourteenth century. It is only at the very end of the thirteenth century, in the period Sherratt terms "post-palatial," that smaller hand-held shields (which could include a boss) are found in archaeological contexts (Sherratt 1990:811–812).

Sherratt's analysis of the conflation of several historical eras in the *Iliad*'s representation of items of material culture demonstrates that in most cases it is not possible to isolate Bronze Age artifacts and conceptions of how to use them from those of later eras. The *realia* of multiple time periods have entered the formulaic diction of the system, with the result that they are all inextricably bound up in and interdependent on one another. Achilles' long "Pelian ash" thrusting spear may well be, like the boar's tusk helmet of *Iliad* 10, an heirloom handed down from an earlier generation, as the archaeological evidence would suggest (see Plate 4), but it can also be thrown at Aeneas like the throwing spears found only in post-palatial contexts (Sherratt 1990:811). Such differing conceptions of how items of material culture function reflect the poem's very long history, with composition in performance taking place over many centuries, in a poetic tradition that would seem to stretch back at least as far as the sixteenth century BCE.

Narrative Layers: How Old Is the Story of the *Iliad*?

The work of Sherratt suggests that epic poetry featuring warriors and weapons was being composed at least as early as the sixteenth century BCE, but were the songs of the Mycenaeans anything like our *Iliad*? I will adduce two different types of evidence, visual and linguistic, that support the idea that the basic narrative structure of not only the Trojan War myth but even of the *Iliad* itself came into existence well before the end of the Bronze Age.[24]

The *Iliad* is an epic poem about a sequence of events that take places in the tenth year of the Trojan War, a war in which Greeks under the leadership of a Mycenaean leader attack and besiege a well-walled city in the Troad. Just such a tale may well be represented in Bronze Age art. Sarah Morris (1989) argued that the frescoes that survive in the so-called West House at the site of Akrotiri on the island of Thera represent a Trojan War–like narrative tradition that very likely would have found expression in verbal art of the time as

---

[24] For some other examples beyond what I discuss here of (Hittite) Bronze Age material seemingly preserved within the Greek epic poetry and myth associated with Troy, see Bachvarova 2016:351–356. She highlights in particular the names Paris and Priam and the close relationship between Apollo (~Apallu) and Troy. Bachvarova, however, sees this material as having entered into the Greek tradition via Near Eastern contact in the early Iron Age, and not as evidence for the antiquity of the *Iliad* or Greek epic poetry about Troy.

well. The frescoes, which date to the seventeenth century BCE,[25] form a border along the upper walls of room 5 of the West House. The east and west segments feature Nilotic landscape scenes with fantastical creatures, including a griffin. The precise subject of the south segment is much debated, but it can generally be described as depicting ships crossing the sea between two towns, one larger than the other. The ships are festively decorated and seemingly peaceful (though they certainly convey warriors, with their boar's tusk helmets hung up on pegs), and people watch them come and go from the walls of each town (see Plate 5). The north wall segment (see Plate 6), however, clearly depicts Mycenaean warriors with oxhide shields and boar's tusk helmets attacking a walled city on a rocky coastline not unlike that of the nearby Anatolian peninsula. An attack from the sea seems to be taking place at the same time, with dead or drowning men depicted in the water near some arriving ships.

Morris interprets the miniature frescoes in the light of other surviving artifacts from the Bronze Age that juxtapose peace and war. She argues that the juxtaposition is an ancient theme that found expression in both the visual and the verbal art of the Bonze Age: "Its images are cognates of epic motifs, without being illustrations of particular episodes. ... The rich repertoire of visual formulae and motifs mirror their proliferation not only in other visual arts but in poetic narratives now believed to be in circulation in the early Mycenaean age" (Morris 1989:515). The city at peace and the city at war featured on the shield of Achilles forged by Hephaistos in *Iliad* 18 may be a verbal attestation of this ancient visual theme, but so too are the many Homeric similes that invoke peaceful activities in the midst of battle and the former peace of Troy (τὸ πρὶν ἐπ' εἰρήνης, *Iliad* 9.403), recalled at several key moments in the *Iliad* (Morris 1989:527–529).

Although Morris does not argue that particular Homeric episodes are being represented in the Theran frescoes (the walled city being attacked need not be Troy, for example), she nevertheless finds remarkable correspondences between the surviving Homeric epics and the stories seemingly depicted in the frescoes. The cities at peace on the south wall show, in Morris's reading, a successful return home from a military expedition. Could the fresco be a visual counterpart to a *nostos*-style song of return like the *Odyssey*? As Morris notes, the harbor towns in this fresco "belong to the world of Aegean topography but also recall the poetic description of that world in Homer," such as the harbors of Ithaca, the land of the Laestrygonians, Aiaia, and Scheria (Morris 1989:518–519). At the very least, the helmets hung up in every boat suggest a successful

---

[25] Bronze Age chronology and the dating of the volcanic eruption that destroyed the island of Thera have long been controversial, but scientific evidence suggests that the eruption took place between 1627 and 1600 BCE (Manning, Ramsey, et al. 2006).

return from a military expedition. Of course, in our *Odyssey*, Odysseus is the only one of his men to return home, after he has lost every one of his ships. But the Theran fresco may tell a tale of homecoming in which many soldiers make it back safely. Morris points to Herakles' expedition against Troy with 6 ships (alluded to in *Iliad* 7.451–453, 20.145–148, 21.442–457) as being of a scale on par with this fresco.[26]

The north wall features the "complementary theme of war" (Morris 1989:522), and parallels with the Iliadic tradition may be found here in virtually all surviving scenes of the combined land and sea attack depicted.[27] A scene that has been previously interpreted to be a ritual gathering at a peak sanctuary may instead be a council of elders and allies who debate what to do about the invading army (or alternatively, an embassy between the attackers and the city leaders). Several mounds and hills are featured as gathering places for the Trojans and their allies in the *Iliad* (e.g. the tomb of Ilos at *Iliad* 10.414–416). People watch the battle from the city walls, as in, for example, *Iliad* 3. The epic theme of the cattle raid (such as that narrated by Nestor in *Iliad* 11.669–684) may be featured in the top right of the surviving portion of the fresco.[28] Warriors with oxhide-covered tower shields, boar's tusk helmets, and long thrusting spears march toward seemingly unsuspecting shepherds, while nearby women carry water in jugs on their heads. Similar episodes of ambush on unsuspecting shepherds are alluded to repeatedly in the *Iliad*; examples include Achilles' ambushes of Andromache's brothers (6.423–424), of Antiphos and Isos (two sons of Priam, 11.101–106), and of Aeneas (20.90–92). The wall depicted in the lower right may be just such a wall as the Achaeans are said to have built upon landing at Troy to protect their ships.[29] Similar collocations of land and sea attack (together with a cattle raid) can be found elsewhere in Bronze Age art, including on a stone rhyton from Epidaurus and a silver rhyton from Mycenae.[30] Close parallels with the fresco can also be seen in the depiction of the city under siege (i.e., the city at war) on the shield of Achilles

---

[26] See also Morris' follow-up article (2000) as well as the work of Shaw (2000), who also interprets the miniature frescoes as a narrative involving departure, voyage, and homecoming, as I do here. For other explanations of what is depicted on the south wall, see Morgan 1988:143–165, Immerwahr 1990:74, Doumas 1992:45–97, and Nagy 2013:633–635 and 2015a.

[27] For still further parallels with the epic tradition besides those adduced here, see Thomas and Conant 2007:44–51.

[28] On the cattle raid as a traditional epic theme see (in addition to Morris 1989:527–528) Martin 2000 and Dué and Ebbott 2010:80–84.

[29] This wall (the ones the Achaeans are said to have built upon landing at Troy) is mentioned in Thucydides (1.11.1) and Herodotus (2.118), and has been the source of much confusion and scholarly debate, especially as it relates to the Achaean wall built in *Iliad* 7. See, eg., Leaf 1900:297, Scodel 1982, Boyd 1995, Porter 2006, and Pache 2014, together with Morris 1989:524–526.

[30] See Morris 1989:523–529 with further references *ad loc.*

(*Iliad* 18.509–540). As Morris concludes: "We can identify half a dozen thematic groups—arrival and departure by sea, council and battle, ambush and defense, the peaceful outskirts of a city, warriors landing and soldiers drowning—that correspond to epic traditions" (Morris 1989: 530).

I would add to Morris's analysis that the thematic pairing of going out on a military expedition (as featured on the north wall; see Plate 6)—be it an attack on a foreign city, an ambush, or a cattle raid—and the successful return (as featured on the south wall) is deeply embedded in the poetics of Homeric epic.[31] Mary Ebbott and I have explored in depth the ancient theme of ambush in Homeric epic, and we have argued (see especially Dué and Ebbott 2010:76–79 and 276–278) that the success or failure of an ambush is expressed in terms of whether the participants return home. Ambush episodes share thematic language and details with the theme of the journey, especially the *nostos*, or journey of homecoming. Spying missions or ambushes were conceived of as having the overall structure of a journey, and the two themes share the particular spatial movements of going out and, more importantly, coming home. If spies do not return, they cannot share the crucial information they were sent to obtain. Moreover, because of the stealth involved, if the warriors on an ambush die, their loved ones may not know where they died or be able to recover their bodies. We see this concern expressed similarly in connection with deaths that happen during a journey. For example, Telemakhos says that if his father had died at Troy, he would have had a proper burial and the *kleos* of a warrior, but since he apparently died before reaching home, he is without *kleos* (*Odyssey* 1.234–243). In *Iliad* 10, the other Achaeans anxiously await the homecoming of Diomedes and Odysseus, reflecting both the necessity of the return and the danger involved in such missions (*Iliad* 10.536–539). When they do arrive, they are greeted in the same language used elsewhere in the epics for welcoming those who have just completed a journey (*Iliad* 10.542). In contrast, when Dolon leaves the Trojan camp, the narrator says that he will not bring the information back to Hektor that he is being sent to gather; since he will not come back, we know immediately that his mission will not be a success (*Iliad* 10.336–337).

The similarities between homecoming journeys and ambush-themed missions are revealed in several places. When Priam is about to set out on a nighttime infiltration into the enemy camp in *Iliad* 24, Hecuba asks him to pray to Zeus for his arrival back home (τῇ σπεῖσον Διὶ πατρί, καὶ εὔχεο οἴκαδ' ἱκέσθαι / ἂψ ἐκ δυσμενέων ἀνδρῶν, *Iliad* 24.287–288). The failure of an ambush, even in

---

[31] Cf. Shaw 2000:272: "In interpreting the arrival of the ships as a return to their base—as I do here—it is important to recall the major role *nostos* played in early Greek literature involving war and naval expeditions."

very compressed versions of ambush narratives, is expressed in terms of a failed return home. For example, in the ambush of Tydeus by fifty Thebans, we hear that "he killed them all, and released only one to return home" (πάντας ἔπεφν’, ἕνα δ’ οἶον ἵει οἶκον δὲ νέεσθαι, *Iliad* 4.397). Similarly, in the failed attempt to ambush Bellerophon, the ambushers never return home (κρίνας ἐκ Λυκίης εὐρείης φῶτας ἀρίστους / εἶσε λόχον· τοὶ δ’ οὔ τι πάλιν οἶκον δὲ νέοντο· / πάντας γὰρ κατέπεφνεν ἀμύμων Βελλεροφόντης, *Iliad* 6.188–190). So, when Diomedes is looking for a partner for the nocturnal spying mission in *Iliad* 10, he chooses Odysseus for the qualities that make him a good ambusher, especially his ability to get home:

> τοῖς δ’ αὖτις μετέειπε βοὴν ἀγαθὸς Διομήδης·
> εἰ μὲν δὴ ἕταρόν γε κελεύετέ μ’ αὐτὸν ἑλέσθαι,
> πῶς ἂν ἔπειτ’ Ὀδυσῆος ἐγὼ θείοιο λαθοίμην,
> οὗ περὶ μὲν πρόφρων κραδίη καὶ θυμὸς ἀγήνωρ
> ἐν πάντεσσι πόνοισι, φιλεῖ δέ ἑ Παλλὰς Ἀθήνη.
> τούτου γ’ ἑσπομένοιο καὶ ἐκ πυρὸς αἰθομένοιο
> ἄμφω νοστήσαιμεν, ἐπεὶ περίοιδε νοῆσαι.

Iliad 10.241–247

Among them in turn Diomedes well-known for his
    battle-cry spoke,
"If you are ordering me to choose a companion myself,
how could I overlook god-like Odysseus,
whose heart and audacious spirit are especially ready
for every kind of labor, and Pallas Athena loves him?
With him accompanying me even from burning fire
we could return home [*nostos*], since he is an expert at devising
    [*noos*]."

Athena, the goddess who loves both Odysseus and Diomedes, tells Diomedes during the ambush to remember his homecoming (νόστου δὴ μνῆσαι μεγαθύμου Τυδέος υἱέ, *Iliad* 10.509). Only that way can the mission be a success.[32]

The mission may also be something other than an ambush or raid, however. When Patroklos commences his fatal impersonation of Achilles in *Iliad* 16, Achilles prays to Zeus that Patroklos will be able to push the Trojans back from the Greek ships in face-to-face combat and return unscathed (ἀσκηθής, 16.247). Zeus grants only part of the prayer, however:

---

[32] Conversely, in the *Odyssey*, Odysseus' men nearly forget about their *nostos* in the land of the Lotus Eaters (νόστου τε λαθέσθαι, 9.97), and it is only Odysseus' intervention by force that allows the men to make it back from that particular mission.

τῷ δ' ἕτερον μὲν ἔδωκε πατήρ, ἕτερον δ' ἀνένευσε:
νηῶν μέν οἱ ἀπώσασθαι πόλεμόν τε μάχην τε
δῶκε, σόον δ' ἀνένευσε μάχης ἐξαπονέεσθαι.

Iliad 16.250–252

The father granted the one [part of his prayer] to him, but denied the
   other:
To push away war and battle from the ships
he granted, but he denied his safe return [*nostos*] from battle.

Patroklos' failure to return home is emphasized in the lamentation that arises
following his death:

αὐτὰρ Ἀχαιοὶ
ἀσπασίως Πάτροκλον ὑπ' ἐκ βελέων ἐρύσαντες
κάτθεσαν ἐν λεχέεσσι: φίλοι δ' ἀμφέσταν ἑταῖροι
μυρόμενοι: μετὰ δέ σφι ποδώκης εἵπετ' Ἀχιλλεὺς
δάκρυα θερμὰ χέων, ἐπεὶ εἴσιδε πιστὸν ἑταῖρον
κείμενον ἐν φέρτρῳ δεδαϊγμένον ὀξέϊ χαλκῷ,
τόν ῥ' ἤτοι μὲν ἔπεμπε σὺν ἵπποισιν καὶ ὄχεσφιν
ἐς πόλεμον, οὐδ' αὖτις ἐδέξατο νοστήσαντα.

Iliad 18.231–238

But the Achaeans
gladly drew Patroklos out from under the arrows
and laid him on a litter. His dear comrades stood around him,
mourning. And among them swift-footed Achilles spoke
shedding hot tears when he saw his trusted comrade
lying on a bier torn by sharp bronze,
(his comrade) whom he sent with horses and chariot
to war, but he never received him back home again.

This same language is used of Achilles himself, who is lamented by his mother
immediately upon Patroklos' death, so closely are the two deaths intertwined:

τὸν μὲν ἐγὼ θρέψασα φυτὸν ὣς γουνῷ ἀλωῆς
νηυσὶν ἐπιπροέηκα κορωνίσιν Ἴλιον εἴσω
Τρωσὶ μαχησόμενον: τὸν δ' οὐχ ὑποδέξομαι αὖτις
οἴκαδε νοστήσαντα δόμον Πηλήϊον εἴσω.

Iliad 18.57–60

After nourishing him like a plant on the hill of an orchard
I sent him forth in the hollow ships to Ilion

to fight with the Trojans. But I will not receive him again
returning back home to the house of Peleus.

These words are echoed by Achilles a few lines later, when he tells Thetis that
he will re-enter battle:

νῦν δ' ἵνα καὶ σοὶ πένθος ἐνὶ φρεσὶ μυρίον εἴη
παιδὸς ἀποφθιμένοιο, τὸν οὐχ ὑποδέξεαι αὖτις
οἴκαδε νοστήσαντ', ἐπεὶ οὐδ' ἐμὲ θυμὸς ἄνωγε
ζώειν οὐδ' ἄνδρεσσι μετέμμεναι, αἴ κε μὴ Ἕκτωρ
πρῶτος ἐμῷ ὑπὸ δουρὶ τυπεὶς ἀπὸ θυμὸν ὀλέσσῃ,
Πατρόκλοιο δ' ἕλωρα Μενοιτιάδεω ἀποτίσῃ.

Iliad 18.88–93

But as it is [it seems that it was all done] in order that there be infi-
nite grief in your heart
for your child who has perished, the one who you may not receive
again
returning back home, since my spirit won't allow me
to live nor go among men unless Hektor
first struck by my spear loses his life,
and pays me for despoiling Patroklos, the son of Menoitios.

Like Patroklos, when Achilles re-enters battle in *Iliad* 20 it is on a mission from
which he will never return home.

Coming back unscathed, ἀσκηθής, is used elsewhere in Homeric epic in
connection with both a return from spying/ambush (*Iliad* 10.212) and a return
home upon completion of a journey. It is used prominently in *Odyssey* 5 of the
need to have both Telemakhos (*Odyssey* 5.26) and Odysseus (*Odyssey* 5.144, 5.168)
return to their fatherland (πατρίδα γαῖαν). At the very beginning of the story of
his wanderings, Odysseus says that he would have returned home unscathed if
the sea currents had not prevented him from making his way to Ithaka (*Odyssey*
9.79–81). As Mary Ebbott and I have argued, arriving unscathed seems especially associated with sailing journeys (Dué and Ebbott 2010:278), as Odysseus
also uses it in one of his Cretan lies, in this case for an easy sailing from Crete
to Egypt (*Odyssey* 14.255).[33] In one additional case in the *Odyssey*, Odysseus tells
Achilles in the underworld that Neoptolemos was very successful in battle and
ambush, and later adds that he was never hurt in the fighting—he was ἀσκηθής
(11.535), never touched by a weapon. Although the context has referred to both

---

[33] Cf. Solon fr. 19 (West), who says that Kypris sent him home unscathed (ἀσκηθῆ) in a fast ship for
a good homecoming (*nostos*) to his own land.

battle and ambush, the word is used to describe Neoptolemos as he boards his ship for the journey home, again displaying its deeply embedded connection to both sailing journeys and *nostos* in the formulaic language of epic.

Do the frescoes of the West House on Thera tell a story featuring a surprise military attack on a walled town together with the all-important safe return of the warriors? If Morris's thesis is correct and the miniature frescoes of the West House really do depict an epic-like narrative, they would be among the oldest-known attestations of narrative in visual art. Moreover, the frescoes would seem to be the creation of Minoan (or Minoan-influenced) craftsmen on the Cycladic island of Thera telling a Mycenaean Greek story (or at least a story featuring Mycenaean Greeks).[34] How are we to understand the relationship between the epic story-telling traditions of the Mycenaean Greeks on the mainland and the artists of Thera at this early date? Morris is perhaps then rightly cautious about asserting specific correspondences to the story of the *Iliad* or the *Odyssey* in the Theran frescoes. Instead she posits that they are evidence for the existence at the time of Thera's destruction of a poetic tradition with formulaic and thematic parallels to surviving Greek epic, a precursor tradition to that in which the *Iliad* and the *Odyssey* were ultimately formed (Morris 1989:530–531).[35] She follows Gregory Nagy (1979/1999:140), Emily Vermeule (1983:142), and others in suggesting that such a poetic tradition (and indeed that of the Trojan War/*Iliad*) may have been inspired ultimately by the activities of the Mycenaeans on the west coast of Anatolia over multiple centuries, as attested in Hittite archives and the material record of the Bronze Age (Morris 1989:531–535).

But there is other evidence to suggest that the deep structure of the *Iliad* is as old or nearly as old as the Theran frescoes. The main story of the *Iliad* as it has been handed down to us is not the taking of Helen, the Trojan War as a whole, or the sack of Troy, but rather Achilles' cosmic wrath in the tenth year of the war, his withdrawal from battle, the devastating consequences, and his ultimate return to battle with knowledge of his own imminent death. The devastating consequences of Achilles' wrath and withdrawal include something he never expected (17.401–411, 19.328–30), the death of his closest comrade, Patroklos, at the hands of Hektor. Building on the work of Whitman (1958), Van Brock (1959), and others, Gregory Nagy has shown that Patroklos is Achilles' *therapōn*, a word which conveys a relationship of ritual substitution (see especially Nagy

---

[34] For the reverse concept—that is, Mycenaean Greeks telling Minoan stories—see Nagy 2015c with further references *ad loc.*

[35] Cf. Betancourt 2007:122: "The scenes are certainly specific enough to suggest that this is a narrative, and those familiar with the story could probably have identified individual ships with known captains and familiar crew members.... Pictorial cycles like this one can best succeed if they are supported by some type of oral or written narratives, like epic poetry."

1979/1999:94–117 and 289–295). This relationship becomes fulfilled when Patroklos leads the Myrmidons into battle in place of Achilles, wearing Achilles' armor. Patroklos' subsequent death, the lamentation for him, and his funeral preview those of Achilles.[36] Achilles' death does not take place within the narrative confines of the *Iliad* itself, but it is nonetheless enacted in the sacrificial death of Patroklos.

The deaths of Patroklos at the hands of Hektor, of Hektor at the hands of Achilles, and of Achilles at the hands of Paris are fundamentally interconnected in the *Iliad*. Achilles' death is prophesied by various characters and foreshadowed repeatedly after the death of Patroklos, including by his mother, Thetis, who tells Achilles at *Iliad* 18.96: "Your own death awaits you straightaway after that of Hektor" (αὐτίκα γάρ τοι ἔπειτα μεθ᾽ Ἑκτορα πότμος ἑτοῖμος). With his dying breath Patroklos foretells the death of Hektor, who in turn with his dying breath foretells the death of Achilles. This interconnectedness is made manifest in the exchange of armor that takes place among these three characters (Whitman 1958:199–203). Patroklos goes into battle wearing Achilles' famous divinely crafted armor in order that he be mistaken for Achilles, Hektor strips Patroklos of this armor upon killing him and puts it on himself, whereupon Achilles must get a new set of divinely made armor, in which he confronts Hektor, who is still wearing his old set. Each of these characters then becomes an embodiment of Achilles; in killing Patroklos, Hektor arguably kills Achilles as well, and in killing Hektor, Achilles kills himself.

It was at one time common in Homeric scholarship to view this sophisticated structure as the finishing touch of the final poet in the tradition, that is, of "Homer," and indeed the character of Patroklos has been interpreted by scholars who conceive of Homer in this way as being the creation of the master poet.[37] It was a central tenet of my 2002 book that such arguments are fundamentally flawed; they misunderstand the way composition in performance within a traditional system operates, and wrongly equate oral methods of composition with simplicity and a lack of both creativity and planning (see especially Dué 2002:83–89). But even setting aside such conceptual arguments about the nature of Homeric composition and the way that tradition operates, there is evidence to suggest that Patroklos' story, especially as it intertwines with Hektor's, is—rather than being the final touch of a master poet at the end of the tradition—in fact incredibly ancient.

---

[36] See also Burgess 2009:72–97 and *passim*. On the interrelationships between Hektor, Patroklos, and Achilles see especially Nagy 1979 and 1997, as well as Whitman 1958:199–203, Sinos 1980, and Lowenstam 1981.

[37] On Patroklos as an invented character, see Howald 1924:411–12 as well as Dihle 1970:159–160 and bibliography *ad loc.* More recent discussions include Allan 2005 and Burgess 1997 and 2006.

The interconnectedness of the deaths of Patroklos and Hektor is reflected in the formulaic language used to tell their story. The same set of three verses marks the passing of each warrior:

Ὣς ἄρα μιν εἰπόντα τέλος θανάτοιο κάλυψε·
ψυχὴ δ᾽ ἐκ ῥεθέων πταμένη Ἄϊδος δὲ βεβήκει
ὃν πότμον γοόωσα λιποῦσ᾽ ἀνδροτῆτα καὶ ἥβην.

Iliad 16.855–857 *and* 22.361–363

When he had thus spoken the finality of death covered him;
His life-breath left his body and flitted down to the house of Hades,
lamenting its sad fate and leaving behind the youth and vigor of its
manhood.[38]

The meter of lines 16.857/22.363 provides an indication of the great antiquity of the verse:

‒ ‒ | ‒ ᴗᴗ|‒ ᴗ ᴗ| ‒ ᴗ ᴗ|‒ ᴗ ᴗ|‒ ‒
ὃν πότμον γοόωσα λιποῦσ᾽ ἀνδροτῆτα καὶ ἥβην.

The first syllable of the word ἀνδροτῆτα ('manhood') must be scanned short, something which is possible only if we assume the verse to have been composed before the linguistic changes that resulted in *anr̥tāta* becoming ἀνδροτῆτα (cf. ἀνδρειπότες at *Iliad* 2.651, where the ἀνδρ- must similarly be scanned short).[39] I quote Calvert Watkins's succinct explanation of the significance here: "Since we know that the change r̥ > or/ro (other dialects ar/ra) had taken place in Greek by the time of the Linear B tablets … the lines with *anr̥tāta* could not have been composed any later than 1400 BC or so. They furnish us with a *terminus ante quem* for the fixation of the formulaic vehicle of a key feature of the thematic structure of the *Iliad*: these two deaths in equipoise."[40]

---

[38]   The translation is based loosely on that of Samuel Butler.

[39]   See Watkins 1995:499 citing Wackernagel 1953:1116n1 and 1170n1 (originally published in 1909), Leumann 1950:221n16, and West 1982:15.

[40]   Watkins 1995:499, citing Ruijgh 1967:69, Wathelet 1970:171ff., Watkins 1987, and West 1988:156–157. Recently Timothy Barnes (2011:10) has argued against this interpretation of the history of the formula, arguing instead for *ἀμ(β)ροτῆτα καὶ ἥβην* "as the model upon which the attested ἀνδροτῆτα καὶ ἥβην was coined, at a relatively recent date, by a poet aiming at an impressive line to close an important scene: the death of Achilles." (Barnes reconstructs this formula, not attested in surviving Homeric epic poetry, on the basis of an Avestan counterpart.) One of Barnes's primary objections to viewing ἀνδροτῆτα καὶ ἥβην as a vestige of Mycenaean hexameter poetry is the implications for our understanding of the composition and history of the *Iliad*. I do not share Barnes's objections and fully embrace the implications. *Contra* Barnes (2011:1–2), I assert the continuity of the Iliadic tradition over more than seven hundred years. The song persisted precisely because it was traditional, while simultaneously flexible, multiform, and ever evolving. These concepts will be explored in more detail in the ensuing chapters.

In sum, two very different kinds of evidence, the frescoes of ancient Akrotiri and linguistic evidence embedded within the formulaic diction of the *Iliad*, suggest that a song tradition similar to our *Iliad* may have existed before the end of the Bronze Age, quite possibly even hundreds of years before. It is not possible to fully reconstruct such an Iliad, nor should we expect that any song performed at this time was fixed and unchanging. Surviving evidence indicates that not only were there numerous competing epics in circulation during the Bronze Age (the epic traditions that eventually resulted in the poems of the Epic Cycle), but very likely there were competing variations on the *Iliad* being composed and performed in different geographical locations.[41] In the introduction I noted the evolutionary models of Nagy and Sherratt, both of whom view the early phases of the *Iliad* and *Odyssey* traditions as being creative and generative, which is to say multiform. The Late Bronze Age would have been an extremely generative period of time for the creation of epic poetry, to use Sherratt's terminology,[42] and, as we will see, it falls fully within period 1 of Nagy's evolutionary model, the period he deems "relatively most fluid."

I propose now to turn to the textual transmission of the poems. As we will see, the earliest textual witnesses of the *Iliad* and the *Odyssey* that have survived, the fragmentary papyri from Egypt (discussed further below), postdate this fluid tradition I have been discussing by nearly a thousand years, but nevertheless contain a great deal of variation that points to a creative and dynamic early history of the poems.

Performance and the Earliest Texts of the *Iliad* and the *Odyssey*

Lack of evidence prevents us from knowing a great deal about the transmission of epic poetry from the end of the Bronze Age through the so-called Dark Ages and into the Archaic period, but once again the poems themselves provide some clues. The song traditions of the Bronze Age continued—which is to say, the system in which epic poetry was created continued to evolve—even as the occasions and circumstances of performance changed. Sherratt views this time period as being one of "active generation and recreation of inherited tradition

---

[41] On the antiquity of the poetic traditions that resulted in the poems we now know as the Epic Cycle (which survive only in fragments and the testimony of ancient witnesses), see especially Burgess 2001 and 2009. For more on the concept of competing Iliads—which is to say, competing epic versions of the mythological story of Achilles' wrath told in our *Iliad*, see Dué 2002:21–36.

[42] Sherratt makes a distinction between the pre-palatial and early palatial periods, which she considers periods of active creation, and the palatial period, which she describes as being one of "active maintenance of inherited tradition with little modification," for which see her arguments at Sherratt 1990:817–819.

in several regions, leaving original remnants" (1990:817). And indeed the material and cultural world of the Iron Age is featured throughout both epics. Iron Age elements identified by Sherratt and others in the poems include the use of cremation for burial, armor (including slashing swords, horned helmets, double throwing spears, and bossed shields), fighting tactics, the use of iron for everyday objects, and architecture (Sherratt 1990:819). The maritime activities described in the stories told by Odysseus and others (which feature raiding, sacking of cities for plunder, slave-taking, and overseas trade) have also been seen to be reflections of an era of colonization and an Iron Age world.[43]

The adaptation of the Phoenician alphabet for the writing down of Greek and the advent of literacy in the Archaic period probably did not have a large impact on the oral poetic tradition and people's reception of it for several centuries, although this is of course a subject of debate among scholars.[44] In Archaic and Classical Greece, the primary access to the *Iliad* and the *Odyssey* for most people would have been in the performances of professional rhapsodes (González 2013 and forthcoming [c]). What "texts" were these rhapsodes performing? And how do their performances relate to the texts we now have? Both Sherratt and Nagy attribute the fixation of the *Iliad* and the *Odyssey* and the loss of multiformity to performance, not the existence of written versions. When the primary venue for the transmission of Homeric poetry came to be the highly regulated competitive performances of the epics, first in regional festivals such as the Panionia and then at Panhellenic festivals, the *Iliad* and the *Odyssey* became "possessions," which is to say, static and unchanging: "The emphasis had shifted from statement to possession. From now on the creative function of the bard (*aoidos*) gave way to the relaying rôle of the rhapsode."[45]

This process took many centuries, however, and multiformity persisted long after the time most scholars generally begin to think of the *Iliad* and the

---

[43]   On the Iron Age reflections in the Homerics epics see Finley 1954, Sherratt 1990:819–820, Morris 1997, Dougherty 2001, Whitley (forthcoming), and Antonaccio (forthcoming).

[44]   See Powell 1991 and 1997a for the view that the Greek alphabet was adapted for the purposes of writing down the Homeric epics. The problem with Powell's thesis, as noted for example by Nagy in his exchange with Powell in the *Bryn Mawr Classical Review* (97.4.18), is that: "Turning an 'oral poem' into a text does not by itself stop the oral tradition that created the 'oral poem.' The oral traditions of composition-in-performance can be independent of a writing technology that turns compositions into texts. This fundamental thesis is evident throughout Albert Lord's last book, *The Singer Resumes the Tale* (1995, especially chapters 1, 8 and 10). It is supported by a wealth of comparative evidence drawn by various scholars from various historical contexts, some of which are adduced in *PP* [= Nagy 1996a]." On Homer and the alphabet see also González (forthcoming [b]).

[45]   Sherratt 1990:821. For the role of performance at festivals in this process see Ebbott (forthcoming) and Nagy (forthcoming). For the Panionia's role in the shaping of the Homeric epics as we now have them see Frame 2009:551–620, §4.20–4.71.

Odyssey as fixed texts.[46] In its most basic form (as outlined in Nagy 2009:4–5) the stages of Nagy's evolutionary model for the text fixation of the *Iliad* and the *Odyssey* are as follows:[47]

> Period 1 of Homer was the relatively most fluid period, with no written texts, extending from the early second millennium BCE to the middle of the eighth century in the first millennium BCE. When I say that this is a most fluid period, I mean that epic was most susceptible to change in this period of its evolution.

> Period 2 of Homer was a more formative, or Panhellenic, period, still without written texts, extending from the middle of the eighth century BCE to the middle of the sixth.

> Period 3 of Homer was a definitive period, centralized in Athens, with potential texts in the sense of transcripts, extending from the middle of the sixth century BCE to the later part of the fourth. Somewhere near the start of this period, there was a reform of Homeric performance traditions in Athens.

> Period 4 of Homer was a standardizing period, with texts in the sense of transcripts or even scripts, extending from the later part of the fourth century BCE to the middle of the second. Somewhere near the start of this period, there was another reform of Homeric performance traditions in Athens.

> Period 5 of Homer was the relatively most rigid period, with texts as scripture, from the middle of the second century BCE onward. This period starts with the completion of the editorial work of Aristarchus of Samothrace on the Homeric texts, not long after 150 BCE or so.

Nagy posits that the Panathenaic festival in Athens, where strictly regulated contests in the performance of Homeric poetry were taking place as early as the sixth century BCE, was the context within which the *Iliad* and the *Odyssey* became crystallized into a relatively fixed form.[48] The resulting "Panathenaic" texts may

---

[46] Scholars differ in their dating of the text fixation, depending on how they conceptualize "Homer." Some imagine a dictating Homer as early as 800 BCE, and others date the text considerably later. The editors of the Homer Multitext, following Nagy's arguments discussed here, understand the process to have been a gradual one. On the concept of a dictating Homer see also Dué 2006b, González 2013:15–70, Ready 2015, and below, note 52.

[47] See also the introduction, pp. 11–12.

[48] On the "Panathenaic bottleneck" see especially Nagy 2001 and 2002:3–35. See also Seaford 1994:151–153. The term "crystallization" is Nagy's, but others have employed the metaphor as well; see, e.g., Sherratt 1990:820 and Cook 1995:5.

have remained in flux for some time, influenced by a variety of factors, including political pressure from those in power (Frame 2009). The tyrant Peisistratos, for example, who is credited with the reorganization of the Panathenaia in 566 BCE and possibly the institution of rhapsodic contests,[49] is cited by several ancient sources as the organizer of a so-called Peisistratean recension, which produced the first written and authoritative text of the Homeric poems.[50] The story has a close affinity with tales in other cultures about how an oral tradition came to be authoritatively fixed in writing (Nagy 1996b:70–75). Nevertheless, there may be a clue here as to how the first written texts of the *Iliad* and the *Odyssey* were commissioned. The other epics that are known to have circulated in antiquity, often referred to collectively as the Epic Cycle, were not performed at the Panathenaia and have not survived in written form.[51]

In any case, at some point during the Archaic or Early Classical period in Athens, texts of the *Iliad* and the *Odyssey* began to be produced.[52] However this was done, it must have required great cost and Herculean effort, since writing would have been a new technology, the materials needed would have been expensive and difficult to acquire, literacy would have been restricted to an elite minority, and the performers would have been unaccustomed to slowing down their composition to meet the needs of a scribe. Milman Parry and Albert Lord faced many of these same obstacles when they attempted to capture in writing the performances of bards in the South Slavic epic song tradition during their fieldwork in Yugoslavia in the 1930s. Whatever texts were produced at this time were copied, and copied again and again for centuries. I have suggested above that a "Panathenaic text" may be the exemplar upon which the written texts of Classical antiquity were based. But our evidence suggests strongly that no single exemplar has reached us from Classical Athens, and there may have been many

---

[49]   The ancient evidence comes from the pseudo-Platonic dialogue *Hipparchus* 228–229.

[50]   See *Anecdota Graeca* 1.6 and Cicero, *De oratore* 3.137. For a parallel myth concerning the reassembly of the Homeric poems by Lycurgus, lawgiver of Sparta, see Plutarch, *Life of Lycurgus* 4.4. For more on the myth of the Peisistratean recension see Nagy 1996b:73–75.

[51]   Summaries of these poems, made in antiquity by a scholar named Proklos, are preserved on folios 1, 4, and 6 of the Venetus A manuscript of the *Iliad*, discussed below. The few, meager surviving fragments of the poems of the Epic Cycle have been edited by Bernabé (1987), Davies (1988), and West (2003). For a discussion of the remaining fragments see Davies 1989. On the relationship of the Epic Cycle to the oral epic tradition in which the *Iliad* and the *Odyssey* were created see Burgess 2001 and Marks (forthcoming).

[52]   It is important to understand that in Nagy's model the presence of such "transcripts" does not put an end to oral tradition or cause the text of the *Iliad* and the *Odyssey* to become fixed. González 2013:15–70 and Ready 2015 are two comprehensive critiques of the so-called "dictation theory" (as set forward first by Lord [1953], then by Jensen [1980], Janko [1982 and 1998], West 1990, and Powell [1991 and 1997a], among others), which attributes text fixation of the *Iliad* and the *Odyssey* to a process of dictation by a master poet. See also Nagy 1996b:30–35, Dué 2006b, and the conclusion.

Panathenaic texts, given that each festival performance was a new composition, even if a highly regulated one.

With the exception of a few ancient quotations that survive in other texts (discussed in chapter 2 below), Homeric papyri are the oldest surviving witnesses to the text of Homer. These papyrus documents are all fragmentary, and range in date from as early as the third century BCE to the seventh century CE. The vast majority of the fragments were discovered in Egypt and now reside in collections located all over the world. The papyrus fragments of Homeric poetry reveal that the texts of the *Iliad* and the *Odyssey* were still somewhat fluid even after the Classical period in Athens. It is only starting around 150 BCE that the texts seem to become standardized, closely resembling the much later manuscripts of the medieval period (Haslam 1997). Because this date coincides with the height of the scholarly activity centered around the great Ptolemaic library in Egyptian Alexandria, it has been theorized that scholars such as Zenodotus, Aristophanes of Byzantium, and Aristarchus played an important role in establishing the relatively standardized text of Homer that is found in the medieval manuscripts of the *Iliad* and the *Odyssey* (Reynolds and Wilson 2014:8). Others have suggested alternate explanations, such as the rise of the book trade around this time, which must have resulted in greater diffusion of a common text (S. West 1967:11–17, Nagy 1996b:96–99, Schironi, forthcoming [a]).

Papyrus fragments are extremely significant for Homeric studies (Dué and Ebbott 2017). First, as already noted, they are ancient witnesses to the text of Homer. The medieval manuscript tradition of Homer begins with the tenth-century CE manuscripts of the *Iliad* known commonly as the Venetus A (Marcianus Graecus Z.454 [=822]) and D (Laurentianus 32.15). The Venetus A is the one upon which modern editions of the *Iliad* are primarily based, but some papyrus fragments predate the medieval tradition by as many as twelve hundred years. The papyrus fragments give us an otherwise irrecoverable picture of the *Iliad* and the *Odyssey* as they were performed and recorded in ancient times. As we will see in chapter 3, Homeric papyri reveal a state of the Homeric texts in antiquity that can be quite surprising. There are numerous verses in the papyri that are seemingly intrusive from the standpoint of the medieval transmission. These additional verses, the "plus verses," are not present in the majority of the medieval manuscripts of the *Iliad*. Other verses that are canonical in the medieval manuscripts are absent from the papyri—these may be termed "minus verses." Also prevalent is variation in the formulaic phrasing within lines. In other words, it seems from this most ancient evidence that the poems were performed and recorded in antiquity with a considerable amount of fluidity.

Because the papyri that predate 150 BCE present such surprising variations from the medieval texts of the *Iliad* and the *Odyssey*, they are often termed "wild." This term, however, is very misleading from a historical point of view. As we will see, the quotations of the *Iliad* and the *Odyssey* that we find in such fourth-century BCE authors as Plato, Demosthenes, and Aeschines likewise present numerous plus verses, minus verses, and other significant variations from the medieval texts of Homer. In other words, the multiformity of the so-called wild texts of the oldest papyri is confirmed by the quotations, which present a similar picture of the *Iliad* and the *Odyssey* in antiquity (Dué 2001a). To put it still another way, the further back in time we go, the more multiform—the more "wild"—our text of Homer becomes. This is the exact opposite of what we should find for an author who composed in writing, where we would expect to see more uniformity in the textual witnesses the closer we came to the author's lifetime.

The so-called wildness of the earliest papyri becomes more understandable and even expected when we take into account the evidence that the Homeric scholia provide from the work of the Alexandrian scholars. Scholia are notes in the margins of medieval manuscripts.[53] They are therefore part of the medieval transmission of Homeric poetry, but the notes derive ultimately from the work of the Alexandrian scholars and especially Aristarchus, the great second-century BCE scholar and editor whose critical work on the text of Homer is referred to throughout the scholia (Nagy 2004:3–24; Schironi 2018 and forthcoming [a and b]). These scholars had available to them at the library of Ptolemaic Alexandria a large number of Homeric texts, and it is clear that there were differences among them—that is to say, they contained multiforms. As Nagy reconstructs it, the editorial process of the great editors and heads of the library, Zenodotus, Aristophanes of Byzantium, and especially Aristarchus, was to comment upon these texts in scrolls of commentary (*hupomnēmata*), which were keyed to a standard text.[54] Such an understanding of Aristarchus' methodology is supported by the following comment in the scholia of the Venetus A at 9.222 (the main text of the *Iliad* here reads αὐτὰρ ἐπεὶ πόσιος καὶ ἐδητύος ἐξ ἔρον ἔντο), which I quote with Nagy's translation (2004:49):

ἄμεινον οὖν εἶχεν ἄν, φησὶν ὁ Ἀρίσταρχος, [εἰ] ἐγέγραπτο "ἂψ ἐπάσαντο" ἢ "αἶψ' ἐπάσαντο," ... ἀλλ' ὅμως ὑπὸ περιττῆς εὐλαβείας οὐδὲν μετέθηκεν, ἐν πολλαῖς οὕτως εὑρὼν φερομένην τὴν γραφήν.

It would have been better, says Aristarchus, if it had been written "ἂψ ἐπάσαντο" or "αἶψ' ἐπάσαντο"; nevertheless, because of his extreme

---

[53] Some papyri also contain scholia. On the relationship between the scholia that survive on papyri and those of the medieval manuscripts see McNamee 1981, 1992, 1995, and 2007.

[54] On Aristarchus' editorial practice see also van Thiel 1992 and 1997, Nagy 1996a:107–152 (with extensive references to earlier scholarship *ad loc.*), Montanari 1998 and 2002, and Schironi 2018 and forthcoming (a).

caution, he changed nothing, having found in many of the texts this attested way of writing it.

It is only in subsequent eras that Aristarchus' preferred readings from the *hupomnēmata* were inserted into editions put together by later scholars (Nagy 1996a:107–152 and forthcoming). Aristarchus himself does not seem to have ever published his own text of Homer with his own preferred readings. But even if he had, we would know from his commentaries about readings in the many other texts that were available to him, and so once again we are forced to confront the multiformity of the Homeric tradition. It is not my intention here to reargue Nagy's theories about Aristarchus, but rather to make clear my own assumption, following Nagy, that the multiforms attributed in the scholia to Aristarchus and other scholars associated with the library of Alexandria are not editorial conjectures of the sort made by nineteenth-century philologists, but observations of multiformity culled from the wide array of texts available to them.[55]

Under Nagy's model, the text of the *Iliad* had become largely fixed by the middle of the second century BCE. This fixation took place over several centuries and occurred primarily within the context of Athenian performance traditions and regulations, especially in connection with the Panathenaic festival (Nagy 2004:25–39), although as Nagy cautions, "the textual evidence allows us to reconstruct a Panathenaic tradition, relatively less multiform than other epic traditions, but this evidence cannot be reduced to a single 'uniform' Panathenaic text" (2004:38). It has been argued that just such an Athenian text is the one upon which Aristarchus commented (Schironi, forthcoming [a]). What we recognize from the scholia of our medieval manuscripts is that the scholars at the library of Alexandria who produced editions of and commentaries on the *Iliad* had access not only to something like a Panathenaic version but also to a wide range of editions from a wide range of people and places, including the so-called city editions (which are attributed to particular cities) and a number of editions attributed to particular individuals. At the same time, there were texts circulating that are referred to in the scholia as the *koinai*, the standard or common texts, and these seem to derive ultimately from Athens (Nagy,

---

[55] There is debate about the extent to which Aristarchus and other Alexandrian scholars consulted other available texts and editions in the preparation of their commentaries, as well as the extent to which they relied upon their own conjectures about the text; for a succinct overview of the debate, see Schironi (forthcoming [a]). In subsequent chapters I argue that attested multiforms in the ancient scholia that are attributed to Aristarchus and others are often just as "Homeric," by any number of criteria, as the readings that survive in the main text in our medieval manuscripts. I will approach them, therefore, as at least potentially performance derived, and will try to understand them as such.

forthcoming). Some groups of texts are referred to in the scholia as being "more refined" (χαριέστεραι) while others are "more common/standard" (κοινότεραι), and a wide variety of other adjectives are employed as well to describe the various kinds of editions to which the Alexandrian scholars had access (see West 2001:37, Nagy 2004:88, and Schironi, forthcoming [a]). For now I only emphasize that even in periods 4 and 5 of Nagy's model, the "standardizing" and "relatively most rigid" periods respectively, there is still considerable evidence for multiformity in the textual tradition, and indeed the bulk of the attested multiforms of the *Iliad* are found in sources deriving from these two periods.

The fact is that even if we accept (as I do) Nagy's theory that by the second century BCE a relatively standard Panathenaic text of the *Iliad* and the *Odyssey* was in circulation, there are still multiple potential performance-derived sources for the multiforms attested in the scholarship of the great Alexandrian editors (such as Zenodotus and Aristarchus) and subsequent ancient scholars. Non-Panathenaic texts from places other than Athens, and possibly even Panathenaic texts from earlier time periods, were in circulation. We do not know the ultimate sources of editions attributed in the scholia to named individuals such as Rhianus of Crete or Antimachus. How were these editions created? Are they perhaps a product of specially commissioned performances? Or could they be the result of collation by an editor of a number of different texts? Because I and my collaborators on the Homer Multitext are not attempting to reconstruct a single text of the *Iliad*, I am interested not in demonstrating that such multiforms should be disregarded or dismissed but rather in what we can learn from them about the performance of the *Iliad* in various places and at various times. It will be my assumption throughout this work that every attested multiform is at least potentially derived from the performance traditions of Nagy's period 4, in which transcripts of epic performances were likely being made and circulated, forming the raw material for the editions that were created by scholars at this time.

This multiformity, as I have argued, can be best understood if we conceive of our earliest texts as the products of a traditional system of composition in performance. The variations recorded in the early Homeric papyri and the Homeric scholia are the vestiges of a once-vibrant performance tradition of the *Iliad* and the *Odyssey*, in which no poem was ever composed, performed, or recorded in exactly the same way twice. In the earliest stages of the tradition that produced the *Iliad*, each performance would have resulted in an entirely new, and entirely traditional, composition. By the time of the earliest surviving papyrus fragments, the oral composition in performance tradition of Homeric epic poetry seems to have died out. But variations in the ancient textual tradition, which are, as I say, reflexes of this once oral and performative tradition, persisted for several more centuries. Moreover, performances of this poetry continued even as written texts were created, sold, and acquired as prestige objects. The variations preserved for us in the Homeric papyri and the scholia are a unique window into the performance tradition that generated them.

Medieval Transmission and Beyond

After papyrus ceased to be used, the *Iliad* and the *Odyssey* were copied onto parchment codices, like the Venetus A.[56] The Venetus A is the earliest-extant complete medieval manuscript of Homer, hand copied and assembled by one or more Byzantine Greek scribes in the tenth century CE. (The few medieval manuscripts that predate it contain commentary on and paraphrases of the poem but not a complete text.) The nearly two hundred Homeric manuscripts that succeed it are remarkable for the relative uniformity of their texts, and in this respect they differ considerably from the ancient witnesses. But although they do not vary in radical ways from one another, it is important to understand that the medieval manuscripts of Homer do not descend from a single exemplar, nor is there a medieval vulgate for the *Iliad* or the *Odyssey*. It is clear that a substantial number of texts survived the transfer from papyrus scrolls to parchment codices and that there were therefore multiple channels of transmission. What is not entirely clear is why the versions that survived resemble each other so closely. As I noted above, it has been postulated that the editorial activities of the scholars associated with the library at Alexandria played a role in the standardization of the Homeric text. But this theory does not entirely account for the continued multiformity of the text in the medieval period.

The Venetus A and several other deluxe manuscripts that survive from the tenth to the thirteenth centuries CE are invaluable to us for much more than their texts of the *Iliad*. As I have noted, these manuscripts contain not only the text of the poem but also excerpts from the scholarly commentaries of these same Alexandrian scholars, which are copied into its margins and between lines of the text. (Of the more than two hundred medieval manuscripts of the *Iliad*, only a small number are deluxe editions complete with scholia like the Venetus A.) These writings contain notes on the text that explain points of grammar and usage, the meaning of words, interpretation, and disputes about the authenticity of verses and the correct text. As we will see in chapter 4, the scholia often preserve examples of the multiformity of the Homeric tradition that are

---

[56] For more on the Venetus A, see Allen 1899, Dué 2009a, and Dué and Ebbott 2014. For an overview of the work of medieval scribes and the medieval transmission of Greek literature in general see Reynolds and Wilson 2014. For more on the differences between papyrus scrolls and parchment codices and the reasons for the transfer, see Ebbott 2009.

attested nowhere else. The material contained in these marginal notes derives from scholarly works that predate the manuscript's construction by a thousand years or more. And like the ancient papyri, which give us their surprising picture of the state of the Homeric text in antiquity, the scholia give us a fascinating historical window into the evolution of the *Iliad*, and will be the source of many of the examples discussed in this book.

Establishing the Text

The first printed edition of the Greek text of the *Iliad* was made in Florence in 1488–1489 (without scholia), and this printing was the first crucial step toward making the *Iliad* widely available to a modern audience. It was edited by Demetrius Chalcondylas, who no doubt consulted several manuscripts available to him at that time (Proctor 1900:66, Sandys 1908:104, and Geanakoplos 1962:57–58). But the application to the Homeric texts of the techniques of textual criticism, in which scholars seek, using a variety of interpretive and deductive methods, to establish the correct text of an ancient author, would not begin in full force for three more centuries. Moreover, the medieval texts on which the early printed editions were based are not the same as the ones that we use now. The Venetus A manuscript of the *Iliad* was not published until 1788, when Jean-Baptiste d'Ansse de Villoison rediscovered it in the Marciana Library in Venice. The manuscript had been there for more than two centuries. It had belonged to the collection of the Greek scholar Cardinal Bassilios Bessarion (1403–1472), whose private library eventually became the core of the Marciana's collection after his death.[57]

Between the early Renaissance and the late eighteenth century, when the Venetus A was published by Villoison, the figure of Homer was consistently the focal point of scholarly controversy. The so-called Homeric Question was in the process of being formulated. The "question" (which was, in reality, many questions) was concerned above all with the authorship and creation of the poems. Did the *Iliad* and the *Odyssey* have the same author? If so, when did he live? Could he write? Did he compose the poems in their entirety, or are parts of them interpolated by later authors? How did the poems come to be in the form that we now have them? Because of the wealth of scholia contained in the Venetus A, with the publication of that manuscript Homeric scholars of the late eighteenth century suddenly found themselves blessed with a treasure trove of information about what scholars of the second century BCE knew about Homer. It seemed that it would now be possible to reconstruct Homer and Homer's original text, and that all of the Homeric questions could be solved (Nagy 2004:3–24).

---

[57] For more on the manuscript's history see Blackwell and Dué 2009.

This was the belief of Villoison, the editor of the *editio princeps* of the Venetus A, who viewed the scholia as an authoritative witness to an authoritative edition of Homer, constructed by the premier textual critic of Homer in antiquity, Aristarchus. But the views of another scholar, Friedrich August Wolf, proved to be more influential. In his 1795 work, *Prolegomena ad Homerum*, Wolf questioned the authoritativeness of the scholia and the work of the Alexandrian critics. Wolf argued, moreover, that the Homeric poems had been transmitted by rhapsodes in an oral tradition that had corrupted the texts irreparably over time. For these reasons, Wolf asserted, the true and genuine text of Homer could never be recovered. Wolf produced his own editions of the Greek texts of the *Iliad* and the *Odyssey* (1804–1807), relying heavily on the medieval transmission of the two poems and disregarding much of the textual work of the Alexandrians of antiquity. Wolf's editions established a kind of notional medieval vulgate that continues to be followed to this day in modern printed editions: the line numbers in use by all modern editors are those of the highly conservative "Wolfian vulgate."

The debates associated with the Homeric Question only intensified after the first publication of the Venetus A and its scholia in 1788 and have continued to dominate scholarly discussions of Homer ever since. Inevitably, how each modern editor of the Homeric poems answers this question has to a large extent determined the text that is printed.[58] When we seek to understand how we have come to have the text of the *Iliad* that we know today, it is important to understand that the debates between Villoison and Wolf and their scholarly successors about the figure of Homer and nature of the Homeric texts still guide the choices of modern editors.

The most recent critical printed edition of the *Iliad* is Martin West's 1998–2000 Teubner edition. It is based on his conception of Homer, the poet and the man, as explained on the first page of his introduction: *Ilias materiam continet iamdiu per ora cantorum diffusam, formam autem contextumque qualem nos novimus tum primum attinuit, cum conscripta est; quod ut fieret, unius munus fuit maximi poetae* ("The *Iliad* contains material diffused through the mouths of singers for a long time, but the form and construction that we now know was first attained when it was written down. In order for this to happen, it was the work of one, very great poet"). West acknowledges here the oral tradition that furnished material on which the *Iliad* is based, but then says that our *Iliad* took its form when it was first written down. This was the work of a *maximus poeta* who could write. That the poet was also the writer is made clear as West continues: *per multos annos, credo, elaboravit et, quae primum strictius composuit, deinceps novis episodiis insertis*

---

[58] I have explored this idea in depth in Dué 2006b.

mirifice auxit ac dilatavit ("Throughout many years, I believe, he labored over it, and what he had at first put together concisely, he later wonderfully expanded and extended by inserting new episodes"). As I have argued already elsewhere, the insertion of *credo* here is telling (Dué 2006b). West is forced to admit, already on the first page, that his conception of Homer is a matter of faith. And because West believes in a *maximus poeta*, his goal is to restore the transmitted text as closely as possible to the composition of that poet. For him, the superfluity of other possible readings that survive from antiquity are of little interest.

Indeed, West's editorial approach is in keeping with what all modern editors over the past three hundred years or so have done. But this methodology is problematic when it is applied to the Homeric texts (Dué and Ebbott 2009, 2010:153–165, and 2017). The practice of textual criticism, as applied to classical Greek texts, has historically had the goal of recovering the original composition of the author. To create a critical edition, a modern editor assembles a text by collating the various written witnesses to an ancient Greek text, understanding their relationship with each other, knowing the kinds and likelihoods of mistakes that can occur when texts are copied by hand, and, in the case of poetry, applying the rules and exceptions of the meter as well as grammar. The final published work will then represent what she or he thinks are the author's own words (or as close to this as possible). An editor may follow one manuscript almost exclusively, or pick and choose between different manuscripts to compile what seems truest to the original. The editor also places in the *apparatus criticus* what she judges to be significant variants recorded in the witnesses. The reader must rely on the editor for the completeness of the *apparatus* in reporting variants. For a text that was composed and originally published in writing, this goal of recovering the original text may be valuable and productive (though the value has been challenged by recent scholarship), even if it may never be fully achieved because of the state of the evidence.[59]

But if, as I have argued, the *Iliad* was not composed in writing, this editorial system cannot be applied in the same way. The evidence outlined at the start of this chapter supports the thesis that the Homeric epics come from a long oral tradition in which they were created, performed, and re-performed, all without the technology of writing. This fundamental difference in the composition and history of this poetry means that we must adjust our assumptions in our understanding of the variations in the written record. What does it mean when we see variations, which still fit the meter and language of the poetry, in the witnesses

---

[59]   What I have described here can be termed the "intentional" model, where "finding an authoritative text [is] based on 'final intentions'" (Price 2008; see also Greetham 1992:347–372, Tanselle 1995:15–16, and Shillingsburg 1996:74–102). Robinson (2009) speaks of this type of editing as being largely in the past, but this is not yet the case in Homeric studies.

to the texts? Instead of "mistakes" to be corrected, as an editor would treat them in the case of a text composed just once in writing, these variations are testaments to the system of language that underlies the composition in performance of the oral tradition.

For these reasons the editors of the Homer Multitext project (http://www. homermultitext.org) do not attempt to answer questions of authorship, nor do they seek a single authoritative text. Rather, the Homer Multitext takes a historical point of departure and has as its central goal to make available an accurate picture of the transmission in all its complexity. The editors of the Multitext assert that poems that were part of a fluid and dynamic performance tradition should not be frozen in a single snapshot view, and instead intend to publish the *Iliad* at many different historical points of transmission. The implications of this approach for the present study are that it allows us to consider the *Iliad* diachronically—that is, as a system evolving over time and space. It allows us to approach each attested ancient "variant" from the medieval sources in the textual transmission of the *Iliad* as at the very least potential *multiforms*, which is to say, genuine products of the Homeric system of composition in performance. The multiforms explored in ensuing chapters can be analyzed within the contexts that produced them, and understood as historical witnesses to the thousand-year-long performance tradition from which they emerged. Rather than hide these witnesses in highly abbreviated Latin in small type at the bottom of the page, I seek in this book to magnify them and investigate what they can tell us about the poetics of the system we call "Homer."

To sum up this wide-ranging historical overview of the history of the *Iliad*, I offer the following schema, which synthesizes the work of myself and the other scholars I have cited in this chapter on the need for a multitextual approach to the *Iliad*:

> Multiformity of oral tradition → bottleneck 1 (Panionia) → bottleneck 2 (Panathenaia) → *koinai* ("standard" or "common" texts) → Alexandrian editorial work (esp. Aristarchus) → multiformity and discussion of multiformity in the surviving textual record → need for a multitext edition

Yes, the Homeric textual tradition is complicated and multiform, and it would be easier for editors if we didn't have to acknowledge it. But as I hope to show in the following chapters, the complexity and multiformity offer us a wealth of riches for more fully and accurately appreciating the poetics of a poem that was over a thousand years in the making.

Chapter 2

Sunt Aliquid Manes

Ancient Quotations of Homer

A MULTITEXTUAL APPROACH TO HOMERIC EPIC acknowledges and even embraces an expected amount of variation between performances of oral poetry. Because this multiformity was generated within a system, the attested variations enable us to appreciate the poetry of the Homeric epics on more than just the level of a single performance. By adopting a multitextual approach, we can, following Albert Lord, train our ears to hear the echoes of many past performances and appreciate the richness and complexity of the Homeric tradition as it evolved through time.[1]

One of the earliest allusions to the text of the *Iliad* in ancient literature contains a well-known and much discussed multiform. The text in question is Aeschylus, *Suppliants* 800–801, in which the chorus sings:

> κυσὶν δ' ἔπειθ' ἕλωρα κἀπιχωρίοις
> ὄρνισι δεῖπνον οὐκ ἀναίνομαι πελεῖν

> A prize for the local dogs
> and a feast for the birds I do not refuse to become.

The passage does not quote *Iliad* 1.4–5, but certainly seems to invoke it for an Athenian audience that would have been well versed in the Homeric epics. Here is the text of the *Iliad* passage as it is transmitted in the Venetus A manuscript:

> ἡρώων· αὐτοὺς δὲ ἑλώρια τεῦχε κύνεσσιν
> οἰωνοῖσί τε πᾶσι· Διὸς δ' ἐτελείετο βουλή·

---

[1] Cf. Lord's formulation from *The Singer of Tales* (1960/2000:65): "Were we to train our ears to catch these echoes, we might cease to apply the clichés of another criticism to oral poetry, and thereby become aware of its own riches."

heroes' [lives], but their selves it made prizes for dogs
and for all birds, and the plan of Zeus was being fulfilled.

But Aeschylus seems to have known a different text.[2] There is no equivalent to
πᾶσι in Aeschylus. And in fact we are told by Athenaeus (*Epitome* 1.12) that the
Alexandrian editor Zenodotus read δαῖτα here at *Iliad* 1.5. It would seem that
δαῖτα is an ancient multiform that was known as early as the fifth century BCE.
Meanwhile, all other sources read the equally Homeric πᾶσι.[3] Gregory Nagy has
written of this passage, "Both variants are traditional multiforms. In a multitextual format of editing Homer, we would have to take both forms into account"
(1996a:134).

Indeed, as this and the following chapters will show, the earliest attestations of the Homeric texts are exceedingly multiform in comparison with the
relatively uniform medieval manuscripts. A brief look at the first ten lines of the
Iliad will provide a sense of the complexity of the transmission that we will be
confronting:

[1] Μῆνιν ἄειδε θεὰ Πηληϊάδεω Ἀχιλῆος
[2] οὐλομένην· ἣ μυρί' Ἀχαιοῖς ἄλγε' ἔθηκεν· [n: v.l. ἔδωκε],
[3] πολλὰς δ' ἰφθίμους ψυχὰς [n: v.l. κεφαλὰς] Ἄϊδι προΐαψεν
– [4] ἡρώων· αὐτοὺς δὲ ἑλώρια τεῦχε κύνεσσιν
– [5] οἰωνοῖσί τε πᾶσι [n: v.l. δαῖτα]· Διὸς δ' ἐτελείετο βουλή·
[6] ἐξ οὗ δὴ τὰ πρῶτα διαστήτην ἐρίσαντε
[7] Ἀτρείδης τε ἄναξ ἀνδρῶν καὶ δῖος Ἀχιλλεύς·
[8] Τίς τάρ σφωε θεῶν ἔριδι ξυνέηκε μάχεσθαι·
[9] Λητοῦς καὶ Διὸς υἱός· ὃ γὰρ βασιλῆϊ χολωθεὶς
[10] νοῦσον ἀνὰ στρατὸν ὦρσε κακήν· ὀλέκοντο δὲ λαοί

Iliad 1.1–10

2: ἔδωκε read by Fulgentius, cf. *Iliad* 18.431 and 24.241   **3:** κεφαλὰς read by
Apollonius of Rhodes et al., cf. *Iliad* 11.55   **4–5:** athetized by Zenodotus   **5:**
δαῖτα read by Aeschylus and Zenodotus [according to Athenaeus *Epitome* 1.12]
and possibly Catullus

---

[2]   I don't mean to imply that Aeschylus was working with an actual text of the *Iliad*, only that he
knew a different *Iliad* (via Panathenaic performance or otherwise) than the one we know from
the medieval transmission.

[3]   The Roman poet Catullus (64.152–153) may also have known δαῖτα (so Zetzel 1978, but see
Thomas's response [1979]). For other possible echoes in Greek tragedy see Pfeiffer 1968:111.
For more discussion of the significance of Aeschylus' apparent reading of δαῖτα, see Ludwich
1885:87–89, Pasquali 1952:236–237, Nagy 1996a:134–135, and Bird 2010:34–40. Janko (1992:23)
calls δαῖτα "an early emendation" (see also Kirk 1985:53). But who did the emending? What
"text" did they emend? And how would Aeschylus have known it? For more on why this kind of
argument in reference to an orally composed poem is inherently problematic, see my discussion
of "interpolation" below.

[1] The anger of Peleus' son Achilles, goddess, perform its song—
[2] disastrous anger that made countless sufferings for the Achaeans,
[3] and many steadfast lives it drove down to Hades,
– [4] heroes' lives, but their selves [n: v.l. heads] it made prizes for dogs
– [5] and for all birds [n: v.l. a feast for birds]; the plan of Zeus was being
    fulfilled—
[6] sing starting from the point where the two first clashed,
[7] the son of Atreus, lord of men, and radiant Achilles.
[8] So, which of the gods was it that pushed the two to clash and
    fight?
[9] It was the son of Leto and Zeus; for, infuriated at the king,
[10] he stirred up an evil pestilence throughout the mass of warriors,
    and the warriors kept on dying

Numerous multiforms for these verses are attested, and they have a good deal of ancient support, both within the formulaic diction of the *Iliad* itself and in the debates of the Alexandrian editors (as preserved in the scholia of medieval manuscripts). The reading κεφαλὰς, for example, in line 3 was read by Aristophanes of Rhodes. At *Iliad* 11.55 we find powerful evidence that κεφαλὰς is perfectly formulaic: there this same verse is attested with κεφαλὰς in place of ψυχὰς. Meanwhile, the Venetus A scholia record that "some" (τινες) write κεφαλὰς instead of ψυχὰς at 1.3, "badly" (κακῶς) in the judgment of the scholiast. The scholia in the Venetus A also tell us that Zenodotus athetized lines 4 and 5, meaning he did not deem them Homeric, but Zenodotus is credited in Athenaeus with reading δαῖτα in the athetized verse 5.[4]

The multiformity does not stop there. An edition known to scholars in the ancient world apparently contained this single verse in place of *Iliad* 1.1–9:

Μούσας ἀείδω καὶ Ἀπόλλωνα κλυτότοξον

I sing of the Muses and Apollo of the silver bow.

This was the edition of Apellicon known by Crates and Nicanor (Erbse 1969:3). Another version of the proem current in antiquity, according to Aristoxenus, consisted of three verses:

ἔσπετε νῦν μοι, Μοῦσαι Ὀλύμπια δώματ' ἔχουσαι,
ὅππως δὴ μῆνίς τε χόλος θ' ἕλε Πηλείωνα
Λητοῦς τ' ἀγλαὸν υἱόν. ὁ γὰρ βασιλῆϊ χολωθείς...

---

4   Athetized verses were not actually removed from the text. The critical sign known as the obelos was placed next to them, indicating that the editor did not think them to be Homeric; on the Alexandrian critical signs that survive in the Venetus A, see Bird 2009.

Tell me now, you Muses who have homes on Olympus,
how anger and fury took hold of the son of Peleus
and the glorious son of Leto. For angered at the king…

The two variant proems come from a scholion found in a manuscript called the *Anecdotum Romanum*, or Ve1 (in the edition of Allen [1931]) or Z (in the edition of West [1998–2000]). Ve1 consists of two manuscripts of scholia on the *Iliad* which were once part of a single whole, one from Rome (Biblioteca Nazionale Vittorio Emanuele 6), and the other from Madrid (Biblioteca Nacional de España 4626).[5] The manuscript is as old as or possibly even older than the Venetus A, dating to the ninth or tenth century CE, but the information contained in it is much earlier, in that it preserves ancient scholarship dating back to Hellenistic and Roman times.

***

As the multiforms in the *Iliad* proem attest, we have a wealth of ancient material, including quotations in ancient authors, papyri, and the scholia of medieval manuscripts, from which we can gain an appreciation of the multiformity of the oral traditional system within which the *Iliad* and the *Odyssey* were composed. In this and the following chapters I propose to proceed chronologically and discuss each of these ancient sources separately, although there will be many points of contact between them. In the remainder of this chapter I seek to point out the possibility and fruitfulness of recovering more fluid stages of the Homeric *Iliad* and *Odyssey* from quotations (especially those of the fourth century BCE). Quotations in fourth-century authors such as Plato and Aeschines are among our very oldest witnesses to the Homeric texts. They are a crucial primary source for any attempt at assessing the state of the Homeric text in the fourth century BCE (Nagy's period 4 in his evolutionary model, the time of our earliest potential transcripts).[6]

The quotations are not only our earliest witnesses but also among the most multiform. It is not uncommon for quotations to contain additional verses (as compared to medieval manuscripts) or fewer verses, or to exhibit multiformity

---

[5] For a more detailed description of these see Allen's *prolegomena* in his *editio maior* of the *Iliad* (= Allen 1931).

[6] Allen (1924:249–70) provides a useful survey of early Homeric quotations and the variants they preserve, building on Ludwich 1898:71–132. For a thorough study of the quotations of Homer in Plato specifically see Labarbe, *L'Homère de Platon* (1949). Labarbe's overall purpose in considering the variation found in Plato is the establishment of the one true text of Homer. As a result his work is fundamentally at odds with my own approach. Nevertheless his discussion is an important contribution to the study of quotations in Homeric textual criticism. On ancient quotations of Homer see also Higbie 1997 and Usher 2000.

within a particular verse. As we will see in chapter 3, the quotations are not unlike the oldest surviving papyrus texts, the ones that have been deemed "wild" in relation to the medieval transmission. In fact, the further back in time we go, the more multiformity we find in our textual witnesses. This is what we should expect to find in the textual transmission of an oral poem, of which there can be no "original."[7]

And yet, two recent critical editions of the *Iliad* and the *Odyssey*, those by H. van Thiel and M. L. West, explicitly disregard the variations presented by ancient quotations. Van Thiel deems ancient quotations and papyri "of minor importance" and treats any multiforms offered by a quotation "as if it were conjecture" (1991:xxi). These scholars are not interested in multiformity for its own sake; they seek rather to establish an authoritative text that can be presented in a printed edition.[8] West understands the multiforms that survive in early quotations to be "interpolations" (1998:vii).[9] Alternatively West and others explain the multiformity of early quotations as lapses of memory, under the common assumption that fourth-century authors like Plato and Aeschines did not have texts before them when quoting Homer.[10] Scholars typically disparage as "banal"[11] or even "inept"[12] (and therefore not worth our consideration) the types of variation that fourth-century quotations and early papyri

---

[7] See above, pp. 45–46.

[8] Van Thiel does not believe that the words of Homer himself can ever be recovered, but he does not claim that the words of Homer never existed. There may have been an authoritative *Iliad*, we simply don't have the means to recover it. The best we can do, in Van Thiel's view, is to work with our medieval sources to reconstruct an authoritative medieval text ("Laurels in textual criticism are not to be won from the text of Homer" [1991:xxiv]). West, by contrast, as we have seen in the last chapter, seeks to recover the words of Homer himself, the *maximus poeta*.

[9] West called the extra verses found in fourth-century quotations "embellishments" by rhapsodes in his *Textual Criticism and Editorial Technique* (1973b), but in his Teubner edition of the *Iliad* (1998–2000) he calls them interpolations (p. vii). West nevertheless does incorporate quotations into his very thorough *apparatus criticus*, which contains a separate band on every page for allusions to and quotations of the Homeric texts in ancient authors. Richard Janko (1992:21) argues that extra verses were later "interpolated" into an originally dictated text. Stephanie West likewise refers to plus verses in the papyri as "interpolations," later adding that these were largely the work of rhapsodes, and compares them to actor's interpolations in Attic drama (1967:12–13; so also Revermann 1998). These scholars make a distinction between "Homer," the creator, and later, non-creative rhapsodes. Following Nagy's evolutionary model, which accounts for the changing creative process of performers as the tradition evolved over time, I do not make such a distinction. For a critical discussion of the use of the term "interpolation" by classicists in reference to performance variants, see Nagy 1996a:28–32.

[10] See West 1998: x. T. W. Allen, on the other hand, attributes to Plato "a designed carelessness of Socrates" that makes him a doubtful witness (1924:254).

[11] Pelliccia 1997:46. See also Finkelberg (2000), who cites Pelliccia as well as S. West (1967) and Powell (1997b) in her argument that the known variants of the *Iliad* and the *Odyssey* are too restricted to be considered multiforms.

[12] Kirk 1985 ad 1.1, on a variant *Iliad* proem.

present.[13] But not only does this criticism do nothing to solve the problem of what to do with this multiformity: it is also untrue.

I and my collaborators on the Homer Multitext are not seeking to establish a single definitive text, and therefore we approach the early quotations from a different perspective. What do the variations preserved in fourth-century quotations tell us about the early textual history of the Homeric poems? What Iliads and Odysseys were audiences at various points in antiquity actually hearing? What impact can the attested multiforms have on our understanding of the poetics of the *Iliad* and the *Odyssey*? I will discuss in this chapter two examples of the kinds of multiformity presented by the early quotations, in order to make a case for their value not only as witnesses to the oral traditional system in which the *Iliad* and the *Odyssey* were composed, but also for their intrinsic value within the history of literature. I would like to begin my discussion of these questions with what may seem to be an extremely, even perversely, minor textual variant, the difference of a single letter in Greek. I will argue that even a variation as small as a single letter has wide-ranging implications for our understanding of the *Iliad* and the transmission and reception of the poem in antiquity. We will get there by way of the Roman elegiac poet Propertius.

***

sunt aliquid manes: letum non omnia finit.

The Shades are something: Death does not end everything.

Propertius IV 7.1

Propertius begins IV 7, a poem that alludes throughout to the dream of Achilles in *Iliad* 23.62–107, with a simple and emphatic declaration: *sunt aliquid manes.* The Shades are something. Commentaries point out that these opening words allude specifically to *Iliad* 23.103–104:

ὢ πόποι ἦ ῥά τις ἐστὶ καὶ εἰν Ἀΐδαο δόμοισι
ψυχὴ καὶ εἴδωλον, ἀτὰρ φρένες οὐκ ἔνι πάμπαν

Iliad 23.103–104

Alas there is indeed someone even in the house of Hades,
a soul and a likeness, but there is no real substance.[14]

---

[13] Cf. Janko's criticism of Van Thiel's decision not to bracket many verses considered by Apthorp (1980) to be interpolated: "This is not progress ... the removal of such lines almost always improves the poem's literary qualities" (1994:293).

[14] I have chosen to translate the lines this way because of the tendency of Homeric verses typically to function as independent units. Another possible translation ("There is a soul, even in the House of Hades, and a likeness...") is discussed further below, but this would be a very

The three words that begin Propertius' poem, moreover, fit within an over-arching structural allusion in which his lover Cynthia, like Patroklos, appears to Propertius in a dream after her death and reproaches him for neglect of her funeral rites. *Sunt aliquid manes* is a verbal echo of the exclamation of Achilles, who, after attempting in vain to embrace the shade of Patroklos, suddenly comprehends the nature of the ψυχή after death.

Propertius alludes directly to *Iliad* 23.65–104 in five more places in the poem:[15]

- *Cynthia namque meo uisa est incumbere fulcro* (3) ~ στῆ δ' ἄρ' ὑπὲρ κεφαλῆς καὶ μιν πρὸς μῦθον ἔειπεν· (*Iliad* 23.68)

- *eosdem habuit secum quibus est elata capillos, / eosdem oculos; lateri uestis adusta fuit* (7–8) ~ ἦλθε δ' ἐπὶ ψυχὴ Πατροκλῆος δειλοῖο / πάντ' αὐτῷ μέγεθός τε καὶ ὄμματα κάλ' εἰκυῖα / καὶ φωνήν, καὶ τοῖα περὶ χροΐ εἵματα ἔστο· (*Iliad* 23.65–67)

- *perfide nec cuiquam melior sperande puellae, / in te iam uires somnus habere potest?* (13–14) ~ εὕδεις, αὐτὰρ ἐμεῖο λελασμένος ἔπλευ Ἀχιλλεῦ. / οὐ μέν μευ ζώοντος ἀκήδεις ἀλλὰ θανόντος· (*Iliad* 23.69–70)

- *mecum eris, et mixtis ossibus ossa teram* (94) ~ μὴ ἐμὰ σῶν ἀπάνευθε τιθήμεναι ὀστέ' Ἀχιλλεῦ (*Iliad* 23.83)

- *haec postquam querula mecum sub lite peregit, / inter complexus excidit umbra meos.* (95–96) ~ Ὣς ἄρα φωνήσας ὠρέξατο χερσὶ φίλησιν / οὐδ' ἔλαβε· ψυχὴ δὲ κατὰ χθονὸς ἠΰτε καπνὸς / ᾤχετο τετριγυῖα· (*Iliad* 23.99–101)

These parallel passages are very close and present no difficulties. They provide a framework that allows Propertius to be in dialogue with the Homeric text and at the same time depart from it.

The allusion in line 1 by which Propertius signals this dialogue with the *Iliad* is not quite exact, however. If the larger context did not make it certain, we might question whether *sunt aliquid manes* should be considered an allusion at all. The Homeric text that I have printed above is that of the Venetus A, as well as that of most modern editions (with some differences of accentuation).[16] The crucial difference between the standard printed text of Homer and the wording that we might expect were we to translate backwards from Propertius

---

unusual construction in Homeric Greek. This portion of the chapter is a revised and somewhat compressed version of Dué 2001b; please see the article for more on the implications of the multiform under discussion for our understanding of Propertius' poem IV 7.

[15] See also the editions Butler and Barber (1933), Camps (1965), and Hutchinson (2006) inter alia, as well as Hubbard 1974:149ff and Papanghelis 1987:145–198.

[16] The one major exception is the edition of Leaf (London, 1900–1902).

is the reading of τις in line 103, rather than the neuter τι. The Homeric text can be translated for the moment as: "Alas there is indeed someone, even in the house of Hades / a soul and a likeness, but there is no real substance." Whereas Propertius reads: "The Shades are *something*: Death does not end everything."

What could account for such a discrepancy? It seems that Propertius indeed had in mind a different text. τις is the majority reading of the manuscripts in the *Iliad* passage, and Eustathius is an early witness. But τι is also a possible reading. It is found in twenty-seven manuscripts of the *Iliad*, and it has strong support in the form of a far earlier witness. This is Plato's *Republic* (386 D). In the Plato passage Socrates discusses the stories that poets tell about the nature of the underworld, concerning which he gives seven citations of Homer in quick succession, including lines 103–104 of *Iliad* 23. Plato's text is considerably closer to that of Propertius: ὦ πόποι, ἦ ῥά τι ἔστι καὶ εἰν Ἀΐδαο δόμοισι, / ψυχὴ καὶ εἴδωλον, ἀτὰρ φρένες οὐκ ἔνι πάμπαν. "There is something, even in the house of Hades, a ψυχὴ and an εἴδωλον…" or, without a sense break after δόμοισι (which is how Propertius must have read it) "the ψυχὴ καὶ εἴδωλον are *something*, even in the house of Hades…."

Now τι is certainly a possible valid reading at *Iliad* 23.103, metaphysical questions aside, and Leaf in fact prints it.[17] There is support in the medieval manuscripts of the *Iliad* for this reading, although it is not the majority reading, nor is it in the oldest manuscripts.[18] Secondly, Plato definitely wrote τι in his citation of these lines. The only support for τις in manuscripts of Plato, the manuscript known as T, is itself an apograph of A, the ninth- or tenth-century manuscript on which modern texts are based, which reads τι. τις is therefore a corruption unique to the manuscript T in Plato.[19] Plato is our earliest witness to the text of Homer at these lines, far earlier than any papyrus and well over a thousand years before the medieval tradition of the text of Homer begins. Another very old witness, a first-century BCE papyrus (511), also reads τι.[20] Finally, Propertius, a first-century BCE witness, seems to have known the reading τι and translated it as *aliquid* in the line *sunt aliquid manes*.

When I first explored this variation in a 2001 article (Dué 2001b), I argued that Propertius may have known both readings. By translating the reading τι

---

[17] Both Lattimore ("Even in the house of Hades there is left something") and Lombardo ("so there is something in Death's house") seem to have chosen to translate τι rather than τις, even though both usually follow Munro and Allen's Oxford Classical Text as the source for their translation.

[18] Cf. Richardson 1993 *ad loc.*, who argues that not only is τι possible, but it is superior to τις, which goes awkwardly with ψυχὴ καὶ εἴδωλον in the following line.

[19] I agree with Labarbe's insistence on this point (1949:169–170).

[20] Papyrus 511 (= P. Mil. Vogl. 3.117 [inv. 425] + 3.118 [inv. 428]). For the publication history of this papyrus see the Mertens-Pack 3 database (http://cipl93.philo.ulg.ac.be/Cedopal/MP3/dbsearch.aspx), s.v. 1002.

found in Plato (and possibly other sources) rather than τις (which may well have been in most texts of Homer, even in the fourth century BCE), Propertius, I argued, was engaging in an Alexandrian method of alluding to Homer. He displays Alexandrian learnedness by alluding to the variant readings of Homer known to him and to the textual problems, or *zētēmata*, encountered in the work of scholars like Zenodotus and Aristarchus on the text of Homer.[21]

I made this argument in part because the first line of Propertius' poem alludes to much more than a minor textual discrepancy. The meaning of the Homeric lines was in fact a major topic of discussion for Homer's readers in antiquity, and the scholia that survive in medieval manuscripts show us that Alexandrian scholars struggled to provide possible explanations.[22] Any interpretation of the lines has to take into account that single sigma that is the difference between τις and τι. First of all, translating τι, how can the εἴδωλον be said to be something anywhere other than in the house of Hades? The same question could be applied to τις: there is a ψυχὴ and an εἴδωλον even in the house of Hades? In both cases the force of the καὶ is awkward. But if we translate τι and take ψυχὴ καὶ εἴδωλον in apposition (a grammatical construction very natural to Homeric Greek), Achilles seems to be wrestling with the exact nature of what remains of life after death. *Something* remains of Patroklos' former self in Hades, that is a ψυχὴ and an εἴδωλον, but then he qualifies it—ἀτὰρ φρένες οὐκ ἔνι παμπαν.

This qualification is just as difficult to interpret. What exactly is the distinction being made between ψυχὴ καὶ εἴδωλον? Patroklos has just given a long speech with no apparent lack of reason, as is noted in the scholia of the Venetus A (ἐμφρόως καὶ συνετῶς διείλεκται πάντα ὁ Πάτροκλος). The intelligence displayed in Patroklos' speech troubled Aristophanes enough for him to suggest that φρένες refers to the physical container of reason—that is, corporeality.[23] Achilles has after all just tried to embrace Patroklos and failed. Aristarchus on the other hand commented that for Homer the souls of the unburied dead still

---

[21] On this very specialized form of allusion, see Rengakos 1993. On Alexandrian allusive techniques and the relationship between the Alexandrian poets and their predecessors, see also Giangrande 1967 and 1970, Bing 1988, and Gelzer 1993. On Roman allusive practice a great deal of work has been done; important studies include Conte 1986, Farrell 1991, Hinds 1998, Thomas 1999, Edmunds 2000, and Barchiesi 2001. For a more recent overview and bibliography see O'Rourke 2012.

[22] On the Alexandrian scholarly debate and the scholia for these lines see also Richardson 1993 *ad loc.* and Van der Valk 1963:540–542. On the awkwardness of these lines in general see Labarbe 1949:170–172

[23] ἢ φρένας λέγει οὐ τὸ διανοητικόν, ἀλλὰ μέρος τι τῶν ἐντὸς σώματος, ὡς καὶ ἀλλαχοῦ "ἔν τε φρένες ἧπαρ ἔχουσι" (~ *Odyssey* 9.301) καὶ πάλιν "ἔνθ' ἄρα τε φρένες ἔρχεται" (= *Iliad* 16.481). ἔστιν οὖν ἀπὸ μέρους τὸ ὅλον σῶμα. οὕτως Ἀριστοφάνης ὁ γραμματικός.

have their intelligence, as opposed to the buried souls whom Odysseus encounters in Hades in *Odyssey* xi.[24]

There are still more explanations to be found in the scholia on these lines in other manuscripts. One is that Patroklos shows lack of φρένες in rebuking Achilles for neglecting his funeral rites.[25] Achilles has indeed already completed the greater part of the preparations for burial and performed most of the rituals on that very day, and the shade of Patroklos visits Achilles on the eve of the planned burial. A final possibility is found in the word πάμπαν, which seems to further qualify Achilles' statement. The shades have sense or intelligence, but it is somewhat diminished.

I do not intend to try to solve the interpretive difficulties here, which have confounded Alexandrian and modern scholars alike.[26] It was sufficient for the purposes of my 2001 article to point out that the meaning of these lines was controversial in antiquity, and there I explored what the poetic significance of that Homeric debate means for our interpretation of Propertius IV 7, which is steeped in poetic traditions about the afterlife and philosophical questions about the nature of the soul. But in that article I was also making a larger point about the Homeric text, namely that both readings, τις and τι, have authority, that both may have been performed in antiquity, and that a multitextual approach to Homer allows us to consider both. If we do not have to privilege one reading over the other, how does that change how we approach the meaning of the passage and its reception at various points in history?

In that same 2001 article I suggested that a poem by Ovid might just prove that Propertius was in fact engaging a known textual issue—that is, he was confronting the multiformity of the Homeric textual tradition—by translating τι. *Amores* III 9, a poem in which critics have found connections with Propertius' fourth book,[27] is a formal lament for the death of Ovid's fellow elegist Tibullus. The thematic connections with Propertius IV 7 (and Lucretius, also discussed in the article) are obvious: the same questions about the immortality of poetry

---

[24] ἡ διπλῆ δέ, ὅτι τὰς τῶν ἀτάφων ψυχὰς Ὅμηρος ἔτι σωζούσας τὴν φρόνησιν ὑποτίθεται. This note immediately follows the previous one in the Venetus A manuscript of the *Iliad*.

[25] κάλλιον δέ, ὅτι φρένας οἱ τεθνεῶτες οὐκ ἔχουσιν· ἐμέμφετο γὰρ ὡς ἠμελημένος. (This comment is preserved in a number of manuscripts, including the Venetus B and the Townley.) This is Leaf's view as well (1902:621).

[26] For Leaf's view see note 16 above. Richardson (1993 *ad loc.*) is inclined to accept φρένες as "physical substance" with Aristophanes.

[27] On Ovid's intertextual relationship with Propertius see Berman 1972:170–172 and Morgan 1977. Early compilations of parallel passages include Zingerle 1869–71/1967, Ganzenmüller 1911, and Neumann 1919. See also Miller 1993, Casali 2009, and O'Rourke 2014.

and the soul are explored.[28] Like Cynthia, Delia and Nemesis will live forever, according to Ovid (31). Homer plays an important role in this poem as well: Ovid's lament is compared to laments for Achilles and Memnon (1–2), and Ovid notes that even Homer had to die, but now his poetry lives on (25–30). Towards the end of the poem, Ovid speculates as to whether a soul lives on after the death of the body. He formulates his question twice, each time as an indirect question within a conditional sentence. The first begins: *si tamen e nobis aliquid nisi nomen et umbra restat...* ("If nevertheless something does remain of us beyond a name and a shade..."). With this formulation Ovid questions whether there is something even beyond the existence of a shade after death. The second formulation is somewhat different: *siqua est modo corporis umbra* ("if only there does exist a shade of the body..."). Here he seems to question the existence of a shade at all after death. And once again, mixed up in the whole philosophical question is the key textual difference between the two formulations: the adjective *aliquis* versus the pronoun *aliquid*. Or, to put it in Greek, τις versus τι.[29]

Whether or not Propertius knew what he was doing when he read τι (and I have tried to show that he did), he set in motion a complex web of allusion and intertext with long-lasting effect.[30] We should wonder then if there is a deeper significance to Propertius' allusion beyond a mere display of Alexandrian learning. Dorothy Lange has suggested that IV 7 is not merely a playful "twist on the amatory elegy" but rather a poetic statement that marks Propertius' farewell

---

[28] See Morgan 1977:94–97, as well as Taylor 1970. Morgan analyzes some of the Propertian echoes in this poem, although she does not discuss IV 7.

[29] Ovid's text goes even further in its engagement of Propertius. For Ovid alludes not only to Lucretius and Propertius IV 7 and the reading of τι instead of τις, but also to Propertius II 34, where Propertius uses *aliquid* in a strikingly similar context: *si post Stygias aliquid restabit undas* (II 34.53). Moreover, *Amores* III 9 isn't the only place where Ovid can be seen to play with *aliquid*. In *Amores* I 12.3 he writes *omina sunt aliquid*. In *Metamorphoses* VI 542 we find: *si numina divum sunt aliquid*. Ovid engages Propertius yet again in *Tristia* IV 10: *si tamen extincti aliquid nisi nomina restat, / et gracilis structos effugit umbra rogos...* (85–86). In this final example there is no *aliqua* to contrast with the *aliquid*, but it seems that there is a play on the two Homeric possibilities that is similar to that of *Amores* III 9.

[30] After Propertius and Ovid the textual debate lives on. We find in Juvenal 2.149 *esse aliquos Manes et subterranea regna* and in Quintilian *negat ullos esse Manes*. The alternative formulations of the question of life after death may have influenced actual epitaphs. Compare the following three quotations from the *Carmina Epigraphica*:
> *si tamen at Manes credimus esse aliquit* (*Carmina Epigraphica* 1190.3)
> *si qui estis Manes* (*Carmina Epigraphica* 132.1)
> *si quae sunt Manes* (*Carmina Epigraphica* 2170)

It is impossible to be certain who is influencing whom, but I am inclined to believe that the epitaphs are modeled on the poetry and not vice versa. This very complex set of allusive relationships (from Homer all the way to Juvenal and Quintilian is, in the language of Hinds, untidy but not, I believe, inert [see especially Hinds 1998:34–47]). On these later echoes of Propertius and Ovid see Shackleton Bailey 1952:331.

to erotic poetry.[31] Achilles' final vision of Patroklos, so full of regret and so tender, is a wonderful metaphor for such a farewell. But by making the shades something, Propertius has given Cynthia (and erotic poetry) the power to come back.

***

I turn now to a more complex example of multiformity, Aeschines' quotation of *Iliad* 23.77–91 in his speech *Against Timarchus* (149).[32] The quotation shows three plus verses and significant internal variation in three separate lines.[33] As we will see, these multiforms are arguably just as "Homeric" as the text preserved in medieval manuscripts such as the Venetus A, and they illustrate, even more so than my first example, the necessity of taking a multitextual approach to Homeric epic.

Throughout his prosecution of Timarchus Aeschines provides carefully selected citations of Homer and the tragedians to support his claim that Timarchus has led the kind of life that, according to Athenian law, precludes him from speaking in the democratic assembly. The following is Aeschines' text of Patroklos' address to Achilles in *Iliad* 23, which the speaker cites in an attempt to refute the defense's claim that Homer highly approved of sexual relationships between men. Aeschines' point is that Homer never explicitly says that Achilles and Patroklos were lovers; rather, the speaker argues, they possessed the noblest of friendships (τὴν ἀρετὴν καὶ τὴν φιλίαν ἄξιον αὐτῶν 146).[34]

οὐ γὰρ ἔτι ζωοί γε φίλων ἀπάνευθεν ἑταίρων	*Iliad* 23.77
βουλὰς ἑζόμενοι βουλεύσομεν· ἀλλ' ἐμὲ μὲν Κὴρ	78
ἀμφέχανε στυγερή, ἥπερ λάχε γεινόμενόν περ·	79
καὶ δὲ σοὶ αὐτῷ μοῖρα, θεοῖς ἐπιείκελ' Ἀχιλλεῦ,	80
τείχει ὕπο Τρώων εὐηγενέων ἀπολέσθαι,	81
+ μαρνάμενον δηίοις Ἑλένης ἕνεκ' ἠυκόμοιο.	81a
ἄλλο δέ τοι ἐρέω, σὺ δ' ἐνὶ φρεσὶ βάλλεο σῇσιν·	82
μὴ ἐμὰ σῶν ἀπάνευθε τιθήμεναι ὀστέ', Ἀχιλλεῦ,	83

---

[31] Lange 1979:336. She notes, among other passages, Cynthia's *laudes desine habere meas* (78). This farewell would be one of many, of course; Propertius renounces both Cynthia and love elegy in general elsewhere (see especially III 24 and 25).

[32] The following arguments have been revised and adapted from Dué 2001a.

[33] For a more general overview of the history of the treatment of plus verses—verses that are attested in quotations and papyri and the scholia, but not in the majority of medieval manuscripts—in Homeric scholarship, see Bird 2010:27–60, and especially 53–56, and chapter 3 below.

[34] See also *Against Timarchus* 151 τὸ σωφρόνως ἐρᾶν. Aeschines is careful to distinguish between sexual relations between men and erotic/romantic love between men and (male) youths (which he calls ἔρωτα δίκαιον, *Against Timarchus* 136). He anticipates that some of his own erotic poetry will be read to the jury along with passages from the poets (*Against Timarchus* 132–136). See Dover 1989:39–54.

+ ἀλλ᾽ ἵνα περ σε καὶ αὐτὸν ὁμοίη γαῖα κεκεύθῃ,   83a
+ χρυσέῳ ἐν ἀμφιφορεῖ, τόν τοι πόρε πότνια μήτηρ,   83b
ὡς ὁμοῦ ἐτράφεμέν περ ἐν ὑμετέροισι δόμοισιν,   84
εὖτέ με τυτθὸν ἐόντα Μενοίτιος ἐξ Ὀπόεντος   85
ἤγαγεν ὑμέτερόνδ᾽ ἀνδροκτασίης ὕπο λυγρῆς,   86
ἤματι τῷ, ὅτε παῖδα κατέκτανον Ἀμφιδάμαντος,   87
νήπιος, οὐκ ἐθέλων, ἀμφ᾽ ἀστραγάλοισι χολωθείς·   88
ἔνθα με δεξάμενος ἐν δώμασιν ἱππότα Πηλεὺς   89
ἔτρεφέ τ᾽ ἐνδυκέως καὶ σὸν θεράποντ᾽ ὀνόμηνεν·   90
ὣς δὲ καὶ ὀστέα νῶιν ὁμὴ σορὸς ἀμφικαλύπτοι.   91

77 οὐ γὰρ ἔτι] οὐ μὲν γὰρ mss.   **82** σὺ δ᾽ ἐνὶ φρεσὶ βάλλεο σῇσιν] καὶ ἐφήσομαι αἴ κε πίθηαι mss.   **84** ὡς ὁμοῦ ἐτράφεμέν περ] ἀλλ᾽ ὁμοῦ ὡς ἐτράφημεν mss.

No longer will you and I, alive, apart from our dear companions	77
sit and make our plans, since the destiny,	78
hateful as it is, that was allotted me when I was born has engulfed me.	79
And you also, Achilles like the gods, have your own destiny;	80
to lose your life under the walls of the prosperous Trojans,	81
+ fighting for the sake of Helen with the beautiful hair.	81a
But I will say another thing, and you cast it in your heart:	82
do not have my bones laid apart from yours, Achilles,	83
+ but where the same earth covers you and me	83a
+ in the golden amphora, which your revered mother gave you.	83b
Just as we grew up together in your house	84
when Menoitios led me as a child from Opoeis	85
to your house because of a grievous killing,	86
on that day when I killed the son of Amphidamas	87
unthinkingly, not intentionally, angered over a game of dice.	88
The horseman Peleus received me there into his house	89
and raised me with kindness and named me your *therapōn*.	90
So let the same vessel hold both our bones.	91

Aeschines *Against Timarchus* 149

Compare the text of the medieval Venetus A manuscript, including line 92 [≈ 83b], which was athetized by Aristarchus and not quoted by Aeschines:

οὐ μὲν γὰρ ζωοί γε φίλων ἀπάνευθεν ἑταίρων	*Iliad* 23.77
βουλὰς ἑζόμενοι βουλεύσομεν, ἀλλ' ἐμὲ μὲν κὴρ	78
ἀμφέχανε στυγερή, ἥ περ λάχε γεινόμενόν περ·	79
καὶ δὲ σοὶ αὐτῷ μοῖρα θεοῖς ἐπιείκελ' Ἀχιλλεῦ	80
τείχει ὑπὸ Τρώων εὐηγενέων ἀπολέσθαι.	81
ἄλλο δέ τοι ἐρέω καὶ ἐφήσομαι αἴ κε πίθηαι·	82
μὴ ἐμὰ σῶν ἀπάνευθε τιθήμεναι ὀστέ' Ἀχιλλεῦ,	83
ἀλλ' ὁμοῦ ὡς ἐτράφην [corr. ἐτράφημεν] ἐν ὑμετέροισι δόμοισιν,	84
εὖτέ με τυτθὸν ἐόντα Μενοίτιος ἐξ Ὀπόεντος	85
ἤγαγεν ὑμέτερον δ' ἀνδροκτασίης ὕπο λυγρῆς,	86
ἤματι τῷ ὅτε παῖδα κατέκτανον Ἀμφιδάμαντος	87
νήπιος οὐκ ἐθέλων ἀμφ' ἀστραγάλοισι χολωθείς·	88
ἔνθά με δεξάμενος ἐν δώμασιν ἱππότα Πηλεὺς	89
ἔτραφετ' ἐνδυκέως καὶ σὸν θεράποντ' ὀνόμηνεν·	90
ὣς δὲ καὶ ὀστέα νῶιν ὁμὴ σορὸς ἀμφικαλύπτοι	91
(–) **χρύσεος ἀμφιφορεύς, τόν τοι πόρε πότνια μήτηρ.**	92

92 athetized by Aristarchus: ἐν πάσαις οὐκ ἦν ὁ στίχος (T scholia). Omitted in papyrus 12.35

Among other variations, this version is shorter than Aeschines' quotation by at least three verses. We do not know if Aeschines' text contained line 92 and its reference to the golden amphora of 83b, because his quotation breaks off at 91.[36]

The arguments typically used to dismiss similar kinds of multiformity in the Ptolemaic papyri will not work here. Aeschines' quotation is a witness older than any papyrus or manuscript, and has not undergone any scholarly editing by the Alexandrians. It has been assumed that this text was provided to a court reporter, who read aloud from it when called upon by Aeschines to do so, starting and stopping where he indicated.[37] Whether that is indeed the case, or some other text was read aloud and included in Aeschines' published speech, a lapse in memory on the part of Aeschines is not a solution to the variation

---

[35] Papyrus 12 (= P. Grenf. 2.4 + P. Hib. 1.22 + P. Heid. 1262–1266). For the publication history of this papyrus see the Mertens-Pack 3 database (http://cipl93.philo.ulg.ac.be/Cedopal/MP3/dbsearch.aspx), s.v. 979.

[36] 83b: **χρυσέῳ ἐν ἀμφιφορεῖ, τόν τοι πόρε πότνια μήτηρ** ~ 92: **χρύσεος ἀμφιφορεύς, τόν τοι πόρε πότνια μήτηρ.** On the possibility that Aeschines' text did contain verse 92 see the discussion below.

[37] Allen (1924:257) supposes that the text is that of the clerk of court's own copy.

within lines. The official nature of the situation in which the quotation took place makes it unlikely that the passage is an eccentric private copy of the sort that a collector might possess, but rather the contrary. A standard wording is what is called for here, and one that was familiar to the jury if it was to carry any weight.

To confront this situation, in which a fourth-century BCE witness challenges the medieval transmission, a scholarly consensus seems to have been reached which asserts that verses 83a and 83b are an interpolation "effecting the equation of the σορός of 91 with the golden amphora which Thetis provides for Achilles' bones at *Odyssey* 24.73–77" (Haslam 1997:76).[38] In this passage from the *Odyssey*, the ghost of Agamemnon in the underworld recalls the funeral of Achilles:

> δῶκε δὲ μήτηρ
> χρύσεον ἀμφιφορῆα· Διωνύσοιο δὲ δῶρον
> φάσκ' ἔμεναι, ἔργον δὲ περικλυτοῦ Ἡφαίστοιο.
> ἐν τῷ τοι κεῖται λεύκ' ὀστέα, φαίδιμ' Ἀχιλλεῦ,
> μίγδα δὲ Πατρόκλοιο Μενοιτιάδαο θανόντος.

Odyssey 24.73–77

> And your mother gave
> a golden amphora. A gift from Dionysos
> she claimed that it was, the work of exceedingly renowned
> Hephaistos.
> In it lie your white bones, radiant Achilles,
> mingled with those of the dead Patroklos, son of Menoitios.

The golden amphora referenced here would appear to be the same one depicted on the so-called François Vase, a large Archaic black-figure vase that prominently features the wedding of Peleus and Thetis, among other scenes connected to the life of Achilles.[39] On that vase, Dionysos can be seen carrying an amphora on his back as he proceeds with the other gods to the wedding (see Plate 7A). Rather than view these multiple attestations of the golden amphora as confirmation of its traditional place in Greek myth and in Homeric poetry, some scholars assert that the *Odyssey* passage actually calls *Iliad* 23.92 into question. Michael Haslam has argued in connection with the *Odyssey* passage: "discussions of the amphora

---

[38] As set forth in two separate places within the Cambridge commentary on the *Iliad*, by Richardson (1993:176) *ad* 23.92 and by Janko (1992:28), as well as by Haslam (1997:76).

[39] On the François Vase see Shapiro, Iozzo, and Lezzi-Hafter 2013. On the relationship of the *Iliad* and *Odyssey* passages to Stesichoros and the François Vase see also Stewart 1983 and p. 79 below.

[on the François Vase] generally fail to realize that the verse [23.92] is an interpolation, and that the jar's only Homeric occurrence—provided we define *Od.* 24 as Homeric—is in *Od.* 24" (Haslam 1991:36). Proponents of this explanation, including Haslam, point to Aristarchus' athetesis of line 92, a verse that is also missing in papyrus 12, a mid-third-century BCE text.[40] They argue that verses 83a, 83b, and 92 are alternative means of bringing the *Iliad* passage into alignment with that of the *Odyssey*. (By this line of reasoning, both 83a–b and 92 are interpolations and therefore not "Homeric.") They therefore maintain that the text from which Aeschines made his citation did not contain 92.

Allen saw long ago that this supposition is by no means demonstrable: "Aeschines' quotation stops at 91; it is therefore impossible to say with certainty that he omitted 92, the sense of which he had already given."[41] And yet most modern scholars do not even admit this possibility, which would weaken the case for interpolation. Giorgio Pasquali argues circularly that the presence of 83a and 83b in Aeschines guarantees that his text did not read 92.[42] Stephanie West declares that 92 is "replaced" by 83a and 83b.[43] Both Janko and Richardson in their respective discussions in the Cambridge commentary state simply— without even hinting that we have no way of being absolutely certain that this is so—that the text of Aeschines omits 92.[44]

In the face of such a unified front, I propose to reformulate, adding some of my own examples, the general argument of Aldo Di Luzio (1969), who has shown persuasively that 83a and 83b are not likely to be interpolations based on the *Odyssey* 24 passage. Di Luzio argues instead that 83a and 83b were originally in the text along with 92. I omit for now but will return later to the question of whether to include 81a or the internal variations in 77 and 82. I also omit for now but will return later to the even larger question of what "interpolation" even means for an orally composed poem.

Di Luzio's presentation of the text reads as follows:

μὴ ἐμὰ σῶν ἀπάνευθε τιθήμεναι ὀστέ᾽ Ἀχιλλεῦ,	83
+ ἀλλ᾽ ἵνα περ σε καὶ αὐτὸν ὁμοίη γαῖα κεκεύθῃ,	83a
+ χρυσέῳ ἐν ἀμφιφορεῖ, τόν τοι πόρε πότνια μήτηρ,	83b

---

[40] Verses 1–85 of *Iliad* 23 are lost in papyrus 12, with the result that we have no direct way of knowing whether it contained 83a–b. See Haslam 1997:76.

[41] Allen 1924:257.

[42] "Il secondo dei versi che in Eschine seguono l' 83 è quello che nei nostri testi noi leggiamo quale Ψ 92: segno certo che nel testo di Eschine Ψ 92 *al suo posto* mancava" (Pasquali 1952:221–222).

[43] West 1967:171.

[44] See citations in n. 38 above. I do not mean to claim that Aeschines ever quoted line 92. I merely point out that we cannot know whether the text from which Aeschines took his quotation contained 92.

ὡς ὁμοῦ **ἐτράφεμέν** ἐν ὑμετέροισι δόμοισιν,   84
εὖτέ με τυτθὸν ἐόντα Μενοίτιος ἐξ Ὀπόεντος   85
ἤγαγεν ὑμέτερον δ' ἀνδροκτασίης ὕπο λυγρῆς,   86
ἤματι τῷ ὅτε παῖδα κατέκτανον Ἀμφιδάμαντος   87
νήπιος οὐκ ἐθέλων ἀμφ' ἀστραγάλοισι χολωθείς·   88
ἔνθά με δεξάμενος ἐν δώμασιν ἱππότα Πηλεὺς   89
ἔτρεφέ τ' ἐνδυκέως καὶ σὸν θεράποντ' ὀνόμηνεν·   90
ὡς δὲ καὶ ὀστέα νῶιν ὁμὴ σορὸς ἀμφικαλύπτοι   91
(–) **χρύσεος ἀμφιφορεύς, τόν τοι πόρε πότνια μήτηρ.**   92

Iliad 23.83–92 mss. (except first half of 84) + 83a and 83b

In this version of the text, there is ring composition as in nearly every speech in Homer. This ring composition is reinforced by the repetition of the reference to the golden amphora in 83b. The ring composition is further enhanced by the parallelism between ὁμοίη in 83a and ὁμή in 91 as well as the ὀστέα of 83 and 91. The verses 83–83a then correspond to verse 91, while 83b corresponds to 92.[45]

Di Luzio's arguments demonstrate that the passage as printed above is just as "Homeric" as the medievally transmitted *Iliad*, and possibly more so. He writes: "con 83ab, il passo 83–92 manifesterebbe una struttura isomorfica con quella di altri discorsi del testo epico in cui le frasi alla fine del discorso sono spesso la ripresa di frasi occorrenti all' inizio di esso" (Di Luzio 1969:83). Not only is the overall structure Homeric, but the individual constructions within this structure correspond to Homeric usage as well. Together 83a and 83b form the familiar pattern of a negative protasis followed by a reinforcing positive apodosis that expresses the same idea. Compare these lines from the *Odyssey*:

οὐ γάρ οἱ τῇδ' αἶσα φίλων ἀπονόσφιν ὀλέσθαι,
ἀλλ' ἔτι οἱ μοῖρ' ἐστὶ φίλους τ' ἰδέειν καὶ ἱκέσθαι
οἶκον ἐς ὑψόροφον καὶ ἐὴν ἐς πατρίδα γαῖαν.

Odyssey 5.113–115[46]

For it is not measured out for him to perish far away from his friends,
but it is still his fate to see his friends and reach
his high-roofed house and his dear fatherland.

The three-verse structure here is nearly identical to that of 83–83b. We can observe the same phenomenon in a more compressed form in the phrase "ἔοικέ τοι, οὔ τοι ἀεικές" (*Iliad* 9.70). Moreover, within this structure Di Luzio

---

45   See further Di Luzio 1969:84–85.
46   On this construction and on these lines from the *Odyssey* see Di Luzio 1969:85 and 110.

distinguishes still further examples of Homeric usage (Di Luzio 1969:84–86). The first half of 83b (χρυσέῳ ἐν ἀμφιφορεῖ) consists of a complementary locative phrase which specifies the preceding clause. The second half of the line is a parenthetical relative clause of a kind that is used frequently in Homeric poetry to designate particular objects. A parallel is *Iliad* 4.215–216: λῦσε δέ οἱ ζωστῆρα παναίολον ἠδ' ὑπένερθε / ζῶμά τε καὶ μίτρην, τὴν χαλκῆες κάμον ἄνδρες. There are numerous other examples.

Di Luzio's compelling analysis illustrates precisely why variants presented by fourth-century quotations and the Ptolemaic papyri cannot be dismissed as inept or unworthy. Thus there is room to disagree with Stephanie West's analysis of this passage. She writes: "The objections to this version are obvious: 83a seems to be based on Σ 329, but barely makes sense; its insertion makes the construction of Patroclus' speech very confused" (West 1967:172). And yet, as we have seen, there is nothing inherently objectionable within the lines themselves. They simply do not survive in the medieval transmission of the text.

Nor does 92 present problems of usage. If we analyze it independently of 83b, we see that it contains an appositional phrase consisting of a synonym that specifies a preceding noun, the σορός of 91 (Di Luzio 1969:84).[47] To this we can compare the following examples:

> μινυνθάδιον δέ με μήτηρ
> γείνατο Λαοθόη θυγάτηρ Ἄλταο γέροντος
> Ἄλτεω, ὃς Λελέγεσσι φιλοπτολέμοισιν ἀνάσσει

Iliad 22.85–86

> To be short-lived did my mother
> bear me, Laothoe, the daughter of the old man Altes,
> Altes, who rules over the war-loving Leleges

> Τρωσὶν δ' αὖ μετόπισθε γερούσιον ὅρκον ἕλωμαι
> μή τι κατακρύψειν, ἀλλ' ἄνδιχα πάντα δάσασθαι
> κτῆσιν ὅσην πτολίεθρον ἐπήρατον ἐντὸς ἐέργει·

Iliad 22.119–121[48]

---

[47] There are several comments by the scholiast concerning the use of three different words (σορός 23.91, ἀμφιφορεύς 23.92, λάρναξ 24.795) to refer to the same sort of object. Di Luzio effectively demonstrates their semantic equivalence in a discussion of the various Homeric uses of these and other words for vessels.

[48] 22.121 is omitted by some manuscripts, including the Venetus A, and West does not print it, but it is attested universally at 18.512, where it likewise follows the phrase ἄνδιχα πάντα δάσασθαι in the preceding line. West and others take the verse's presence in 18.512 as an indication that 22.121 is an interpolation, based on the earlier passage. A Parry/Lord approach would see the

[If I] afterwards take an oath sworn by the elders from the Trojans
not to hide anything, but to divide up everything in two
as much property as the lovely citadel holds inside

ἀλλὰ σὺ μὲν χαλκόν τε ἅλις χρυσόν τε δέδεξο
δῶρα τά τοι δώσουσι πατὴρ καὶ πότνια μήτηρ

Iliad 22.340–341

But you accept the bronze and sufficient gold,
gifts which my father and lady mother will give you

In the first example the name Altes is repeated in the same case in order to introduce a specifying relative clause. In the second example there is a similar construction, but πάντα of line 120 is further specified by the apposition of κτῆσιν at the beginning of line 121. I adduce the last example because of its striking similarity to 23.92, the very verse in question. Like 83a and 83b, it seems that on its own 92 presents no difficulties.

The problem must originate in the existence of both 83a–b and 92 together at some pre-Alexandrian stage of the text. As Di Luzio points out, this sort of doubling, though unquestionably Homeric, was just the sort of thing that troubled Alexandrian critics. It is only to be expected that one or the other would have been omitted by Aristarchus' time in many texts. And indeed it seems that 83a and 83b had almost completely dropped out of the tradition, in deference to 92, by Aristarchus' day but that remnants of an alternative excision of 92 still remained. The T scholiast states: ἐν πάσαις οὐκ ἦν ὁ στίχος. καὶ Ἀρίσταρχος ἐκ τῆς Νεκυίας αὐτὸν ἐσπάσθαι φησίν ("The verse is not in all. And Aristarchus says that it was taken from the Nekuia"). Di Luzio suggests that Aristarchus conjectured that verse 92 was an interpolation based on the *Odyssey* only after he felt compelled to explain why it was not present in all the texts available to him (Di Luzio 1969:83). This scenario is all the more likely if some of Aristarchus' texts no longer contained 83a and 83b.

Nor is it surprising that verses 83a and 83b lost out so decisively to verse 92 when we consider that *Iliad* 22.121, discussed above, has likewise disappeared from a large majority of manuscripts (including papyrus 27).[49] Di Luzio's examples exhaustively demonstrate that this sort of construction is Homeric, yet its repetitive quality troubled editors enough to jeopardize the place of these

---

presence of both 18.512 and 22.121 as evidence for the formulaic nature of the poetry. In such a system, repetition is not problematic, and the poet would be free to use the verse following ἄνδιχα πάντα δάσασθαι or not, as he saw fit.

[49] Papyrus 27 (= P.Oxy. 558). For the publication history of this papyrus see the Mertens-Pack 3 database (http://cipl93.philo.ulg.ac.be/Cedopal/MP3/dbsearch.aspx), s.v. 989.

verses in the tradition. Verses 83a and 83b had double reason to be suspect in the eyes of the Alexandrians: they contained the repetitive negative and positive formation like that of 22.121 on the one hand, and on the other they nearly duplicated 92.

My formulation of the history of the passage is the opposite of that of Haslam, West, Janko, and Richardson. I posit the loss of 83a–b or 92 in all or most texts between the fourth and second centuries BCE rather than their insertion sometime prior to Aeschines' quotation of them. It is easier to understand the loss of such lines that we know to have been troublesome for scholars of the Hellenistic era than to postulate an interpolation in a text as early as that of Aeschines. The attribution of interpolation to such an early text indeed stretches the limits of the term, for there could have been scant means and little motive to interpolate in a time when literacy was limited and performance was still alive and well as the primary means of access to the Homeric epics for most people. T. W. Allen hit the nail on the head in 1924 when he wrote, "The origin of additions and omissions cannot be referred to anything except to the recitation of rhapsodes, and therefore the phenomenon must have existed and presumably been most frequent during the period when a reading public hardly existed" (267). If we understand "performance" in place of Allen's "recitation" (which implies memorization) we have here an early formulation of what Parry and Lord would later demonstrate by way of fieldwork. What Allen could not have realized is that these additions and omissions are not interpolations but genuine performance-derived multiforms no less "Homeric" than those that survive in the medieval transmission.

Not only is there no reason to theorize that 83a–b/92 is an interpolation, such a theory does nothing to explain other multiforms in the passage that are equally difficult to explain by conventional text-critical methods. The first words of the first line of the passage are not the same as we find in medieval manuscripts: οὐ γὰρ ἔτι versus οὐ μὲν γὰρ (ζωοί γε φίλων ἀπάνευθεν ἑταίρων). The phrase οὐ γὰρ ἔτι is certainly Homeric; it occurs four times in our *Iliad* and *Odyssey*. The phrase οὐ μὲν γὰρ, on the other hand, occurs forty-three times. Van der Valk objects to Aeschines' reading, stating simply: "It is obvious that the solemn formula of the Homeric mss. οὐ μὲν γὰρ represents the original text" (1964:327n230). It is not obvious at all: the number of occurrences suggests that οὐ γὰρ ἔτι is the more marked form and arguably the more solemn. But by far the most remarkable evidence in support of Aeschines' reading is the fact that the A scholia attest that this was the reading in some of the "city editions" (ἔν τισι τῶν πολιτικῶν). An old attestation with ancient authority, it deserves at least as much consideration as the text transmitted into medieval times.

Line 81a, another plus verse, holds up to similar scrutiny. This line is perfectly formulaic. The phrase μάρνασθαι δηΐοισιν occurs in verse-initial position four times in our *Iliad* (9.317, 11.190, 11.205, 17.148). The participle μαρνάμενον is likewise attested in various cases in verse-initial position throughout the *Iliad*: μαρνάμενον 3.307, 6.204; μαρνάμενοι 6.257, 6.328, 14.25; μαρναμένων 12.429, 13.579, 16.775; μαρναμένοισι 13.96. The phrase Ἑλένης ἕνεκ' ἠυκόμοιο is also found at *Iliad* 9.339, and there are six instances of the phrase Ἑλένης πόσις ἠυκόμοιο, all in verse-final position.[50] Others have viewed the formulaic nature of verse 81a as proof of interpolation.[51] But this view is fundamentally at odds with the findings of Lord that in the system within which the *Iliad* and the *Odyssey* were composed, every line is formulaic.[52] Stephanie West (1967:13) is sympathetic to the idea of interpolation, but acknowledges:

> Some of these [verses] may have been composed for interpolation, but it is equally possible that they come from lost hexameter poetry. Obviously none of these plus-verses is indispensable, but since there are many equally dispensable lines in our texts of Homer which no one would excise, this would not in itself be a sufficient reason for rejecting them.

West here distinguishes between two types of interpolation: those composed by the "interpolator," and those taken out of their original context and inserted improperly by the "interpolator" into another passage. West's own analysis suggests that the plus verses are as "Homeric" as medievally transmitted verses, but she nevertheless treats them as "interpolations" that have no place in our texts of the *Iliad* and the *Odyssey*.

Line 23.82 of Aeschines' quotation presents a comparable difficulty for those who insist on the aberrance of the fourth-century quotations of Homer. The Venetus A at this line reads ἄλλο δέ τοι ἐρέω καὶ ἐφήσομαι αἴ κε πίθηαι. As with 77, the variation is internal to the line and therefore is not a question of plus or minus verses (or the *numerus versuum*, as it is often referred to by scholars).

---

[50] Cf. Richardson 1993 *ad* 23.81.

[51] As evidenced by such statements as Allen's "a dispensable line ... constructed of two Homeric pieces" (1924:257). Allen's remark is a typical response to plus verses, even today.

[52] See Lord 1960/2000:47 (Lord is speaking of the South Slavic tradition here, but he goes on to apply his findings to the Homeric epics by analogy). Textual critics of Homer today seem no less reluctant to accept this formulation than those of Parry's time. See Parry's comments (written in 1928) in Parry 1971:8–9. Parry cites Antoine Meillet, whose *Origines indo-européennes des mètres grecs* (1923) had appeared five years earlier: "Homeric epic is entirely composed of formulae handed down from poet to poet. An examination of any passage will quickly reveal that it is made up of lines and fragments of lines which are reproduced word for word in one or several other passages. And even lines, parts of which are not found in another passage, have the character of formulae, and it is doubtless pure chance that they are not attested elsewhere" (1923:61, as quoted in Parry 1928:10 [= Parry 1971:9]). In asserting that Homeric diction is formulaic I do not deny Homeric artistry. Cf. Parry 1932:14 [= Parry 1971:335]: "The fame of a singer comes not from quitting the tradition but from putting it to the best use." See Dué and Ebbott 2010 for a demonstration of the complex levels of meaning that are possible in oral traditional poetry.

Line 82 is the only instance of this verse in Homer, although the construction is a familiar one. (Cf. *Iliad* 1.207: ἦλθον ἐγὼ παύσουσα τὸ σὸν μένος, αἴ κε πίθηαι.) The phraseology of Aeschines' reading, on the other hand (ἄλλο δέ τοι ἐρέω **σὺ δ' ἐνὶ φρεσὶ βάλλεο σῇσιν**), is attested eleven times in the medieval texts of the *Iliad*. I do not suggest that Aeschines' reading is superior or more "Homeric": I merely propose that it is no less so.

On this point the positions taken by editors break down. The work of Di Luzio, Labarbe, Haslam, and others has challenged the negative assumptions scholars make about the validity of ancient multiforms. But where the intent of Di Luzio, for example, is to find the *ipsissima verba* of the one true Homer, the editor of a printed edition must necessarily privilege one reading over another in every case. Gennaro D'Ippolito (1977), to cite another example, prides himself on being the only editor to include plus verses in his text of *Odyssey* 5,[53] but his acceptance of the authenticity of plus verses does not solve the question of what to do with variation such as what we find in *Iliad* 23.82, or the situation in which a papyrus or quotation presents an entire formulaic line in place of another.[54] Within the model of the single monumental composer that D'Ippolito proposes, they cannot both be accepted. Janko and others, on the other hand, accept the idea of an Aristarchean *numerus versuum*, but do not admit that the textual variants that Aristarchus records can be genuine performance variants and worthy of inclusion in the text.[55] Like D'Ippolito, they have no solution for multiple readings, mutually exclusive in their view, that occur in the same line or formular unit—other than the elevation of one reading at the expense of others which may be equally genuine.[56]

---

[53] D'Ippolito 1977 *ad Odyssey* 5.24a.

[54] See, for example, *Odyssey* 5.21 τὴν δ' ἀπαμειβόμενος προσέφη νεφεληγερέτα Ζεύς. Papyrus 30 (= *P. Tebt.* 3.697) has in place of this line τὴν δ' ἠμείβετ' ἔπειτα πατὴρ ἀνδρῶν τε θεῶν τε (as restored by D'Ippolito), which also occurs at *Iliad* 1.544. D'Ippolito does print the alternate line in his *apparatus*. For the publication history of Papyrus 30 see the Mertens-Pack 3 database (http://cipl93.philo.ulg.ac.be/Cedopal/MP3/dbsearch.aspx), s.v. 1056.

[55] Janko 1992:22. For arguments against Janko's position, see Nagy 1996a:138–140.

[56] Haslam's position on plus verses and variations found in the Ptolemaic papyri is more subtle than the other positions surveyed here but still problematic. He notes: "Whatever kind of a history they have behind them, the verses existed, and while editors whose quest is the original Homer may not see fit to admit them or even to report them, the fact remains that they were just as much a part of the Homeric text as verses whose subsequent life was longer" (1997:68). I am much in agreement on this point. But Haslam reveals a prejudgment when he says, "From a transmissional point of view, however, it is easier to view plus-verses as accretions which did not gain a sufficiently firm hold to be perpetuated than as pristine material which has dropped" (1997:68). See also his 1991 article in which he calls *Iliad* 23.92 an "interpolation" and not "Homeric." The distinction between "accretions" and "pristine material" is still contingent upon an original text. Haslam's model, like those of the other scholars I have cited, excludes the possibility of a multiform text that does not privilege any single performance-based textual tradition.

The substitution of one formula for another is part of the poetics of the oral-formulaic system. Parry (1932:15 [= 1971:336]) demonstrated the significance of this for the text of Homer. He writes:

> The formula thus is by no means the unit of the singer's poetry, but it nevertheless ever tends to become so, for no singer ever tells the same tale twice in the same words. His poem will always follow the same general pattern, but this verse or that will be left out, or replaced by another verse or part of a verse, and he will leave out and add whole passages as the time and mood of his hearers calls for a fuller or briefer telling of a tale or of a given part of a tale. Thus the oral poem even in the mouth of the same singer is ever in a state of change; and it is the same when his poetry is sung by others.

Variation is a clear sign of the oral poetics of recomposition in performance and no one formula is more or less Homeric than another. Here we come to the crux of the problem. What do textual critics of Homer mean when they say that a verse has been interpolated?[57] For Parry the term "interpolation" would be applicable neither to plus verses nor to variations such as that found in line 82 of Aeschines' quotation.

This passage challenges the way we deal with multiforms, particularly those that are demonstrably formulaic and in strict accordance with Homeric usage. The variations take the form of both internal variation within lines and fluctuation in the *numerus versuum* resulting from expansion and compression at the performance level.[58] Many of the features that are Homeric in 83–92 are present in a more compressed form even if 83a, 83b, and 92 are eliminated from the text. Let us consider:

μὴ ἐμὰ σῶν ἀπάνευθε τιθήμεναι ὀστέ' Ἀχιλλεῦ,	83
ἀλλ' ὁμοῦ ὡς ἐτράφημεν ἐν ὑμετέροισι δόμοισιν,	84
εὖτέ με τυτθὸν ἐόντα Μενοίτιος ἐξ Ὀπόεντος	85
ἤγαγεν ὑμέτερον δ' ἀνδροκτασίης ὕπο λυγρῆς,	86
ἤματι τῷ ὅτε παῖδα κατέκτανον Ἀμφιδάμαντος	87
νήπιος οὐκ ἐθέλων ἀμφ' ἀστραγάλοισι χολωθείς·	88
ἔνθά με δεξάμενος ἐν δώμασιν ἱππότα Πηλεὺς	89
ἔτραφέ τ' ἐνδυκέως καὶ σὸν θεράποντ' ὀνόμηνεν·	90
ὣς δὲ καὶ ὀστέα νῶϊν ὁμὴ σορὸς ἀμφικαλύπτοι	91

---

[57] See also the similar arguments made by Bird (2010:86), who asks the same question.
[58] On fluctuation of the *numerus versuum* and expansion/compression see Nagy 1996a:138–140, with citations, Bird 2010:49–49, and chapters 3 and 4 below.

The variation found within verse 84, caused by the fluctuation between the shorter and longer version, has been eliminated. There is still ring composition and verbal repetition of ὀστέα in 83 and 91. Verses 83–84 alone are a somewhat elliptical version of the construction featuring a negative protasis / positive reinforcing apodosis—if we understand an ellipse of τιθήμεναι in 84. The presence of 83a–b and 92 expands and reinforces these features. The textual critic who wishes to print an edition of the *Iliad* is forced to choose between these two quite different texts, either of which is defensible in terms of Homeric usage.

For the Alexandrian editors, that choice was nearly always in favor of the shorter of two variants. As Di Luzio points out, many characteristics of oral poetry such as the adding of description, specification, recapitulation, and repetition, all connected paratactically or in apposition, were antithetical to the aesthetics of the day in much the same way that they are now.[59] Verses that contained these features met with a very difficult reception. The plus verses which are so weakly attested and other verses which have survived medieval transmission but which we know to have been athetized or omitted by Alexandrian editors are proof of this. Their possession of these same features surely accounts for the disappearance of plus verses from most texts that survived to Aristarchus' day.

***

How does the presence or absence of the golden amphora in this passage affect our larger *Iliad*? If we take a step beyond the history of transmission and interpret the significance of Aeschines' quoted multiforms from an artistic or "literary" perspective, we can see that in fact the issue is neither minor nor banal. Homeric multiforms can and do present vastly different narrative consequences. These narrative consequences are not accidental, nor are they *ad hoc* inventions; rather, multiformity can signal alternative performance traditions that are not incorporated into our *Iliad* and *Odyssey*. In this case, the presence or absence of the golden amphora has not only a literary but also a cultural and religious consequence: it is a case of signaling or not signaling the reassembly of Achilles' bones into an immortalized hero.[60]

Throughout the *Iliad* there is reference to a larger event that will take place outside of the confines of the epic, and that is the death of Achilles. We are constantly reminded of his short life and impending doom, close on the heels of Hektor's.[61] The presence here of the golden amphora, which Achilles' mother gave him in anticipation of his approaching death, evokes in Patroklos' reminder

[59]   Di Luzio 1969:142–143. See also D'Ippolito 1977:246–247.
[60]   See especially Nagy 1979:208–209 and Stewart 1983:64.
[61]   Cf. *Iliad* 1.352, 416; 18.59–60, 89–90, 95–96; 19.416–417; 22.359–360; 23.80–81; 24.132.

not only that impending death but its aftermath.[62] Our awareness of the presence or absence of the golden amphora in the narrative of Achilles' death indicates whether he will achieve immortality through cult or pass into obscurity in the underworld.[63] Although the *Iliad* centers on Achilles' mortality, here we have a glimpse of the immortality that is so important in the tradition outside of the *Iliad*.[64] Andrew Stewart (1983) has argued that the golden amphora is the focal point for the two conceptions of Achilles on the François Vase as well: he understands the compositional unity of the François Vase to be centered on the golden amphora depicted on it. The wedding of Peleus and Thetis is set amidst narratives that explore the tensions between mortality and immortality, peerless excellence and savage wrath, and mighty prowess and terrible hubris in the figure of Achilles. Stewart notes: "Appropriately, all these themes intersect in the motif of Dionysos' amphora and its twin promises of death and immortality" (1983:66). The golden amphora points to a critical dichotomy in how the Achilles story ends.

***

Fourth-century quotations of Homer are some of our oldest witnesses and preserve information about the various epic traditions that we have otherwise lost. In one of those traditions, Achilles was not left to dwell in Hades, lamenting the choice he had made to re-enter the fight and now preferring a life of servitude to death with κλέος (as in *Odyssey* 11.487–491). Instead his bones were assembled and placed in a golden amphora along with those of Patroklos, thereby securing his immortality in cult. A multitextual approach can embrace both possibilities, as well as demonstrate the reality of oral performance and transmission, which requires that no oral text will ever be composed, performed, and recorded the same way twice.

Many of the issues raised by the two quotations examined here will need to be confronted again in connection with the Homeric papyri, which are discussed in the next chapter and which are similarly multiform. I would like to conclude the present chapter by making two final points about how we treat the multiforms preserved in the quotations.

First, the question of just what text a court reporter would have read out to the jury in the fourth century BCE is a good one. We have no direct evidence

---

[62] On the significance of Patroklos' reminding Achilles of his own death see also Di Luzio 1969:85 and Pestalozzi 1945:33.

[63] For a discussion of Hades-type narrative closure vs. "Elysium"-type narrative closure, see Nagy 1979, chaps. 9–10.

[64] On the hero cult of Achilles in the area of the Black Sea, where Achilles was believed to live as an immortal on the island of Leukē ("the White Island"), see Hedreen 1991.

that an official state text existed for Homer or any other poetry at this time.[65] Elsewhere I have suggested that the later Lycurgan law that called for official state copies of the tragedies of Aeschylus, Sophocles, and Euripides to be placed in the Metroon had little to do with the establishment of the text and more to do with symbolically elevating the poetry to the status of law (Dué 2000). We simply cannot assume—nor should we expect—that at this transmissional stage any one text of Homer was canonical.

Nevertheless, on principle I do not believe, as has been asserted by Van der Valk, that Aeschines could have or would have deliberately altered the text either on the occasion of delivering the speech or in its subsequent publication.[66] Wherever ancient citations of Homer differ from the medieval transmission, I submit that there are generally reasons other than deliberate alteration by the quoter. Aeschines argues with the defense about the *interpretation* of the cited text, not about which text is the correct one. Altering Homer to suit an argument and paraphrasing (as sometimes occurs in Plato) are different matters entirely.[67] Quoting Homer is not the same as quoting the Bible, as Andrew Ford (1999) has pointed out, but Homeric poetry carried an undeniable authority that makes the notion of interpolation—even overlooking the difficulty of identifying a canonical text to be interpolated—extremely problematic.[68]

The preceding analysis shows that the multiformity presented by Aeschines' quotation of *Iliad* 23 is of a formulaic nature that is in no way incompatible with what we know of the system as a whole. Rather than try to find ways to dismiss, denigrate, or otherwise obfuscate such multiformity, I submit that it is better to treat each of the surviving quotations as valid, even if fragmentary, instantiations of the *Iliad* or the *Odyssey* in their own right. Allowing each instantiation to enter our awareness and our appreciation of the *Iliad* and the *Odyssey* as orally created poems is problematic only for those who insist that there is one text alone that can be authoritative, that composed by the postulated "Homer" himself. Albert Lord explains why this is not the right approach for oral poetry (1960:100–101):

---

[65] See chapter 1 (with citations *ad loc.*) on the role that the state-sponsored Panathenaic festival played in the formation of the Homeric text as we now have it. I don't mean to imply otherwise here; I mean only that there were not official state copies of the poems kept for the purposes of fixing the text in a particular form.

[66] Van der Valk argues that Aeschines has inserted 83a–b in place of 92 early in Patroklos' appeal in order to support his argument that Patroklos and Achilles are the archetypal pair of "chaste" lovers (1964:326–331). I do not agree with Van der Valk's argument that the text of Aeschines' citation supports his argument more than the medievally transmitted text does.

[67] See, e.g., *Apology* 28c–d and further examples collected in Labarbe 1949:340–360.

[68] On the authority of Homer for ancient disputes see also Perlman 1964 and Higbie 1997.

Our real difficulty arises from the fact that, unlike the oral poet, we are not accustomed to thinking in terms of fluidity. We find it difficult to grasp something that is multiform. It seems to us necessary to construct an ideal text or to seek an original, and we remain dissatisfied with an ever-changing phenomenon. I believe that once we know the facts of oral composition we must cease trying to find an original of any traditional song. From one point of view each performance is an original.... The truth of the matter is that our concept of "the original," of "the song," simply makes no sense in oral tradition.... In an oral tradition the idea of an original is illogical. It follows then that we cannot correctly speak of a "variant," since there is no original to be varied! Yet songs are related to one another in varying degrees; not, however, in the relationship of variant to original, in spite of the recourse so often made to an erroneous concept of "oral transmission"; for "oral transmission," "oral composition," "oral creation," and "oral performance" are all one and the same thing. Our greatest error is to attempt to make "scientifically" rigid a phenomenon that is fluid.

By imposing an authorial model on what has survived of Homeric poetry from antiquity, modern editors necessarily exclude an abundance of alternative instantiations of the *Iliad* and the *Odyssey*, and so a wealth of data about the system in which those two poems were composed.

Just as problematic is the fact that this same authorial approach is the one taken by the vast majority of editors of *all* Greek and Roman authors, not just Homer. At the outset of this chapter we saw that Plato, like Propertius, read τι at *Iliad* 23.103. But until relatively recently few modern scholars could know it. When I wrote my 2001 article on this multiform, I noted that although the A and F manuscripts of Plato on which modern texts are based read τι, all modern editors of Plato that I could locate at that time printed τις. These editions make this slight but significant change in order to bring Plato's text into alignment with the medievally transmitted *Iliad*, whose reading of τις, I stress, is by no means certain. In addition, only one of the editors of the more than ten editions of the *Republic* that I consulted indicates in the *apparatus criticus* that they have done so. This is a dangerous practice, and it is based on two flawed assumptions: that fourth-century quotations are not reliable witnesses to the text of Homer and that somehow the same editorial principles that apply to the rest of the text of Plato do not apply to quotations. Fortunately, the practice appears to be changing. S. R. Slings's 2003 edition of the *Republic* prints τι, while noting in the *apparatus* that most Homer manuscripts have τις.

It is not a defensible editorial practice to alter Plato's text here or elsewhere to bring it into alignment with our concept of a Homeric "vulgate." No such vulgate existed during the fourth century BCE at least.[69] This can be proven from the numerous fourth-century quotations of Homer in Plato and orators such as Aeschines that do not accord with our medievally transmitted manuscripts. Moreover, the surviving papyri, the next-oldest witnesses we possess (chapter 3), as well as the ancient scholia (chapter 4), confirm that the kind of variation presented by fourth-century quotations remained a feature of Homeric texts for several centuries after Plato. When combined, the picture they present of the earliest written forms of the *Iliad* and the *Odyssey* is one of fluctuation in the number of verses and considerable variation within lines. There is no justification for insisting that Plato's text correspond exactly with the medieval manuscripts, whose relative uniformity, as we have seen already in chapter 1, cannot be entirely explained, nor can it be traced back to a single historical source. At any rate, certainly the *apparatus criticus* is the appropriate place to note or comment on discrepancies such as this one. Ancient quotations, papyri, and the scholia are our only sources for variant readings that were at one time a part of the living oral tradition but dropped out. When editors not only change the reading of Plato but also fail to indicate that they have done so in the *apparatus*, they hide from students of Homer a window into the vibrant oral tradition that is now mostly lost to us.[70]

---

[69] As was seen as early as 1906 by Grenfell and Hunt (68). For more on the concept of a "vulgate," see Dué 2001a.

[70] Martin West, for example, does not seem to have known that Plato read τι at 23.103 when he compiled his 1998–2000 critical edition of the *Iliad*, citing only the Propertius passage in his *apparatus*.

Chapter 3

"And Then an Amazon Came"
Homeric Papyri

IN THE PREVIOUS CHAPTER WE SAW that the earliest witnesses to the text of the *Iliad*, in the form of early quotations, are multiform. Additional verses and variations within verses are not uncommon, and the attested variations are often of a demonstrably formulaic nature, by which I mean they are perfectly in keeping with what we know of Homeric diction. The fragmentary texts of the *Iliad* and the *Odyssey* that survive on papyrus are the next-oldest witnesses to the text of Homer. Some papyrus fragments predate the medieval tradition by as many as twelve hundred years, and like the early quotations, they are multiform—so much so that they have been labeled "wild" by the scholars who work with them. In papyrus texts from the third and second centuries BCE, we find differences on the level of entire lines of the poetry. Also prevalent is variation in the formulaic phrasing within lines, such as the presence of one noun-epithet formula in place of another. As in the quotations, there are also numerous verses attested in the papyri that are seemingly intrusive from the standpoint of the medieval transmission. These additional verses, the so-called plus verses, are not present in the majority of the medieval manuscripts of the *Iliad*. Other verses that are canonical in the medieval manuscripts are absent from the papyri. It is not until about 150 BCE, in the era of Aristarchus, that the papyrus texts begin to present a relatively more uniform text that more closely resembles the medieval manuscripts, and multiformity persists even after this date.

Graeme Bird has been closely affiliated with the Homer Multitext since its earliest days, and his 2010 book, *Multitextuality in the Homeric Iliad: The Witness of the Ptolemaic Papyri*, advocates for an understanding of the multiformity attested in the Homeric papyri that is similar to my own. Drawing on the work of Milman Parry and especially Albert Lord, Bird emphasizes the natural multiformity of poetry composed in performance and the ways in which live performances necessarily contributed to the transmission of the text of the *Iliad*. In this respect Bird's work differs considerably from most earlier studies. Stephanie West's (1967) work on the Ptolemaic papyri of Homer is dismissive of most multiforms transmitted in the papyri, as is Michael Haslam in the *New Companion to Homer* (1997).[1] Derek Collins, by contrast, takes an approach similar to Bird's:

> The question of the authenticity of these variations is also misleading to the extent that it presupposes an "original" text against which the variations ought to be judged. Instead, it makes more sense to view the variations as stemming from or produced for live performances during which variations were expected—which also means they must all be regarded as "authentic." (Collins 2004:216)

Both Bird and Collins see the multiformity attested in the Ptolemaic papyri as being in some way connected to performance, either directly (in the sense of transcripts of lives performance) or indirectly (in the sense that the textual transmission still reflects, even in later eras, the multiformity that is natural to poetry composed in performance). In this brief chapter then I will strive not to simply repeat the work of Bird or Collins, though I have certainly been influenced by it, and instead to build on some of the implications of my previous chapter as well as Bird's findings, using some of my own examples.[2]

The fieldwork of Parry and Lord showed that composition in performance allows for the expansion or compression of the theme or episode that the singer is performing, as well as a certain degree of variability from performance to performance (Bird 2010:48–49). The multiformity of the papyri and the plus and minus verses they transmit are evidence of what any given Homeric performance might have included, the operation of the system underlying the performance, and what the epic tradition as a notional totality comprised. I and my collaborators on the Homer Multitext assert that these examples of multiformity and compression and expansion—coming late as they do in the performance tradition, yet at the same time early from the standpoint of the transmission of the text—provide crucial insight into the system in which the Homeric poems were composed as well as the means by which they were trans-

---

[1] For more on West's and Haslam's views see above, pp. 69–76. For more on the Homeric papyri and the multiformity of they exhibit, see Dué and Ebbott 2010:169–191, where three papyri containing text from *Iliad* 10 from different eras are compared to the Venetus A manuscript.

[2] Bird's findings are, as to be expected, quite similar to those expressed in Dué 2001a and Dué and Ebbott 2009, 2010, and 2017.

mitted.[3] Finally, attested multiforms also very likely reveal to us the Homeric poems as they were actually experienced by ancient audiences, information which is in many ways just as valuable and worth preserving as any notional "original" text.

***

I noted at the beginning of chapter 2 that the first ten lines of the *Iliad* exhibit considerable multiformity when all ancient sources are taken into account, in keeping with what we would expect of an oral-derived text. I'd like to begin my discussion of the papyri with a well-known example that concerns the final line of the poem.[4] The medieval manuscripts and all modern editions, such as that of Munro and Allen's 1920 Oxford Classical Text, end this way, at *Iliad* 24.804:

[804]   ὣς οἵ γ' ἀμφίεπον τάφον Ἕκτορος ἱπποδάμοιο.
[804]   Thus they celebrated the burial of Hektor, tamer of horses.

This is a deeply meaningful ending that brings closure to the story of the *Iliad*, while at the same time powerfully looking ahead to the death, lamentation for, and funeral of the *Iliad*'s central figure, Achilles. As Thetis makes clear in *Iliad* 18.95–96, Achilles' death will come "straightaway after Hektor" (αὐτίκα γάρ τοι ἔπειτα μεθ' Ἕκτορα), and the two are inextricably linked.[5] But it seems that

---

3   We should be careful to note that even though the Ptolemaic papyri are, as I have stated, "late" in terms of the performance tradition of these poems, the texts they preserve are not necessarily late. Some papyrus texts are clearly not hastily made transcripts of performance, but rather carefully assembled editions, whose ultimate source is not known to us. It has been argued by Ready (2015:2) on the basis of comparative evidence that "the textualized versions of Homeric epic that stemmed from a process of dictation should be understood as co-creations of the poet, scribe, and collector." My own understanding of the textualization process differs in some ways from that of Ready, however. While I see scribes as editors and in many cases scholars and poets in their own right, I do not believe that the multiformity that survives in texts of the *Iliad* on papyrus usually results from the intervention of scribes or collectors. Certainly the circumstances of performance, including any patronage associated with them, may have played a shaping role in the overall structure of the performance and no doubt affected the choices of the composer as he performed. But in the vast majority of cases, attested multiforms in the Ptolemaic papyri conform to what we know of the system as a whole and are clearly a product of it. (See chapter 2, above, and further below for examples.) I see therefore no reason to treat these Ptolemaic multiforms as in any way less "Homeric" than those that survive in the medieval manuscripts.

4   For discussion of the attested variations on the final line of the *Iliad* and their relationship to the *Aithiopis* see the edition of Bernabé 1996 (*Aithiopis* fragment 1) as well as Burgess 2001:140–142 and Davies 2016:46–52 with additional bibliography and primary sources discussed *ad loc.*

5   See chapter 2 above, p. 78.

not every Iliad ended this way. A note in the scholia of the eleventh-century CE Townley manuscript (Burney 86) states that "some write" (τινὲς γράφουσιν):

[804] ὣς οἵ γ᾽ ἀμφίεπον τάφον Ἕκτορος· ἦλθε δ᾽ Ἀμάζων,
[804a] Ἄρηος θυγάτηρ μεγαλήτορος ἀνδροφόνοιο

[804] Thus they celebrated the burial of Hektor, and then an
Amazon came
[804a] the daughter of great-hearted man-slaying Ares

We might be tempted to dismiss this comment as resulting from some sort of confusion involving the *Aithiopis* in the Epic Cycle. We know that by the time the poems of the Cycle came to be summarized by Proklos (the primary form in which we now know them), they had been edited to fit around the *Iliad* and the *Odyssey* and to flow relatively seamlessly from one to the next (Burgess 2001:132–143). This is how Proklos describes the initial episodes of the *Aithiopis*:

Ἀμαζὼν Πενθεσίλεια παραγίνεται Τρωσὶ συμμαχήσουσα· Ἄρεως μὲν θυγάτηρ Θρᾷσα δὲ τὸ γένος· καὶ κτείνει αὐτὴν ἀριστεύουσαν Ἀχιλλεύς· οἱ δὲ Τρῶες αὐτὴν θάπτουσι. Ἀχιλλεὺς Θερσίτην ἀναιρεῖ λοιδορηθεὶς πρὸς αὐτοῦ καὶ ὀνειδισθεὶς τὸν ἐπὶ τῇ Πενθεσιλείᾳ λεγόμενον ἔρωτα·[6]

The Amazon Penthesileia comes to Troy as an ally of the Trojans. She is the daughter of Ares and Thracian by birth. In the middle of her *aristeia*, Achilles kills her, and the Trojans bury her. Achilles slays Thersites, fter having been reviled by him and reproached for his alleged love for Penthesileia.

If we can trust Proklos, the *Aithiopis* began with the arrival of Penthesileia (though it is by no means certain that we can trust Proklos). Could this attested multiform really be a verse from the *Aithiopis*, wrongly added to the *Iliad*?

If that were our only evidence, we might be tempted to think so. But a similar variation at the end of the *Iliad* is also attested on a first-century CE papyrus (104):[7]

[804] ὣς οἵ γ᾽ ἀμφίεπον τάφον Ἕκτορος· ἦλθε δ᾽ Ἀμάζων,
[804a] Ὀτρήρ[η]<ς> θυγάτηρ εὐειδὴς Πεντηεσίλ<ε>ια

---

[6]   The text is taken from folio 6r in the Venetus A, printed here as written.
[7]   Papyrus 104 (= P. Lond. Lit. 1.6 + P. Ryl. 3.540 + P. Lib. Cong. inv. 4082b + P. Morgan inv. M662[6b] + [27k] + P. Giss. Univ. inv. 213). For the publication history of this papyrus see the Mertens-Pack 3 database (http://cipl93.philo.ulg.ac.be/Cedopal/MP3/dbsearch.aspx), s.v. 643.

[804]   Thus they celebrated the burial of Hektor, and then an
            Amazon came
[804a] the daughter of Otrera, beautiful Penthesileia.[8]

A plausible explanation is that even as late as the first century CE, the division between the *Iliad* and the *Aithiopis* was not so cut and dried. It could certainly be the case that the *Aithiopis* began before the traditional end of our *Iliad*, and that the *Iliad* tradition and the *Aithiopis* tradition overlapped in content.[9] Likewise the *Iliad* may well have extended further in more fluid phases of the epic tradition. Even after the poem had crystallized into the shape in which we now know it, in nonregulated contexts a versatile singer with a broad repertoire should have been able to pick up and leave off where he saw fit (as time, occasion, and audience response guided him). Only highly regulated festival contexts would have required a particular ending to the *Iliad*. Even if what we know from medieval manuscripts as verse 24.804 was the usual way to end the *Iliad*, there was nothing to stop a skilled singer from continuing the story if he and his audience desired it.

The *Odyssey* gives us a glimpse of this flexibility in its opening invocation: the poet asks the Muse to tell the story of Odysseus' wandering, starting from whatever point she chooses (τῶν ἁμόθεν γε, θεά, θύγατερ Διός, εἰπὲ καὶ ἡμῖν). In *Odyssey* 8, the Muse inspires the singer Demodokos to pick up a story thread (μοῦσ' ἄρ' ἀοιδὸν ἀνῆκεν ἀειδέμεναι κλέα ἀνδρῶν / οἴμης τῆς τότ' ἄρα κλέος οὐρανὸν εὐρὺν ἵκανε 8.73–74). In other words, Demodokos, inspired by the Muse, dips into the epic tradition and pulls out from among the many tales he could tell the story of the quarrel of Agamemnon and Odysseus. Where a singer starts and stops in such a tradition is significant, not least because there was more than one place to do so.[10]

The introduction of Penthesileia into a story that has been up to now a tale of the consequences of Achilles' wrath, which was provoked by his grief at the taking of Briseis, changes the arc of the poem considerably. But just because we prize the thematic closure that *Iliad* 24 brings does not mean that the poem always had to be sung that way. The addition of Penthesileia to the poem would bring to the fore a theme associated with Achilles that is for the most part not emphasized in our *Iliad*, namely his erotic associations with a wide variety of female

---

[8]   Otrera was a queen of the Amazons. For more on Penthesileia, her lineage and alliance with the Trojans, and her fatal battle with Achilles, see Mayor 2014:297–304.
[9]   On this point see again Burgess 2001:140–142, discussing the work of Kopff (1981 and 1983). Kopff argues on the basis of surviving visual representations that the *Aithiopis* tradition at one time included the ransom of Hektor.
[10] On the concept of a story thread, see *Odyssey* 8.73–74 with Nagy 1979:18n3.

characters beyond Briseis, including Deidameia on Skyros, various women of the towns he sacked throughout the Troad, Polyxena, and even Helen.

This is a theme that I explored in my 2002 study of Briseis, where I suggested on the basis of surviving tales about Achilles in a variety of sources that there were local, Aeolic epic traditions in which Achilles has a love interest who helps him storm Pedasos and/or Methymna (and possibly other towns as well). I further suggested that the *Iliad* associates Briseis with these women on some level (Dué 2002:57–65). Archaic vase paintings too depict Briseis and Achilles together in a way that suggests a romantic encounter in which Briseis falls in love with and aids Achilles in the pattern of Ariadne and Theseus or Medea and Jason (Dué 2002:33–36). The *Iliad* would be likely to screen out such an erotic narrative, but I argue that it does not do so entirely. In *Iliad* 1 Briseis leaves Achilles "unwillingly" (ἀέκουσα 1.348), and in *Iliad* 9 Achilles proclaims that he loves her as a man loves his wife, even though he won her in war (ἐκ θυμοῦ φίλεον δουρικτητήν περ ἐοῦσαν 9.343). In Briseis' lament for Patroklos in *Iliad* 19 we learn of her hope to become Achilles' *kouridiē alokhos* (19.298) in Phthia.

The existence of an erotic component to Achilles' killing of Penthesileia in the *Aithiopis* is supported by several Archaic vases, including a black-figure amphora signed by Exekias (ca. 540/530 BCE, British Museum B 210; see Plate 8) that appears to depict the moment Achilles falls in love with Penthesileia, as he is killing her. Their locked eyes (very unusual in Archaic vase painting) convey this moment of erotic connection.[11] As Marco Fantuzzi notes in his wide-ranging study of Achilles in love: "It is a love which lives only for a few moments on the battlefield and is, in a way, a product of Achilles' martial valour; for it is only after he has inflicted the mortal wound that Achilles is able to gaze on the face of his great foe, Penthesileia, thus falling in love" (Fantuzzi 2012:268).

The *Iliad* that we know mostly omits these erotic narratives, which seem to have been more prevalent in the poems of the Epic Cycle, perhaps because of the *Iliad*'s focus on Achilles' wrath in connection with Agamemnon's seizure of Briseis, and his subsequent grief for Patroklos. As Fantuzzi observed: "The limited presence of eros in the *Iliad*, and in particular the limitation of its narrative relevance to the female sphere, cannot be satisfactorily explained just by the fact that the poem was a martial epos. Tailoring the role and features of eros to this particular aspect of heroic life may have been a choice of poetics pursued by the oral tradition that generated the *Iliad*. In fact, in the *Aethiopis* ... we find that eros and martial prowess are treated as interrelated and overlapping

---

[11] See also Fantuzzi 2012:270 and Nagy 2013:75–77. For more on the visual representations of Achilles and Penthesileia see Kossatz-Deissmann 1981, Ahlberg-Cornell 1992:69–70, and Mayor 2014:298–301.

aspects of the heroic world" (Fantuzzi 2012:267). The themes of the *Iliad*, as I noted in chapter 1, center around Achilles *mēnis* and *akhos*, not *eros*.

There are still other themes that such a performance might have highlighted by including the story of Penthesileia. As Fantuzzi has explored in his study, the plot of the *Aithiopis* and the Penthesileia narrative in particular involve "a series of mirror repetitions of the structure of the *Iliad*," beginning with an attack on Achilles' honor (by Thersites) in connection with a woman and his temporary withdrawal from the army. Following the work of Burgess (2009), I see such repetitions as the result of deeply entrenched traditional patterns at play in the epic poetry associated with the life of Achilles rather than an intentional mirroring of the *Iliad*. But by including the story of Penthesileia, a poet necessarily juxtaposes her storyline with that of the *Iliad*, and thereby highlights their shared structures and themes.

One such thematic parallel concerns the very name of Penthesileia, as Gregory Nagy has shown:[12]

> A big question remains: why would Achilles fall in love with the Amazon Penthesileia in particular? A key to the answer is the name of this Amazon, Penthesileia, which means 'she who has *penthos* for the people [*lāos*]'. This name is a perfect parallel to the name of Achilles, the full form of which can be reconstructed linguistically as **Akhi-lāos* and which is understood in the specialized language of Homeric poetry to mean 'he who has *akhos* for the people [*lāos*]'. Not only the names of these epic characters but even the characters themselves are beautifully matched. When Achilles and Penthesileia are engaged in mortal combat, as we see in the vase paintings, their eyes meet at the precise moment when he kills her. And what Achilles sees in Penthesileia is a female reflection of his male self. All along, Penthesileia has been his other self in the feminine gender, as even her name shows, and now he has killed her. The death of Penthesileia thus becomes a source of grief, sorrow, and overwhelming sadness for Achilles, this man of constant sorrow. Both these epic names—and the epic characters that are tied to them—have to do with themes of lament, as signaled by the words *akhos* and *penthos*. (Nagy 2013:76–77)

As we saw in chapter 1, the theme of Achilles' sorrow or *akhos* is a deeply ingrained theme in the *Iliad*, perhaps as old or older than his wrath (as Nagy's

---

[12] For fuller discussion of Nagy's reconstruction of the names of Achilles and Penthesileia see Nagy 1979:94–117 and 2004:131–137.

reconstruction of his name suggests). A performance of the *Iliad* that included Penthesileia might well have emphasized this theme even further.

The traditional way of ending the *Iliad*, within the "poetics pursued by the oral tradition that generated the *Iliad*," and especially in regulated contexts such as the Panathenaia, may well have been with the funeral of Hektor. And the Panhellenic *Iliad* could have evolved in such a way as to for the most part pass over Achilles' romantic exploits (except where it concerns Briseis). But as papyrus 104 and the Townley scholion show, there is really no reason why a poet versed in both the Iliadic tradition and that of the *Aithiopis* could not have segued from one to the other, as the occasion allowed or the audience requested. That audience then would have a experienced a different Iliad than the one we know.

***

Not every example of multiformity preserved in the papyri has such dramatic narrative consequences. Most of the early papyri exhibit the fairly standard forms of variation that I noted above as being typical of oral-derived texts. The Ptolemaic papyri as a group have been labeled "wild" and "eccentric" by papyrologists and editors of the Homeric poems alike. But they are only "wild" from the perspective of the medieval transmission. The variations themselves present little that is surprising when considered from the viewpoint of the system as a whole. Papyrus 40 (P. Hibeh 19) is one such "wild" papyrus, dating to the first half of the second century BCE (West 2001:90). It is a lengthy papyrus with quite a few plus verses as well as multiformity within individual lines. The following is an excerpt from fragment L of this papyrus:

> *Iliad* 3.302–310 (fragment L, column I of P. Hibeh 19 [= papyrus 40])[13]
> [302]   <ὣς ἔφαν εὐχό>μενοι, μέγα δ' ἔκτυπε μητίετα Ζεὺς
> [302a] [ca. 10 letters]   φων ἐπὶ δὲ στεροπὴν ἐφέηκεν·
> [302b] <θησέμεναι γ>ὰρ ἔμελλεν ἔτ' ἄλγεά τε στοναχάς τε
> [302c] <Τρωσί τε καὶ> Δαναοῖ<σι> διὰ κρατερὰς ὑς<μί>νας.
> [302d] <αὐτὰρ ἐπεί ῥ' ὄ>μοσέν τε τελεύτησέν <τε> τὸν ὅρκον,

---

[13]   The text and supplements are taken from the digital edition of this papyrus made by Joseph Miller, who follows S. West's 1967 edition in most respects. Note that text within angle brackets is not present on the fragmentary papyrus and has been supplied by the editor based on what is attested in the medieval manuscripts. Letters with dots underneath are visible but unclear on the papyrus. For 302a M. West (1998) suggests ['Ίδης ἔκ κορυ]φῶν ἐπὶ δὲ στεροπὴν ἐφέηκεν ("from the peaks of Ida he let fly lightning"). On this section of the papyrus see also Bird 2010:86–89. For the publication history of the papyrus see the Mertens-Pack 3 database (http://cipl93.philo.ulg.ac.be/Cedopal/MP3/dbsearch.aspx), s.v. 640.

[303] [   ]<Δαρδανί>δ<η>ς Πρίαμος πρὸς μῦθον ἔειπ<ε·>
[304] <κέκλυτέ μευ Τ>ρῶες καὶ Δάρδανοι ἠδ' <ἐ>πίκ<ουροι>
[304a] <ὄφρ' εἴπω> τά μ<ε θυ>μὸς ἐνὶ στήθεσσιν ἀν<ώ>γε<ι.>
[305] <ἤτοι ἐ>γὼν εἶμι πρ<ο>τὶ Ἴλιον ἠνεμόεσσαν·
[306] <ο>ὐ γάρ κεν τλαίην <ποτ' ἐν ὀφθα>λμοῖσιν ὁρᾶ<σθαι>
[307] <μα>ρνάμ<ε>νον φίλο<ν> υἱὸν ἀρηϊφίλῳ Μενελάῳ.>
[308] <Ζεὺς μέν που> τό <γ>ε <οἶδε καὶ ἀθάνατοι θεοὶ ἄλλοι>
[309] <ὁππότέρῳ θα>νάτοιο τέλ<ος πεπρωμένον ἐστίν.>
[310] <ἦ ῥα καὶ ἐς δίφρο>ν ἄρ<νας θέτο ἰσόθεος φώς>

302: <ὣς ἔφαν εὐχό>μενοι, μέγα δ' ἔκτυπε μητίετα Ζεύς] ὣς ἔφαν, οὐδ' ἄρα πώ σφιν ἐπεκραίαινε Κρονίων mss.   303: πρὸς] μετὰ mss. 304: Δάρδανοι ἠδ' <ἐ>πίκ<ουροι>] ἐϋκνήμιδες Ἀχαιοί mss. 306: <ο>ὐ γάρ κεν τλαίην <ποτ' ἐν ὀφθα>λμοῖσιν ὁρᾶ<σθαι>] ἄψ, ἐπεὶ οὔ πω τλήσομ' ἐν ὀφθαλμοῖσιν ὁρᾶσθαι mss.

[302] So they spoke, praying, and Zeus the deviser thundered loudly
[302a]   and he let fly lightning.
[302b] For he was about to place still more sufferings and groans upon
[302c] the Trojans and the Danaans in powerful combat.
[302d] Next, once he [Agamemnon] had sworn the oath and completed the sacrifice,
[303] To them Priam, descendant of Dardanos, spoke words,
[304] "Hear from me, Trojans and Dardanians and allies,
[304a] let me say what my heart in my chest tells me to say:
[305] I will go to wind-swept Ilion,
[306] for I would never bear to watch with my own eyes
[307] my dear son fighting with Menelaos, dear to Ares.
[308] Zeus, I suppose, knows this, as well the rest of the immortal gods,
[309] to which of the two the fulfillment of death has been allotted."
[310] He spoke, and into the chariot he, a man equal to a god, placed the lambs

At verse 302, the papyrus seems to read ὣς ἔφαν εὐχόμενοι, μέγα δ' ἔκτυπε μητίετα Ζεύς ("So they spoke, praying, and Zeus the deviser thundered loudly") in contrast to the medieval manuscripts, which read ὣς ἔφαν, οὐδ' ἄρα πώ σφιν ἐπεκραίαινε Κρονίων ("So they spoke, but not yet did Zeus bring it to fulfillment for them"). Following that verse, there are four plus verses that are not attested in the medieval manuscripts. At verse 303, the papyrus reads πρὸς where the medieval manuscripts have μετά.[14] At verse 304, the papyrus reads Δάρδανοι ἠδ’ <ἐ>πίκ<ουροι> ("Dardanians and allies") where the manuscripts read ἐϋκνήμιδες Ἀχαιοί ("well-greaved Achaeans"). After 304 there is another plus verse. At verse 306, the papyrus appears to read <ο>ὐ γάρ κεν τλαίην <ποτ’ ἐν ὀφθα>λμοῖσιν ὁρᾶ<σθαι> ("for I would never bear to watch with my own eyes") whereas the manuscripts have ἄψ, ἐπεὶ οὔ πω τλήσομ’ ἐν ὀφθαλμοῖσιν ὁρᾶσθαι ("back, since I will not yet dare to watch with my own eyes").

As we can see in this small segment, this particular papyrus text differs from medieval texts of the *Iliad* in its number of lines and often within lines (with one verse almost entirely different at 302), but the variations are formulaic in nature, with the kind of compression and expansion and differences in choice of formula that are natural for oral-derived texts. Verse 302 on the papyrus does not happen to survive in any other manuscript or papyrus in this particular location within the epic, but it *is* found at *Iliad* 15.377, indicating that it is a perfectly Homeric line. Verse 302 in the manuscripts (οὐδ’ ἄρα πώ σφιν ἐπεκραίαινε Κρονίων) is also attested elsewhere in the poem (at *Iliad* 2.419). Both, then, are equally acceptable within Homeric diction. Here is another case where a multitextual approach can accommodate both without excluding one or the other.

There are five so-called plus verses in a span of fourteen lines, but four of these have close parallels elsewhere in the *Iliad*. Verses 3.302b–302c on the papyrus closely resemble *Iliad* 2.39–40:

[2.39] θήσειν γὰρ ἔτ’ ἔμελλεν ἔπ’ ἄλγεά τε στοναχάς τε
[2.40] Τρωσί τε καὶ Δαναοῖσι διὰ κρατερὰς ὑσμίνας.

[2.39] For he was about to place still more sufferings and groaning upon
[2.40] the Trojans and the Danaans in powerful combat.

Verse 3.302d on the papyrus can be found at *Iliad* 14.280:

[14.280] αὐτὰρ ἐπεί ῥ’ ὄμοσέν τε τελεύτησέν τε τὸν ὅρκον
[14.280] Next, once he had sworn the oath and completed the sacrifice

And finally, verse 3.304a on the papyrus can be found at *Iliad* 19.102. In fact, this particular passage from *Iliad* 19, in which Zeus addresses the other gods, is contextually similar to the one we are exploring in *Iliad* 3:

---

[14] As Leonard Muellner points out to me, and as West (1967) observes as well here, the beginning of the verse, which is not preserved, must likewise differ from what is attested in the medieval manuscripts. πρός could be used with a reading like Τρῶας, but not with the manuscripts’ τοῖσι δέ.

[19.100] ἤτοι ὅ γ᾽ εὐχόμενος μετέφη πάντεσσι θεοῖσι·
[19.101] κέκλυτέ μευ πάντές τε θεοὶ πᾶσαί τε θέαιναι,
[19.102] ὄφρ᾽ εἴπω τά με θυμὸς ἐνὶ στήθεσσιν ἀνώγει.

[19.100] Making a solemn statement, he spoke among all the gods,
[19.101] "Hear from me, all you gods and goddesses,
[19.102] let me say what my heart in my chest tells me to say."

We can see that verse 2.304 on the papyrus is likewise parallel to 19.101, with the substitution of the contextually appropriate Τρῶες καὶ Δάρδανοι ἠδ᾽ ἐπίκουροι for πάντές τε θεοὶ πᾶσαί τε θέαιναι.

These differences are not a case of a rogue scribe inserting lines from elsewhere in the *Iliad* into *Iliad* 3. Rather, each of the variations presented by papyrus 40 are the kind of multiforms that are natural to oral poetry composed in performance, as shown by the fieldwork of Milman Parry and Albert Lord. Following Parry and Lord, the editors of the Homer Multitext view the early Homeric papyri much as we do such early quotations as Plato's and Aeschines' quotations of *Iliad* 23.[15] They are the vestiges of a once-vibrant performance tradition of the *Iliad*. A multitextual approach does not seek to privilege the papyri in any special way over the medieval transmission; rather it simply makes the readings they contain readily available to scholars and anyone interested in the transmission of the Homeric poems. There is great historical value in the picture they present of the state of the Homeric texts in the earliest stage at which we have them. And of course there are literary implications as well.

***

As in the previous chapter, I propose to explore now a particular passage as an example of how a multitextual approach to the multiformity attested in the papyri helps us to better understand the poetic system in which the *Iliad* and the *Odyssey* were composed. The passage I have chosen to focus on comes from the excursus on the shield of Achilles in *Iliad* 18, and as with other passages discussed in this book, we will need to draw on a number of different kinds of witnesses to fully appreciate the multiformity attested. I will begin with the text as preserved in the medieval manuscripts, and then work backward from there until we get to a particular papyrus, the papyrus known as papyrus 51.[16]

---

[15] And in fact, as we have seen already in chapter 2, the multiforms exhibited in early quotations often find support in surviving papyrus texts.

[16] Papyrus 51 (= BKT 5.1.18 + 20 [P. Berol. inv. 9774] + BKT 5.1.19 [P. Berol. inv. 9774]). For the publication history of this papyrus see the Mertens-Pack 3 database (http://cipl93.philo.ulg.ac.be/Cedopal/MP3/dbsearch.aspx), s.v. 962. The multiforms exhibited in the passage are also discussed by Nagy (2015d, part IV), but without reference to this papyrus.

At *Iliad* 18.603–606, near the end of the recital of Hephaistos' decoration of the shield of Achilles, and following a long passage describing the dancing of young men and women on a dancing floor "like the one which once in broad Knossos Daidalos made for Ariadne of the beautifully braided hair" (18.591–592), the Venetus A and all medieval manuscripts read as follows:

πολλὸς δ᾽ ἱμερόεντα χορὸν περιίσταθ᾽ ὅμιλος
τερπόμενοι· δοιὼ δὲ κυβιστητῆρε κατ᾽ αὐτοὺς
μολπῆς ἐξάρχοντες ἐδίνευον κατὰ μέσσους.

A great crowd stood around the lovely dancing place
delighting in it. And two tumblers throughout them
leading off the song and dance whirled in the middle.

As Martin Revermann has pointed out in his analysis of the lines, this version of the text has not only universal manuscript support, but also the support of five papyri and a quotation of the passage in Dionysius of Halicarnassus (Revermannn 1998:29). And yet this seemingly canonical version of the text is not the only possibility. Friedrich Wolf, whose conservative edition set the standard numbering of verses that all modern editions adopt, prints this longer version of the passage, as attested in Athenaeus (181b):[17]

[18.603] πολλὸς δ᾽ ἱμερόεντα χορὸν περιίσταθ᾽ ὅμιλος
[18.604] τερπόμενοι· μετὰ δέ σφιν ἐμέλπετο θεῖος ἀοιδὸς
[18.605] φορμίζων· δοιὼ δὲ κυβιστητῆρε κατ᾽ αὐτοὺς
[18.606] μολπῆς ἐξάρχοντες ἐδίνευον κατὰ μέσσους.

[18.603] A great crowd stood around the lovely dancing place
[18.604] delighting in it. And among them a divine singer sang and
          played
[18.605] on the phorminx. And two tumblers throughout them
[18.606] leading off the song and dance whirled in the middle.

Because the line numbers of Wolf's edition have been adopted by all subsequent editors, Athenaeus' version of these verses receives the canonical line numbers 603, 604, 605, and 606. Modern editors who choose to leave out the expansion due to insufficient textual support must format their edition in such a way as to

---

[17] See Revermann 1998:39n29 for earlier bibliography. Wolf's edition (1804–1807) is generally conservative in that he does not typically include plus verses or readings from outside the medieval manuscript transmission. This passage is an exception.

preserve the line numbers of Wolf, but not the parts of verses 604 and 605 that are attested only in Athenaeus.

What do we gain in Athenaeus' longer version of the passage? First and foremost we gain a divine singer, who also plays the phorminx as the young people dance. In this final image from the shield of Achilles (at least as it has survived in the medieval transmission) we find a link between the current occasion of performance of the poem and the internal occasion depicted on the shield. The shield, so famously full of movement and activity and dynamic energy on an object that should be static, picks up on the earlier scenes involving festive music and singing (491–495, 526, 569–572) and concludes with the sound not only of the phorminx but also the voice of an *aoidos*. Gregory Nagy has argued that the metalworking of the shield passage as a whole is a metaphor for the composition of Homeric poetry via the metaphor of pattern-weaving (*poikillein*; cf 18.590). The *aoidos* on the shield then becomes a manifestation of the external *aoidos* of the poem ("Homer"), who calls attention to his own status as the leader of the singing and the dancing in the current festival context (Nagy 2015d:4§§9–17).

The context within which Athenaeus cites these verses is actually an argument about the correct text of the *Odyssey*. Athenaeus says that those in Aristarchus' circle (οἱ περὶ Ἀρίσταρχον 180c) and Aristarchus himself were deceived by verse 4.3 (in which Menelaos is found giving a wedding feast) and inappropriately added to the text verses that come from the description of the shield of Achilles in the *Iliad*:

ἀλλ' ἐξαπατηθέντες ὑπὸ τοῦ πρώτου ἔπους:
[4.3]   τὸν δ' εὗρον δαινύντα γάμον πολλοῖσιν ἔτῃσιν...
προσσυνῆψαν τοιούτους τινὰς στίχους
[4.15]   ὣς οἱ μὲν δαίνυντο καθ' ὑψερεφὲς μέγα δῶμα
[4.16]   γείτονες ἠδὲ ἔται Μενελάου κυδαλίμοιο,
[4.17]   τερπόμενοι: μετὰ δέ σφιν ἐμέλπετο θεῖος ἀοιδὸς
[4.18]   φορμίζων, δοιὼ δὲ κυβιστητῆρε κατ' αὐτούς,
[4.19]   μολπῆς ἐξάρχοντες, ἐδίνευον κατὰ μέσσους.
μετενεγκόντες ἐκ τῆς Ὁπλοποιίας σὺν αὐτῷ γε τῷ περὶ τὴν λέξιν ἁμαρτήματι.

But having been deceived by the first verse
[4.3]   They found him giving a wedding feast for his many kinsmen...
They fastened on in addition such verses as follows
[4.15]   So they feasted throughout the great high-roofed house

[4.16] the neighbors and kinsmen of the outstanding Menelaos,
[4.17] delighting in it. And among them a divine singer sang and
       played
[4.18] on the phorminx. And two tumblers throughout them
[4.19] leading off the song and dance whirled in the middle.

having transferred them from the "Making of the Arms" together with
the error concerning the text.

Athenaeus, much like a modern critic, accuses the scholars associated with
Aristarchus of taking lines that belong in *Iliad* 18 and inserting them in *Odyssey*
4. This argument is part of a larger discussion about the appropriate mix of
wine, song, and dance, in which Athenaeus claims that in Homer it is mainly
the suitors and the Phaeacians who indulge in this kind of activity. But the fact
is that in both passages song and music are thematically and formulaically
appropriate—and even expected, from what we know of Homeric diction—as
Revermann has shown and as I will discuss below. Just as in the case of the
golden amphora of *Iliad* 23 and *Odyssey* 24, which I discussed in chapter 2, we
should not have to choose between the *Iliad* and the *Odyssey* here. Both poems
make use of the formulaic language associated with feasting and festivals where
it is thematically called for.

But the problem goes deeper than a mere accusation of interpolation,
because the verses that Athenaeus quotes from the *Odyssey*, the ones he accuses
the circle of Aristarchus of having transferred from book 18 of the *Iliad*, are not
the same as the ones we find preserved in the medieval transmission of the *Iliad*
18 and in the papyri. In the process of making one argument about the text of
the *Odyssey*, Athenaeus creates an entirely different problem for the text of the
Iliad. What is an editor of the *Iliad* to make of the multiformity presented by
Athenaeus? Do we simply ignore the fact that in the course of making an argument about the correct text of the Odyssey such an early witness as Athenaeus
challenges our text of the *Iliad*?

To make matters even harder than they already are for the modern editor,
there are additional issues in the text addressed by Athenaeus, which lead to
further evidence of multiformity in the textual transmission as it was known
to Athenaeus. Athenaeus, for example, objects to the reading ἐξάρχοντες
at *Odyssey* 4.19 (this is what he means by "the error concerning the text").
Athenaeus argues that the tumblers are not the ones who lead off the song
and dance but rather the ἀοιδός, suggesting that the correct reading should
be ἐξάρχοντος (180d). In the *Odyssey* passage, as Athenaeus quotes it, there is
an ἀοιδός who could in theory lead off the singing. But when Athenaeus then
quotes the *Iliad* passage once again (181a–181b), the ἀοιδός is not present! (μετὰ

δέ σφιν ἐμέλπετο θεῖος ἀοιδὸς / φορμίζων is omitted, just as it is in our medieval manuscripts of the *Iliad*.) The omission appears to be an accidental one. Later in the discussion (181d), Athenaeus quotes the text again, and again without μετὰ δέ σφιν ἐμέλπετο θεῖος ἀοιδὸς / φορμίζων, but he attributes this version of the text to Aristarchus, who, he says, "removed" (ἐξεῖλεν) the singer from the *Iliad* passage. Athenaeus objects to the removal, because without an ἀοιδὸς, it is not possible to read ἐξάρχοντος.

It would be tempting to dismiss Athenaeus' longer text as it is first quoted altogether, given its lack of support in the manuscripts and the textual difficulties present in Athenaeus' own discussion of the passage. Moreover, we have no reason to dismiss the shorter passage, as it has been transmitted in all manuscripts. Nagy has argued, *pace* Athenaeus, that both the shorter and the longer versions of the passage discussed by Athenaeus have support within the formulaic diction of Homeric epic (see Nagy's arguments in Nagy 2015d:4§§26–38, drawing on the scenes featuring Demodokos in *Odyssey* books 8 and 13). In other words, both versions are legitimate multiforms generated within the system of Homeric diction. But Revermann makes a persuasive case that there is indeed something missing from the more compressed shield passage as transmitted in the medieval manuscripts of the *Iliad*. He studies all available passages that depict dancing in ancient epic, including two others on the shield (at 18.491–496 and 18.561–572), and concludes that in every case music, musical instruments, and/or singing are explicitly mentioned:

> To sum up: as the text stands, the final group dance on the Shield of Achilles is not only unaccompanied but, apart from the mention of μόλπη, even silent. The near-silence and the absence of any form of accompaniment are unparalleled on the Shield, in the Homeric epics as a whole, in Ps.-Hesiod, and in the Homeric Hymns.... I conclude that the description of a festive ἱμερόεις χορός of young men and women on the Shield, the most elaborate scene of its kind in the Homeric epics, is incomplete without more noise and an explicit mention of instruments and/or instrumentalists. Thus, a lacuna of uncertain length is to be postulated. (Revermann 1998:32)

Revermann's arguments clearly show that something is missing, but the lacuna he postulates, in his view, cannot be filled by the citation in Athenaeus, which he finds too problematic.[18]

---

[18] S. West (1967:134) likewise dismisses Athenaeus, suggesting that the longer version of the passage comes from a "wild" text of book 18, which Athenaeus assumed to have been excised by Aristarchus but believed to be genuine. Because West's understanding of the Homeric text is

***

Revermann goes on to discuss (and ultimately dismiss) another possible source for filling in the postulated lacuna on the shield, a first-century BCE papyrus known as papyrus 51. It is this papyrus that I now propose to examine. In what follows I am indebted to the edition of Stephanie West (1967:132–136), on whose papyrological observations and expertise I rely (as does Revermann), even, as mentioned above, when I have disagreements about the significance of attested multiforms for our understanding of the the Homeric epics.

West sums up the importance of papyrus 51 this way (1967:132): "This is one of the most remarkable of the eccentric papyri: it is the latest in date, it contains a lengthy interpolation from the Hesiodic *Scutum*, and it is liberally provided with critical signs, its most problematic feature." The papyrus once contained two columns of at least seventeen verses each, but the first column is now almost completely missing except for a few letters at the end of some of the verses. Still, in what remains it is clear that plus verses were present (West 1967:132). Column II also contains plus verses, including one (18.606a) that is highly relevant to our discussion of Athenaeus, and four (18.608a–d) that closely resemble the Hesiodic *Shield* (verses 207–215).

The portion of column II relevant to our discussion reads as follows (as edited by West). There is a *diplē* next to each verse at 603, 605, and 608a–d, and a possible *obelos* along with the *diplē* at 608a. There is a *stigmē* next to 607.[19]

[603]   πολλὸς [δ' ἱμε]ρόεντα χ[ο]ρὸν περιίστα[θ' ὅ]μιλ[ος
[604/5] τερπόμ[ενοι·] δοιὼ δὲ κυ[β]ιστητῆρε κ[α]τ' αὐτ[οὺς
[606]   μολπῆ[ς ἐξ]άρχοντες ἐδίνευον κατ[ὰ] μέσ[σους.
[606a] ἐν δ' ἔσ[αν σ]ύριγγε[ς, ἔσ]αν κίθαρίς τ[ε] καὶ α[ὐλοί.
[607]   ἐν δὲ τ[ίθει] ποταμοῖο μέγα σθένος Ὠκε[ανοῖο
[608]   ἄντυγα πὰρ πυμάτην σάκεος πύκα π[οιητοῖο.
[608a] ἐν δὲ λιμὴν ἐτέτυκτ[ο] ἐανοῦ κασσιτέρ[οιο

---

so different from my own (she finds reasons to dismiss or disregard the multiformity of early witnesses, while I seek to show that it was the norm and in fact to be expected), it is difficult for me to be in dialogue with her arguments. Nevertheless I do aim to build on her work even while operating within a different paradigm. For West, a "wild" text (which as I stress throughout this book, is only "wild" in hindsight, from the perspective of the medieval transmission) is not likely to preserve what she would consider a genuine reading. But since my definition of "genuine" depends not on a single composer or a single authoritative text, and instead encompasses all the poetry composed within a system that evolved over many centuries, I can argue for the acceptance of Athenaeus' text as a "genuine" multiform.

[19]   On the critical signs preserved in medieval manuscripts such as the Venetus A see Bird 2009. For signs in the papyri see McNamee 1981, 1992, and 2007. See also West 1967:132–133 with further bibliography on the use of signs on this particular papyrus.

[608b] κλυζ[ομ]ένωι ἵκε[λο]ς· δοίω δ' ἀναφυσιόω[ντες
[608c] ἀργύ[ρεοι] δελφῖνες [ἐ]φοίνεον ἔλλ[ο]πας [ἰχθῦς·
[608d] τοῦ δ' [ὕπ]ο χάλκε[ιοι] τρέον ἰχθύες· αὐτὰ[ρ ἐπ' ἀκταῖς

[603]   A great crowd stood around the lovely dancing place
[604/5] delighting in it. And two tumblers throughout them
[606]   leading off the song and dance [μολπή] whirled in the
        middle.
[606a] And on it were panpipes and a lyre [*kithara*] and flutes [*auloi*].
[607]   And on it he placed the great might of the river Okeanos
[608]   next to the outermost rim of the intricately made shield.
[608a] And on it was wrought a harbor of beaten tin
[608b] and it was like as if rising from the waves. And drawing deep
        breaths two
[608c] silver dolphins reddened the scaly fish.
[608d] And beneath it the bronze fish trembled. Meanwhile on the
        shore

For the moment I call attention only to verse 606a on the papyrus. This verse is attested in no other manuscript and is not found elsewhere in what survives of Homeric poetry. As West points out, the text as she has reconstructed it is problematic metrically, but there are no likely alternatives to her supplement. Clearly, at some point in the history of composing this passage in performance it was felt that musical accompaniment was called for here, and Revermann's research confirms that we should expect to find it. In terms of what we know of Homeric diction, however, the verse is problematic, and it is not surprising that it did not gain a stronger foothold in the textual transmission.[20]

Even thornier is the question of the remaining plus verses on the papyrus. These verses are almost universally regarded as an "interpolation" or "contamination" from the Hesiodic *Shield*, verses 207–215.[21] Here is the Hesiodic passage, with overlapping phrases underlined:

[207]   <u>ἐν δὲ λιμὴν</u> ἐύορμος ἀμαιμακέτοιο θαλάσσης
[208]   κυκλοτερὴς <u>ἐτέτυκτο</u> πανέφθου κασσιτέροιο

---

[20] Lord points out that in his fieldwork not every performance resulted in perfectly composed verses from a metrical standpoint: "Under the pressure of rapid composition in performance, the singer of tales, it is to be expected, makes occasional errors in the construction of lines. His text may be a syllable too long or a syllable too short. This does not trouble him in performance, and his audience scarcely notices these lines" (Lord 1960:38).
[21] See West 1967:136 with citations of earlier scholarship.

[209] κλυζομένῳ ἴκελος· πολλοί γε μὲν ἂμ μέσον αὐτοῦ
[210] δελφῖνες τῇ καὶ τῇ ἐθύνεον ἰχθυάοντες
[211] νηχομένοις ἴκελοι· δοιὼ δ᾽ ἀναφυσιόωντες
[212] ἀργύρεοι δελφῖνες ἐθοινῶντ᾽ ἔλλοπας ἰχθῦς.
[213] τῶν δ᾽ ὕπο χάλκειοι τρέον ἰχθύες· αὐτὰρ ἐπ᾽ ἀκταῖς
[214] ἧστο ἀνὴρ ἁλιεὺς δεδοκημένος· εἶχε δὲ χερσὶν
[215] ἰχθύσιν ἀμφίβληστρον ἀπορρίψοντι ἐοικώς.

[207] And on it a harbor with good mooring of the monstrous sea
[208] was wrought in a circle of pure tin
[209] like as if rising from the waves. In the middle of it many
[210] dolphins darted here and there fishing
[211] like as if swimming; and drawing deep breaths two
[212] silver dolphins feasted on the scaly fish.
[213] And beneath them the bronze fish trembled. Meanwhile on
        the shore
[214] sat a fisherman watching. And he held in his hands
[215] a casting net, seeming like one about to cast it.

Revermann uses the presence of these verses on the papyrus to condemn 606a, even though 606a contains the music that he argues is lacking from the medievally transmitted shield of Achilles:

> The overall impression is that the verse is awkwardly squeezed in to supplement what is felt to be lacking. The way in which the papyrus elsewhere indulges in what are unmistakably interpolations shatters its trustworthiness as a whole, and clinches the question of the authenticity of 606a. (Revermann 1998:33)

West likewise speaks of the plus verses on the papyrus as being an "interpolation" from the Hesiodic passage. But a comparison of the two passages arguably shows something quite different. The passages make use of similar formulaic language to describe a similar image on a shield, but one need not be an "interpolation" of the other, if we take into account that both shield passages were composed within a long oral tradition of such passages. The Iliadic shield of Achilles and the Hesiodic shield of Herakles are only two such compositions that happen to survive. We simply cannot know how many more may have existed and how prone such compositions may have been to expansion and compression in performance. Papyrus 51's additional verses are almost certainly not the work of a miscreant scribe intentionally "contaminating" the *Iliad* with verses from the Hesiodic corpus. Rather, both passages draw on the traditional formulaic language associated with shield poetry, language that was evidently readily available to poets of the Homeric and Hesiodic *corpora* alike.[22]

Indeed, the presence of critical signs on the papyrus, what West calls the papyrus' "most problematic feature," point to this text being a critical edition, and not some carelessly made transcript of an unusual performance. We cannot know the source for the text that has been preserved, but we can see that it has been annotated and is keyed to a commentary, which would have been published in a separate scroll.[23] So while the additional verses on papyrus 51 may be the result of a particular performance in which a singer drew on thematically appropriate formulaic diction in order to extend his performance of the making of Achilles' shield, as Revermann (1998:37) suggests later in his article, they have been taken seriously enough to be included and commented upon in this critical edition. It is worth noting that this particular edition did indeed mark verse 606a for athetesis, but 608b–608d (and possibly 608a) received only a *diplē*. The *diplē* indicates merely that they were discussed in the accompanying commentary, not outright condemned. And in fact it is this very lack of condemnation that West finds so problematic about these signs. She notes that there is no difference in ink color or anything to indicate that the signs were inserted later by someone else, but wonders if "it is perhaps not necessary to assume that they were inserted by the original scribe" (1967:132). Her reason is that the signs do not match up with her expectations of the Homeric text here: "the only sign which would be at all appropriate before 608a, b, c, d is the obelos" (1967:133). For West, working within a model in which there is a single, correct text to be found, athetesis of 608a–608d is the only conceivable option. But it seems the editor of this particular papyrus in the first century BCE did not feel that way. They are unusual enough to be commented upon, but they were included nonetheless.

***

Instead of taking this passage on the shield of Achilles as an example of why a multitextual approach to the *Iliad* might be fruitful and instructive, Revermann explicitly rejects such an approach:

---

[22] For the relationship between Hesiodic poetry and Homeric poetry (and their interconnectedness with other Archaic song traditions) see González (forthcoming [a] and Martin (forthcoming). I would adduce the descriptions of the shields of the Seven in the *Seven Against Thebes* of Aeschylus as another, later manifestation of a longstanding tradition of shield poetry.

[23] See chapter 1 above, p. 46 and Ebbott 2009:42.

If the considerations put forward in this paper are correct, they point to the peculiarities of the transmission of the Homeric poems. Performance and written versions co-exist at least up to the fifth century, and performances continue to leave their imprint on the texts. The ending of the description of Achilles' Shield was particularly liable to fluctuations owing both to the attraction which the dancing-scene climax exerted on the performers and to the fact that the ecphrasis as a whole was perceived as a self-contained unit, presumably one of the jewels of any performance of the *Iliad*.

This result may bring to mind the theory of transmission of the Homeric poems advocated by Nagy, especially his notion of 'fluidity' and 'rigidity'. I nevertheless disagree with most aspects and implications of this theory, in particular the attempt to identify different stages of 'fluid' transmission in a 'multitext edition' of the Homeric poems. The passage at the end of Shield description on which I concentrated is an isolated and special case, in which the evidence from a 'wild' papyrus and the secondary transmission allows for a glance at the 'fluidity' to which the text could be exposed. But beyond noting the 'fluidity', the overall result is, alas, negative. Comparison with the relevant textual and archaeological evidence available suggests that our tradition of a particular passage of this ecphrasis is lacunose. There are, however, no means of recovering the 'genuine version' of this passage. In fact the quest for it would be misguided in principle.

Revermann's analysis, by his own admission, uncovers an instance of fluidity (or multiformity) in the textual transmission, only to reject such fluidity as interesting or worthy of further examination. He describes as being a "special case" something that, as we have seen, is not particularly special or unusual. The earliest quotations and papyri reveal that the Homeric text existed and was presumably performed in shorter and longer versions throughout antiquity. Revermann's penultimate sentence highlights the difference between the approach of many scholars and that which I and my fellow editors (following Nagy, and ultimately Albert Lord) advocate for. We are not attempting to recover the "genuine version," nor do we think that there is only one "genuine version" to be had. [24] A multitextual approach can accept that formulaic language asso-

---

[24] Much like Revermann, Janko (2016:104) rejects a multitextual approach to Homer on principle, almost as a matter of faith: "Indeed, textual criticism was developed in order to spare ourselves from having to read through 'multitexts', which may, in a case like Homer's *Iliad*, amount to thousands of verses in thousands of sources. Homeric studies have for years been bedevilled by some scholars' rejection of the idea of an authoritative archetype, even for this oral dictated text, in favour of a multitextual chimera." My collaborators and I, however, do not assume the

ciated with shield poetry could have been used in performance to further extend the shield passage. It can also accept that different performances of the shield of Achilles might have included varying numbers of verses devoted to describing the musical accompaniment of the dancers. It can accept the presence or absence of an *aoidos* in the passage, while acknowledging that there are poetic implications of each multiform that should be taken into account in any analysis of the passage.

My point in writing about this passage and its attested multiforms has not been to disagree with Revermann's core arguments; in fact I agree with almost every point that he makes. Where we diverge is in our understanding of the implications of his analysis, and of multiformity more generally. Because the editors of the Homer Multitext are not interested in identifying a single correct or pristine text, we can appreciate papyrus 51 in a different, more historically contextualized, way:

- We can find evidence for the formulaic diction connected to Shield poetry in the larger epic tradition.

- We can find evidence pointing to a thematic preference for musical accompaniment in passages that depict dancing, something that seems to have dropped from the medievally attested text of the shield of Achilles.

- We can find evidence for how the Homeric poems were being performed and circulated and received in the first century BCE.

The performers whose songs are the ultimate source for papyrus 51 evidently were not always quite ready to end the making of the shield of Achilles at verse 18.608, and might keep going. Likewise it seems plausible that the ultimate source of the multiform ending of the *Iliad* preserved on papyrus 104 were performers who were not ready to end the *Iliad* with the burial of Hektor. They too kept going, and brought Penthesileia onto the scene. The choice to keep going, and not end with the burial of Hektor, or to include an *aoidos* on the shield or not, necessarily affects our understanding and reception of the *Iliad*, as it did for audiences in the first centuries BCE and CE.

The presence of such multiformity in our earliest sources complicates many traditional forms of literary analysis, but our response to that complexity

---

existence of a single dictated text, and in fact a core aim of this book is to show that our evidence simply does not support the notion. We *are* interested in the thousands of verses in thousands of sources that Janko rejects. The existence of an abundance of evidence for multiformity is precisely why we think it is important to present the Homeric epics as multiform compositions with a very complicated transmission, and not monolithic entities with recoverable archetypes.

need not be to hide or dismiss it. Rather, in embracing multiformity we can attempt to recover some of the richness and creativity of a poetic tradition in which compositional possibilities abounded for performers even while they worked within a highly traditional medium. What may be surprising about the papyri is that this kind of creativity persisted within the system long after the time in which scholars have typically conceived of the *Iliad* and the *Odyssey* as being fixed and unchanging. Even within Nagy's evolutionary model, a text like papyrus 51 comes quite late in the process of crystallization. Many scholars would be comfortable with an oral tradition that remained in flux until "Homer's time," a time typically conceptualized as being in the late Iron Age or early Archaic period. But to embrace or even acknowledge that multiformity persisted long past this date requires abandoning modern notions of authorship and genius. Indeed, it requires us to abandon "Homer." It requires us to blur the line between the creative *aoidos* and the replicating rhapsode (González, forthcoming [c]). I will return to this idea in my conclusion.

Chapter 4

The Lost Verses of the *Iliad*

Medieval Manuscripts and the Poetics of a Multiform Epic Tradition

IN THIS CHAPTER WE SKIP AHEAD MANY CENTURIES, to the medieval manuscript tradition. The medieval manuscripts are our best source of information about the texts known to the Hellenistic scholars who were in charge of the library of Alexandria, including Zenodotus, Aristophanes of Byzantium, and Aristarchus. The scholia in the margins of such manuscripts as the tenth-century CE Venetus A, the eleventh-century manuscripts Venetus B, Townley, Escorialensis Y.1.1 and Ω.1.12, and the thirteenth-century Genavensis discuss a variety of grammatical and literary topics, and they record debates about the correct text of the *Iliad*, with reference to the texts of the poem that were circulating in the third and second centuries BCE.[1] The result is that even though they are preserved in much later documents, the disputes about the text being discussed in the scholia are in some cases as old as the Ptolemaic papyri. And like the papyri, they preserve a treasure trove of multiformity.

In some ways, after nearly two decades of working on the Homer Multitext, my collaborators and I are only just beginning to scratch the surface of the multiformity hinted at and in many cases explicitly discussed in the scholia of our medieval manuscripts. My coeditors and I have made a complete edition of the text and scholia of one manuscript—arguably the most important manuscript for understanding the textual transmission of the *Iliad*, the Venetus A—but there is much work still to be done to create similar editions of other manuscripts and papyri, and still more to understand the implications of their

---

[1] For more information about these manuscripts, please see the Homer Multitext website at http://www.homermultitext.org, where there is a page devoted to each and images can be accessed.

contents. Nevertheless, the aim of this chapter is to provide an overview of what we have come across so far and what we have learned during the course of our work with the Venetus A and other manuscripts. I will collect in this chapter some of the more remarkable multiforms we have encountered (some of which are already quite well known to scholars and/or have been explored in depth elsewhere), drawing on my research and writing about the multiformity of the epic tradition over the last twenty years.[2] The next step from here, now that we have created a complete edition of the Venetus A and have begun to work on other manuscripts, will be to study the contents of these documents systematically, using modern forms of computer-assisted analysis.

The five examples I will discuss here span the entire narrative arc of the *Iliad*, and so I will proceed through them in order of their place in the poem as we now know it. In each case, I will try to convey how the multiformity in question informs our understanding of the composition and the poetics of the system in which the *Iliad* was composed, especially if we take a diachronic view that appreciates the evolution of the poem over many centuries. We will see that our *Iliad* cannot be separated from or understood independently of the vibrant and dynamic mythological and poetic tradition that was, in its earliest phases, always in flux and evolving in performance even as it presented itself as fixed and authoritative. The *Iliad* certainly became at some point the essentially fixed poem we now know, but it was not always so, and as a result it must be appreciated differently if we want to recover any sense of the poetics of this oral-traditional work and its reception by ancient audiences.

The Alexandrian editors whose scholarship is preserved in the scholia were attempting to recover a single authoritative text from an oral tradition in which, to paraphrase Albert Lord, there was quite simply no original to be found.[3] As we saw in chapter 2, their highly learned and literate Hellenistic and Roman aesthetics were in many ways incompatible with the oral poetic tradition to which they devoted so much intellectual energy in the attempt to understand it. But it is in their struggles with a wide array of mutually incompatible oral-derived texts that we find preserved the echoes of an *Iliad* that was at one time far more flexible than the one we know, an epic that was created within a fluid poetic system from which poets could pick up a story thread, and begin to sing wherever the Muse saw fit to inspire.[4] It is this more fluid *Iliad* that I wish to explore via the following examples.

---

[2] The examples discussed in this chapter offer a "big picture" view of multiformity. For a sustained analysis involving more typical examples of the multiformity that survives in the medieval transmission of the *Iliad* see Dué and Ebbott 2010:208–221 and Dué 2012.

[3] Modern editors make the same mistake. See chapter 2 above, pp. 80–81.

[4] See chapter 3 above, p. 87.

"The daughter of Brises, whom the sons of the Achaeans gave me"

Because Achilles' captive prize-woman Briseis speaks only ten verses in the *Iliad*, one might be tempted to think that she is not a traditional character or, to put it another way, that she does not have her own epic backstory. On the other hand, she plays a crucial role in the plot: it is the taking of Briseis that initiates Achilles' *mēnis*, which is the first word and driving theme of the poem (Muellner 1996). I wrote my dissertation (which later became Dué 2002) on this very question of Briseis' backstory, and during the course of my research, I discovered that not only does Briseis have a story, but there was more than one way to tell that story in epic. I propose to recap that research here, since it was greatly informed by evidence preserved in the scholia of medieval manuscripts.

Even within the *Iliad* there are detectable variations on Briseis' history, but there are traces in other sources too (including the now-lost poems of the Epic Cycle) of narratives associated with her. Briseis' role in the *Iliad* is indeed enormously compressed, to use a term of Albert Lord, in comparison to the more expanded narratives we can reconstruct using all available sources. As we will see both here in the case of Briseis and in my next example involving the Catalogue of Ships, it is important to understand that the *Iliad*, as expansive as it is (at over fifteen thousand verses), is far from being a totality of the epic poetry about Troy. It is a narrative about the anger of Achilles during a brief span in the tenth year of the Trojan War. Even though it might take as many as three days and nights to perform, the *Iliad* is nevertheless a compression of the full potential extent of epic poetry about Troy—what we might call the ultimate expansion of the *Iliad*. I have argued that one result of this compression is that the *Iliad* gives us only a glimpse of the figure of Briseis, whose role in the larger epic tradition must have been much greater at one time.

In addition to the *Iliad* and the poems of the Epic Cycle (as best as we can reconstruct them), there are a number of ancient vase paintings that depict Briseis, paintings which in some ways match closely our poetic sources and in other respects do not, as we saw already in chapter 1 with reference to the taking of Briseis from Achilles by Agamemnon in *Iliad* 1 (see also Dué 2002:21–36). Plate 2 shows her being taken from the tent of Achilles by Agamemnon. This event is narrated (with important differences) in book 1 of the *Iliad*, where the text says, tantalizingly, that she went "unwillingly."[5] In *Iliad* 9 Achilles proclaims that he loves Briseis as a man loves his wife, even though he won her in war (ἐκ θυμοῦ

---

[5] See above, p. 88. In the *Iliad*, Agamemnon does not come in person to take Briseis, but sends two heralds. On the relationship between vase paintings and epic narratives see Dué 2002:29–36 (with further references *ad loc.*) and Lowenstam 2008.

φίλεον δουρικτητήν περ ἐοῦσαν 9.343). And in Briseis' lament for Patroklos in *Iliad* 19 we learn of her hope of becoming Achilles' wedded wife in Phthia. And so we see that compressed but not entirely hidden within the *Iliad* there is also a love story, one that implies episodes before our *Iliad* begins, and at least one episode after, when Achilles dies and Briseis becomes a widow again.[6]

In the *Iliad* Briseis does not even really have a name—her name means, presumably, "daughter of Brises," just as Chryseis (for whom she is interchanged as the prize of Agamemnon in *Iliad* 1) is the "daughter of Chryses." Yet elsewhere there are hints that her name was Hippodameia, and that she was part of another story—or other stories. In Erbse's edition of the Homeric scholia, we find this note at *Iliad* 1.392, where Achilles calls Briseis κούρην Βρισῆος ("daughter of Brises"):

ἔοικε πατρωνυμικῶς – δὲ Ἱπποδάμεια. | ὁ δὲ τρόπος ἀντωνομασία. **A**

The presence of a dash is an indication that Erbse has skipped over a section of the scholion. Because he chose not to include in his edition material in a category that he and others call the D-scholia, which often treat mythological subjects, he has abbreviated the scholion in his edition. But if we look at the full scholion in the Venetus A at 1.392 (folio 19v), we find this:

ἔοικε πατρωνυμικῶς τὰ ὀνόματα αὐτῶν σχηματίζειν ὁ ποιητὴς καὶ οὐ κυρίως. ὡς γὰρ ἄλλοι ἀρχαῖοι ἱστοροῦσι ἡ μὲν Ἀστυνόμη ἐκαλεῖτο, ἡ δὲ Ἱπποδάμεια. ὁ δὲ τρόπος ἀντωνομασία.

It is likely that the poet forms the names [of Briseis and Chryseis] patronymically and not by proper name. For as other ancient [poets] relate, Chryseis was called Astynome, and Briseis was called Hippodameia. And the figure of speech is *antonomasia*.

As I noted in my 2002 book, the term *arkhaioi* in the scholia refers to Homer and earlier poets in contrast with more recent poets (*hoi neōteroi*), who can include Hesiod, the Archaic poets, the tragedians, and Alexandrian poets like Callimachus.[7] The scholion thus suggests that there were Archaic poetic traditions as old as or older than our *Iliad* in which Briseis had not only a name, but a greatly expanded story.

---

[6] On the love story, see now Fantuzzi 2012 and chapter 3 above. For more on these earlier and later components of the Achilles and Briseis story, see Dué 2002, where later literary sources that do narrate some of this material are explored for their possible relationship to the earlier epic tradition.

[7] For *hoi arkhaioi* vs. *hoi neōteroi* in the scholia see Henrichs 1993:189n44. For the poets of the Epic Cycle as *neōteroi* see Davies 1989:4.

It seems likely that there were at least two variations on the story of Briseis in antiquity, because of the two-fold pattern she fulfills in the surviving ancient references. Our sources are scanty, but it appears that in at least one tradition she is very much a young (or at least unmarried) girl, the daughter of King Brises of Pedasos, whom Achilles receives as a prize along with Diomedē, the daughter of King Phorbas of Lesbos.[8] But according to *Iliad* 2.688–694, 19.295–296, and elsewhere she was captured by Achilles in the sack of Lyrnessos, and in her lament for Patroklos (*Iliad* 19.292–302) Briseis says that she was married and that Achilles killed her husband, who may have been King Mynes. Our *Iliad* primarily assumes the latter story, but in fact alludes to multiple variations on these two basic themes.

Having even just a skeletal understanding of Briseis' epic backstory allows us to appreciate even more fully than we otherwise would the formulaic language that unites Briseis in her lament for Patroklos in *Iliad* 19 with the soon-to-be captive women of Troy, or with the unnamed widow to whom Odysseus is compared in his weeping in *Odyssey* 8. When Briseis sees the body of Patroklos "torn by the sharp bronze" (δεδαϊγμένον ὀξέϊ χαλκῷ 19.283), she recalls her own husband, who died in just this way (δεδαϊγμένον ὀξέϊ χαλκῷ 19.292). Briseis' lament for Patroklos reenacts the lament that she must have performed for her husband upon learning of his death, perhaps just before Briseis herself was led off into slavery (like the woman in the simile of *Odyssey* 8). Thus in just two lines (19.283–284), traditional resonances that are contained in the phrases themselves evoke a whole range of epic narratives—a phenomenon that Egbert Bakker has termed "interformularity."[9]

The lines that follow these are likewise extremely rich in traditional cross-references. In line 19.288 Briseis mentions her departure from the tent of Achilles, an event narrated at 1.345–348. It was Patroklos who led her from the tent. Patroklos, Briseis laments, was always kind to her (19.300). The kindness of Patroklos is important, as lines 19.291–294 go on to explain. Briseis is a captive woman in a foreign camp; she is the concubine of the man who killed her husband. Her brothers are also dead:

ἄνδρα μὲν ᾧ ἔδοσάν με πατὴρ καὶ πότνια μήτηρ
εἶδον πρὸ πτόλιος δεδαϊγμένον ὀξέϊ χαλκῷ,

---

[8] Cf. the Townley scholia at *Iliad* 16.57: τὴν Πήδασον οἱ τῶν Κυπρίων ποιηταί, αὐτὸς δὲ Λυρνησ‹σ›όν ("The poets of the *Cypria* say [that she was taken from] Pedasos, but Homer says Lyrnessos"). For more on the Pedasos version of Briseis' story, see my reconstruction at Dué 2002:49–65. Note that in *Iliad* 9.665 the daughter of Phorbas is called Diomedē, while in Dictys of Crete she is called Diomedea.

[9] See Bakker 2013:157–169.

τρεῖς τε κασιγνήτους, τούς μοι μία γείνατο μήτηρ,
κηδείους, οἳ πάντες ὀλέθριον ἦμαρ ἐπέσπον.

Iliad 19.291–294

The husband to whom my father and mistress mother gave me
I saw torn by the sharp bronze before the city,
and my three brothers, whom one mother bore together with me,
beloved ones, all of whom met their day of destruction.

Patroklos proves to be an ally for a vulnerable woman who no longer has the protection of her father, husband, or brothers.

These lines not only refer us to epic traditions outside of the *Iliad* and to a raid that was narrated in the *Cypria*, but they also make a meaningful connection to another part of the *Iliad* itself. Lines 19.291–294 evoke Andromache's words to Hektor in *Iliad* 6, in which she laments the death of her brothers:

οἳ δέ μοι ἑπτὰ κασίγνητοι ἔσαν ἐν μεγάροισιν
οἳ μὲν πάντες ἰῷ κίον ἤματι Ἄϊδος εἴσω·
πάντας γὰρ κατέπεφνε ποδάρκης δῖος Ἀχιλλεὺς

Iliad 6.421–423

I had seven brothers in the palace
all of whom went to Hades in one day.
For the swift-footed Achilles slew all of them.

The sacks of Lyrnessos (the city in which Briseis was captured) and Thebe (in which the brothers of Andromache were killed) took place on a single campaign. In this same sack of Thebe Chryseis was taken and given as a prize to Agamemnon.[10] Andromache was already living in Troy as Hektor's wife at the time of the raid. She thus escapes capture, but only temporarily: through Chryseis and Briseis we are reminded that Andromache (and all of the Trojan women) will soon be captives. As J. W. Zarker notes in his study of allusions to the raid on Thebe in the *Iliad*: "The fate of both Hector and Andromache is the same, as is that of Thebe and Troy. What happened at Thebe and the other cities of the Troad will happen to Troy. What happened to Chryseis, Briseis, and other

---

[10] On the connection between Chryseis and Andromache and her mother in this passage see Taplin 1986 and Robbins 1990. Lyrnessos, Pedasos, and Thebe are thought to be located very close to one another, near Mount Ida, not far from the Gulf of Adramyttium. All of these cities are located near the coast opposite Lesbos. Lyrnessos and Thebe in particular are closely related in the ancient sources. Aeschylus' *Phrygians* (as cited in the scholia to Euripides' *Andromache*) refers to Lyrnessos as the birthplace of Andromache, even though everywhere else in Greek literature she is said to come from Thebe (fragment 267). For a complete compendium of all ancient testimonia regarding the location of Lyrnessos, Pedasos, and Thebe, see Stauber 1996:91–175.

captive women will happen to Andromache.... Achilles' taking of Thebe is the dramatic foreshadowing of the fall of Troy" (Zarker 1965–66:114).

From the standpoint of Homeric narrative, the past and future are joined and brought to life in Briseis' lament. In the context of the broader epic tradition, these verses hint at other tales in which the given events traditionally took place, like the *Cypria* or the *Aethiopis*. In lines 19.295–299 we can see once again how Homeric poetry connects its own tale to other epic traditions:

> οὐδὲ μὲν οὐδέ μ' ἔασκες, ὅτ' ἄνδρ' ἐμὸν ὠκὺς Ἀχιλλεὺς
> ἔκτεινεν, πέρσεν δὲ πόλιν θείοιο Μύνητος,
> κλαίειν, ἀλλά μ' ἔφασκες Ἀχιλλῆος θείοιο
> κουριδίην ἄλοχον θήσειν, ἄξειν τ' ἐνὶ νηυσὶν
> ἐς Φθίην, δαίσειν δὲ γάμον μετὰ Μυρμιδόνεσσι.
> κουριδίην ἄλοχον

Iliad 19.295–299

Nor did you allow me, when swift Achilles killed my husband,
and sacked the city of god-like Mynes,
to weep, but you claimed that you would make me the
wedded wife of god-like Achilles, and that you would bring me in the
ships
to Phthia, and give me a wedding feast among the Myrmidons.

The allusion to Mynes raises the interesting possibility that Briseis was the queen of Lyrnessos, and that her husband was Mynes.[11] If this interpretation is right, with this one detail the story of Briseis comes together and we can piece together the narrative of her life as it is implied in the *Iliad*. As I have reconstructed it, she was born in Brisa on Lesbos and married to King Mynes of Lyrnessos. When Achilles went on his series of raids in and around Lesbos, he sacked not only Briseis' hometown, where presumably her brothers were killed, but also Lyrnessos. Achilles killed Mynes and enslaved the women of the town, winning Briseis as his prize. Because of the hypertext-like power of traditional poetry, in these few lines Briseis can allude elliptically to all of these events, indeed her entire life history up to the present moment.[12]

---

[11] The syntax of 19.295–296 seems to express paratactically what in English prose would be subordinated: that Achilles killed Briseis' husband Mynes, who was the ruler of the city (Lyrnessos). This is the interpretation of the scholia in the Venetus B and the Townley. It is possible, however, that her husband was a man of Lyrnessos other than Mynes. See also Leaf 1912:246; Edwards 1991, *ad loc.*; and Pucci 1993:263–264.

[12] For the Homeric tradition as a "hypertext," see Tsagalis 2010a and below, p. 155. On this dynamic interplay between the current performance and the broader tradition see also Scodel 2002.

Moreover, in these same lines we hear the hopes Briseis has for the future. She says that Patroklos always promised she would be Achilles' wife, his *kouridiē alokhos,* and that he would give a wedding feast for them in Phthia after the war. But a traditional audience knows that Achilles will never go back to Phthia. The death of Patroklos means the death of Hektor, which in turn, as Achilles hears from his mother, Thetis, in 18.96, means the death of Achilles. Briseis will become a widow once again and the captive of some other man. Briseis' vain hopes for the future recall Achilles' own speculation on a marriage back in Phthia: ἢν γὰρ δή με σαῶσι θεοὶ καὶ οἴκαδ' ἵκωμαι, / Πηλεύς θήν μοι ἔπειτα γυναῖκά γε μάσσεται αὐτός, "For if the gods save me and I return home, then Peleus will get me a wife himself" (9.393–394). When Achilles makes that statement in *Iliad* 9, return is still a possibility, from the standpoint of the narrative. In *Iliad* 19, however, we know that Achilles will never marry.

The words of Briseis in *Iliad* 19 therefore bring together a monumental sequence of events in one highly compressed and expressive song. This sequence of events may not have been narrated in full on any one occasion, but, as I have argued, the traditional mechanics of expansion and compression can incorporate—by way of allusion, reference, and even the resonance of formulaic diction—complex narratological relationships that span a vast continuum of poetic and artistic traditions. In this brief sketch, we have seen how any one performance of an Iliad can assume and refer to events of other songs in the Epic Cycle. A traditional system such as the one described here, moreover, contains a built-in poetic structure of stories within stories. As the narrative proceeds, these stories within stories are incorporated in more or less expanded form. The least expanded narrative—that is, the most compressed—could be as small as an epithet or a patronymic. The *Iliad* itself is an extreme example of expansion, but, as I have been arguing, it is not the ultimate expansion. We might think of the entire Epic Cycle, if it survived as fixed and complete poems, as an ultimate expansion of the poetry about Troy—or, better, as a variation on such an ultimate expansion.

Knowing that Briseis had a name—that she is not simply the "daughter of Brises" but Hippodameia, a traditional character with her own story to tell—not only opens up a deeper understanding of Briseis' role in the *Iliad*, but helps us to better appreciate how the poetics of an oral traditional poem like the *Iliad* work. In such a system, characters are not invented *ad hoc* for clever literary purposes, but rather are invoked and deployed in ways that reverberate far and wide and powerfully within their tradition.[13] Knowing that Briseis' story is not only

---

[13]   Cf. Graziosi and Haubold 2005:9 on the "resonance" of epic, that is, epic poetry's "ability to evoke a web of associations and implications by referring to the wider epic tradition." The poetics I attempt to describe in this chapter by way of examples are very much in accordance with the work of Graziosi and Haubold, though their focus is not on the multiformity of the epic tradition, as mine is here.

traditional but multiform enhances our understanding of the system further still. When, in the absence of Briseis, Achilles goes to sleep with "the daughter of Phorbas, Diomedē of the beautiful cheeks" in *Iliad* 9.663–665, we catch a glimpse of another tradition about Briseis that our *Iliad* has not included. There were audiences in antiquity who no doubt knew it and felt its absence.

"Of the Boeotians Peneleos and Leitos were the leaders"

In chapter 1 we saw that the Catalogue of Ships in book 2 of the *Iliad* contains information that would seem to reflect, at least in places, a Bronze Age Greek world, and hence it is likely to preserve some of the oldest material in the poem. But the Catalogue of Ships is missing entirely from several manuscripts of the *Iliad*, including a third-century papyrus, the eleventh-century Townley, and the thirteenth-century Genavensis. The Venetus A, the Venetus B, and the Escorial manuscripts Y.1.1 and Ω.1.12 all include the Catalogue, but in every case it is formatted in such a way that sets it apart visually.[14] What does this formatting signify? Might it reflect, in some dim way, an ancient performance tradition, in which the Catalogue was performed on its own as a unit, as has been suggested for the individual books of the poem?[15] Consider, for example, Aelian, *Varia Historia* 13.14, where the Catalogue of Ships is named explicitly as one of the episodes that "the ancients" (οἱ παλαιοί) used to perform separately. Is it one of many genres of speech and song, like lament, that had their own independent occasions for performance, but whose form and poetics have been incorporated into those of epic? Could it be that the Catalogue was sometimes not performed in antiquity? Might it have required special skill that not all performers possessed? Or is its omission in some manuscripts the result of scholarly decisions in antiquity, debates that may have deemed the Catalogue un-Homeric or else not meant to be part of the *Iliad*? Surviving sources do not provide a definitive answer, and my questions are highly speculative.

But whatever the answer, visual inspection reveals what is otherwise obscured in a traditional edition. The Venetus A, Venetus B, and the Escorial manuscripts Y.1.1 and Ω.1.12 preserve copious scholia on this portion of the text, which make it clear that the Catalogue was intensely scrutinized in antiquity. If we did not have these images and had to rely solely on the reporting of editors, we would know only that A, B, Y.1.1, and Ω.1.12 include the Catalogue of Ships while the Townley and Genavensis do not, and we would not see that it

---

[14] Images of these manuscripts can be accessed at http://www.homermultitext.org. See, for example, folio 34r of the Venetus A.

[15] See further below on the shield of Achilles as another such unit.

has been carefully set apart from the rest of book 2 in each manuscript that does include it. It would also be more difficult to appreciate the density of scholarly commentary on this portion of the poem.[16]

What do we lose if we omit the Catalogue of Ships? Edzard Visser (1997) and Benjamin Sammons (2010) are two of the more recent scholars to explore the poetics of the Catalogue and its relationship to the larger poem.[17] Visser's exhaustive work shows above all that while political geography is certainly an important component, myth is a driving force in the composition of the Catalogue as we now know it. That is to say, attached to the place names of the Catalogue is a host of poetic narratives and mythological associations whose importance came to outweigh geographical and political considerations for poets composing in performance. Sammons's study examines the artistic principles at work within the Catalogue, and while his study is built on a different theoretical foundation from that of the Homer Multitext (he prefers to see the artistry he articulates as being the work of a master poet, whereas I and my collaborators view it as the result of an oral poetic system that developed organically over a very long period of time), it does important work in establishing catalogue poetry as a sophisticated genre in its own right, one that allows a poet to situate his own performance within the context of the much larger epic tradition. In other words, if we lose the Catalogue of Ships, we lose the multiplicity of connections outward to the larger tradition that are made possible by this remarkable assemblage of heroes and their highly compressed epic stories. Sammons would argue that we lose much more than that—we lose the poet's personal commentary on his own poetic narrative by way of such outward-looking references.

I could not hope to replicate the monumental work of Visser or that of Sammons here in this brief chapter, but I think it is worth exploring in a bit more detail how the presence or absence of the Catalogue of Ships affects our understanding of the *Iliad* and the epic tradition as a whole, as I see it, from a multitextual perspective. In so doing, I hope to show, as I did in the case of Briseis, how some of the long-standing questions about the Catalogue (noted above in chapter 1), can be approached differently if we build on the work of Parry and Lord and those who have come after them. Once again we will see an evolving oral tradition at work, one that relies heavily on the poetics of compression and expansion within a traditional medium.

---

[16] For more on the special treatment of the Catalogue of Ships in our surviving manuscripts see the Homer Multitext research blog at http://homermultitext.blogspot.com/2012/02/catalogue-of-ships.html.

[17] See also Tsagalis 2010b.

Let's begin with the place of the Catalogue within the poem. Why narrate a roster of the combatants in the tenth year of the war? Indeed, the seeming inappropriateness of the Catalogue's placement in the *Iliad* may well be what led to its omission in some texts. This is an objection that has been raised time and again in connection with a number of episodes in the *Iliad*, including the duel between Paris and Menelaos for Helen in book 3 and the *teikhoskopia* ("viewing from the walls," also in book 3), in which Helen points out and describes, as if for the first time, the Greek soldiers fighting before the walls of Troy. Many scholars of prior eras (especially those of the Analyst and Neoanalyst schools of thought) have wanted to see such episodes as borrowings by the poet of our *Iliad* from the poems of the Epic Cycle. Mabel Lang (1995) has offered a different explanation for these seeming chronological inconsistencies. In her argument, the *Iliad* has its origins in a linear telling of the Trojan War. Over time it came to be a song about Achilles' wrath, and parts of the earlier tradition were arranged to fit it. For example, the so-called *teikhoskopia* by Helen and Priam seems to belong more naturally to the beginning of the war than its tenth year, according to Lang, but this scene was then fitted to the "restart" of the fighting after Achilles' withdrawal.

Lang's arguments are more in keeping with my own understanding of the *Iliad* as a poem that evolved over the course of many centuries—one that is not the creation of one particular poet, who "borrows" material from other poems, but is rather the collective creation of the sum total of generations of singers, all composing in performance within the same traditional system. I would formulate the process slightly differently from Lang, in that I see the transformation of the linear narrative as being natural and organic, occurring gradually as the poem was recomposed in performance over the course of centuries, rather than an inorganic process by which earlier episodes were "made to fit." (In saying this, I don't mean to deny that certain cultural forces or institutions, such as the regulated performances of the *Iliad* at the Panathenaia, contributed to the shaping of the *Iliad* as we now have it.) I think we need to try to understand the Catalogue of Ships, regardless of how it may have functioned in an earlier stage of the tradition, as an organic component of the *Iliad* as we have it (and in this respect my views overlap very well with those of Sammons), one that developed as the poem evolved over the centuries.

As many have noted, our Catalogue is aware of what has come before and what will come after in the narrative. The entry for Achilles is a perfect example:

Νῦν, αὖ, τοὺς ὅσσοι, τὸ Πελασγικὸν Ἄργος ἔναιον
οἵ τ' Ἄλον οἵ τ' Ἀλόπην· οἵ τε Τρηχῖν' ἐνέμοντο
οἵ τ' εἶχον Φθίην ἠδ' Ἑλλάδα καλλιγύναικα
Μυρμιδόνες δὲ καλεῦτο καὶ Ἕλληνες καὶ Ἀχαιοὶ.
τῶν αὖ πεντήκοντα νεῶν ἦν ἀρχὸς Ἀχιλλεύς.

ἀλλ' οἵ γ' οὐ πολέμοιο δυσηχέος ἐμνώοντο·
οὐ γὰρ ἔην ὅς τί σφιν ἐπὶ στίχας ἡγήσαιτο·
κεῖτο γὰρ ἐν νήεσσι ποδάρκης δῖος Ἀχιλλεὺς
κούρης χωόμενος Βρισηΐδος ἠϋκόμοιο
τὴν ἐκ Λυρνησσοῦ ἐξείλετο πολλὰ μογήσας
Λυρνησσὸν διαπορθήσας καὶ τείχεα Θήβης·
καδ δὲ Μύνητ' ἔβαλεν καὶ Ἐπίστροφον ἐγχεσιμώρους
υἱέας Εὐηνοῖο, Σεληπιάδαο ἄνακτος·
τῆς ὅ γε κεῖτ' ἀχέων. τάχα δ' ἀνστήσεσθαι ἔμελλεν·

Iliad 2.681–694

Now however many inhabited Pelasgian Argos,
and those who possesed Alos and Alope and Trachis,
and those who held Phthia and Hellas of the beautiful women,
and were called Myrmidons and Hellenes and Achaeans,
of these Achilles was the leader of fifty ships.
But they did not have in mind grievous war.
For they did not have anyone to lead the troops.
For swift-footed radiant Achilles lay among his ships
furious over the girl Briseis with the beautiful hair,
whom he took from Lyrnessos with great toil,
when he sacked Lyrnessos and the walls of Thebe
and he slew the spear-fighters Mynes and Epistrophus,
the sons of the lord Euenus, who was the son of Selepius.
He lay grieving because of her, but he was soon to rise up.

I have written about these lines elsewhere as an illustration of the way that epic narratives can be greatly expanded (to a poem the scale of the *Iliad*) or highly compressed (as here) within an oral performance tradition (Dué 2002:8–9). If the *Iliad* did not survive and these lines were found in another epic about another warrior at Troy, today's readers would find the references to Achilles' anger and the capture of Briseis at Lyrnessos obscure. But for a traditional audience, the *mēnis* of Achilles would be called before their eyes and that compressed narrative would resonate within its context. Briseis' own personal history is now largely lost to us, but as I have already argued, ancient audiences of the *Iliad* most likely knew at least one expanded version, and very possibly more than one version, of her story, and that story reverberates throughout the poem.

We can see that the entry for Achilles within the Catalogue of Ships connects both backwards and forwards and outwardly to the larger tradition. The Myrmidons are without a leader because of the events of *Iliad* 1. It is also noted that Achilles is going to return—an event that will not occur for another seventeen books. At the same time, events outside the scope of our *Iliad* are likewise referenced, namely the sack of Lyrnessos and the capture of Briseis. The sack of Lyrnessos (and/or Pedasos and Thebe) and the taking of Briseis were narrated in the *Cypria*, according to our ancient sources. The *Iliad* can refer to this poetic tradition and it can be assumed that the audience will be familiar with the expanded narrative.

As I have suggested already in chapter 1, I find it helpful to think of each entry in the Catalogue—and indeed all named figures in the *Iliad*—as being like an index entry, with the epic tradition as a whole being the work to which it refers. (Compare, for example, Milman Parry on traditional epithets such as πολύμητις Ὀδυσσεύς: "δῖος and πολύμητις, for the audience, describe the Odysseus of all the epic poems which sang his deeds" [Parry 1928/1971:171].) The audience has, at least as a notional entity, read the entire "book." Because we are so far removed from the historical performance contexts of the *Iliad* and the *Odyssey*—and all other epics that existed in antiquity—we modern readers of the epics have, in most cases, read only the index entry.

Keeping this notion of the index in mind, I would like to turn now to the first named characters in the Catalogue, the leaders of the Boiotians, Peneleos and Leitos (Βοιωτῶν μὲν Πηνέλεως καὶ Λήϊτος ἦρχον *Iliad* 2.494). These heroes play only a small role in the *Iliad* as a whole, meaning they are "walk-on characters," so to speak. They appear again together in book 13 (91–125), where Poseidon, after first inspiring the two Ajaxes, exhorts Peneleos and Leitos to fight, along with Teucer, Thoas, Deipyros, Meriones, and Antilokhos, all of whom are resting near the ships. Their inclusion among some of the foremost fighters of the Achaeans is suggestive, but there is otherwise little to be learned about them in this passage.

In 14.487–505, however, Peneleos avenges the death of the warrior Promakhos at the hands of Akamas.[18] Akamas retreats unharmed, but Peneleos kills the Trojan Ilioneus, an only son whose head Peneleos lifts up "like the head of a poppy," boasting over it:

> Πηνέλεῳ δὲ μάλιστα δαΐφρονι θυμὸν ὄρινεν·
> ὁρμήθη δ' Ἀκάμαντος· ὃ δ' οὐχ ὑπέμεινεν ἐρωὴν
> Πηνελέωο ἄνακτος· ὃ δ' οὔτασεν Ἰλιονῆα
> υἱὸν Φόρβαντος πολυμήλου, τόν ῥα μάλιστα
> Ἑρμείας Τρώων ἐφίλει καὶ κτῆσιν ὄπασσε·
> τῷ δ' ἄρ' ὑπὸ μήτηρ μοῦνον τέκεν Ἰλιονῆα.
> τὸν τόθ' ὑπ' ὀφρύος οὖτα κατ' ὀφθαλμοῖο θέμεθλα,

---

18 It would appear that Promakhos and Peneleos are related, on which see the scholia of the Venetus B *ad* 2.494 and Kirk's commentary *ad* 14.449.

ἐκ δ' ὦσε γλήνην· δόρυ δ' ὀφθαλμοῖο διὰ πρὸ
καὶ διὰ ἰνίου ἦλθεν, ὃ δ' ἕζετο χεῖρε πετάσσας
ἄμφω· Πηνέλεως δὲ ἐρυσσάμενος ξίφος ὀξὺ
αὐχένα μέσσον ἔλασσεν, ἀπήραξεν δὲ χαμᾶζε
αὐτῇ σὺν πήληκι κάρη· ἔτι δ' ὄβριμον ἔγχος
ἦεν ἐν ὀφθαλμῷ· ὃ δὲ φὴ κώδειαν ἀνασχὼν
πέφραδέ τε Τρώεσσι καὶ εὐχόμενος ἔπος ηὔδα·
εἰπέμεναί μοι Τρῶες ἀγαυοῦ Ἰλιονῆος
πατρὶ φίλῳ καὶ μητρὶ γοήμεναι ἐν μεγάροισιν·
οὐδὲ γὰρ ἣ Προμάχοιο δάμαρ Ἀλεγηνορίδαο
ἀνδρὶ φίλῳ ἐλθόντι γανύσσεται, ὁππότε κεν δὴ
ἐκ Τροίης σὺν νηυσὶ νεώμεθα κοῦροι Ἀχαιῶν.

Iliad 14.487–505

But he [Akamas] especially stirred the heart [*thumos*] in keen-spirited
    Peneleos
and he started for Akamas. But he [Akamas] did not wait for the
    onrush
of the lord Peneleos. And he [Peneleos] wounded Ilioneos,
the son of Phorbas of many flocks, whom especially
of the Trojans Hermes loved and granted property.
To him his mother had born Ilioneos as an only child,
and him at that moment he [Peneleos] wounded under the eyebrow
    in the roots of the eye
and he pushed the eyeball from it. Right through the eye came the
    spear
and it went through the occipital bone, and he [Ilioneos] sat down,
    stretching out his hands,
both of them, while Peneleos drew his sharp sword
and drove it in the middle of his neck, and to the ground he struck
    off
his head together with its helmet. The mighty spear still
was in his eye. And he [Peneleos], holding it up like the head of a
    poppy,
signaled to the Trojans and boasting spoke a word:
"Tell for me, Trojans, illustrious Ilioneus'
dear father and mother to lament in their halls.
For the wife of Promakhos the son of Alegenor
will not be gladdened by her dear husband coming home, whenever
the sons of the Achaeans return from Troy with their ships."

Even though the account of Ilioneos' death is followed by a boast, in which the grief of his parents is treated as just compensation for the grief of the widow of Promakhos, we see in it a kind of mourning for Ilioneos and great compassion for the suffering of his Trojan parents. This passage closely resembles others found throughout the *Iliad* that introduce warriors just before they die. As Mary Ebbott and I have argued elsewhere, these highly compressed biographies would likely have served a commemorative function, and, abbreviated though they are, often share themes and imagery (especially botanical imagery) with traditional laments performed by women, such as those sung by Andromache, Briseis, and Achilles' mother, Thetis, in the *Iliad* (Dué and Ebbott 2010:322–323). Many of these compressed biographies seem to be focalized through the eyes of a mother or widow. In *Iliad* 11.221–228, we hear the story of Iphidamas, who leaves behind his bride and half-built house to "go after the *kleos* of the Achaeans." In *Iliad* 4.473–489, we learn how Simoeisios comes to be named by his parents, and that he dies before he can repay their care in raising him. He is compared to a felled poplar, a use of plant imagery that is also common in lament.

The death of Gorgythion at *Iliad* 8.302–308 is another particularly beautiful example of this kind of passage, for which we may cite the evocative translation of Samuel Butler:

> ὃ δ' ἀμύμονα Γοργυθίωνα
> υἱὸν ἐῦν Πριάμοιο κατὰ στῆθος βάλεν ἰῷ,
> τόν ῥ' ἐξ Αἰσύμηθεν ὀπυιομένη τέκε μήτηρ
> καλὴ Καστιάνειρα δέμας εϊκυῖα θεῇσι.
> μήκων δ' ὡς ἑτέρωσε κάρη βάλεν, ἥ τ' ἐνὶ κήπῳ
> καρπῷ βριθομένη νοτίῃσί τε εἰαρινῇσιν,
> ὣς ἑτέρωσ' ἤμυσε κάρη πήληκι βαρυνθέν.

The arrow hit Priam's brave son, faultless Gorgythion, in the chest. His mother, fair Kastianeira, lovely as a goddess, bore him after she had been married from Aisyme, and now he bowed his head as a garden poppy in full bloom when it is weighed down by showers in spring— even thus heavy bowed his head beneath the weight of his helmet.

We can easily imagine these words spoken in the first person by Kastianeira upon learning of the death of her son in battle. Indeed, epic poetry is infused with the imagery, themes, and language of lament, so much so that a number of scholars have speculated that women's lament traditions played a crucial role in the development of epic. Epic poetry narrates the glory of heroes, the *klea andrōn*, but it also laments their untimely deaths and the suffering they cause. That these lament-filled passages are more often than not sung for the death of the Trojans and their allies is a testament to the remarkable parity of compassion that underlies the *Iliad*. Both sides are mourned equally.[19]

I have dwelled for so long on Peneleos' killing of Ilioneus simply to point out that we have ample evidence for the traditionality of such passages, and that although his role is small, Peneleos (and for that matter, Ilioneus) is as integrated into the poetics of this system as any other warrior. We may compare *Iliad* 6.35–36, where this time Leitos kills Phylakos in the midst of a list of warriors who get their man (Φύλακον δ' ἔλε Λήϊτος ἥρως / φεύγοντ'). Much as in the Ilioneus passage, in the lines just before the death of Phylakos we find yet another highly compressed biography for a fallen warrior:

> Ἔλατον δὲ ἄναξ ἀνδρῶν Ἀγαμέμνων·
> ναῖε δὲ Σατνιόεντος ἐϋρρείταο παρ' ὄχθας
> Πήδασον αἰπεινήν.

> And lord of men Agamemnon killed Elatos
> who inhabited the banks of the wide-flowing river Satnioeis
> sheer Pedasos.

Here we are not told anything about Elatos' parents or any other details of his life (such as we find in the other passages cited), but his hometown is remembered along with some geographical details that connect him to a particular place and add to the sense of loss that accompanies his death.

In book 16 (335–344) Akamas and Peneleos are once again to be found in close proximity to one another on the battlefield. This time Peneleos kills Lykon, while Meriones chases down Akamas and kills him. In book 17 (597–621), however, Peneleos' and Leitos' role in the fighting comes to an end: both Peneleos and Leitos are wounded, one right after the other. Leitos, wounded at the wrist, is permanently disabled, while Peneleos is struck by Polydamas with a deep wound to the shoulder. Neither warrior is mentioned again in our *Iliad*.

As with the warriors they kill, I would argue that Peneleos' and Leitos' roles in the poem are typical, but they are not generic. Like Briseis, Peneleos and Leitos each has a story, one that is known to the larger epic tradition, from which the poet draws the details of his narrative. Neither is a major character in our *Iliad*, but that does not mean that they never were—or that they did not play a larger role in other epic narratives. And in fact, it seems very likely that these two did play such a role in another epic tradition: they are included in a list

---

[19] See Dué and Ebbott 2010:323 for additional bibliography on the relationship between lament and epic, women's songs and men's songs, the mortality of the hero as a central theme of epic, and passages that lament the death of heroes in a highly compressed form, such as the one quoted from *Iliad* 8 here. See also Tsagalis 2004:179–187.

of the Argonauts at Apollodorus 1.9.16 (Lang 1995:161). If the early Argonautic epic tradition (referred to as "a concern for [i.e., known to] all" at *Odyssey* 12.70) survived for us today along with the *Iliad* and the *Odyssey*, we would no doubt have a much better understanding of their expanded story, and we would not have to wonder why these two of all the warriors who fought at Troy are named first in the Catalogue. And so once again I return to the idea of the index. A traditional audience, like the oral epic poet, has access to the notional totality of the epic tradition, and unconsciously connects to the expanded narrative each time that Peneleos and Leitos appear, however briefly. Without knowing more about their Argonautic exploits, it would be difficult for us modern readers to reconstruct how such knowledge on the part of the audience would have affected the poetics and the reception of the scenes in which they appear, but I submit that they are necessarily affected.[20]

Each entry in the Catalogue signals to the audience an awareness of and respect for a whole host of epic narratives associated with those names and places. As Lang has written (1995:161): "Speculative in the extreme? Yes, but sensible if one sees the Catalogue of Ships not as a survey of actual political geography, but as a poetic attempt to list as many famous heroes as might possibly have fought in the Trojan War, although in the *Iliad* at least, several have little or no part. These heroes must have been known to the bards, complete with epithets and epitheted place-names, from their local exploits." Not every warrior named will play a major role in the epic, but the role they play in other traditions, be they local or more Panhellenic in nature, adds to the richness of the narrative and the poetic resonance of every scene in the *Iliad* in which they appear.

And what of the "epitheted place-names" to which Lang refers? How do they fit into the poetic system I have been describing? Let's continue from where we left off, at *Iliad* 2.494:

> Ἀρκεσίλαός τε Προθοήνωρ τε Κλονίος τε,
> οἵ θ' Ὑρίην ἐνέμοντο καὶ Αὐλίδα πετρήεσσαν
> Σχοῖνόν τε Σκῶλόν τε πολύκνημόν τ' Ἐτεωνόν,
> Θέσπειαν Γραῖάν τε καὶ εὐρύχορον Μυκαλησσόν,

---

[20] Cf. Tsagalis (2010b:323), who writes: "By selecting a name the bard opens a path to the hypertextual web of myth." Tsagalis concludes: "catalogues have no end, only 'endings,' whose plurality is an invitation to the audience to go on in their own mind, to conjure up more information from other traditions or sources, to be alert to the existence of a totality that song can never fully achieve" (2010b:347). A nice example of this phenomenon outside of the Catalogue of Ships can be found in the Venetus A scholia at 7.9, where Menesthios the son of Areithoos is killed by Paris. The scholia provide a history of Areithoos' exploits and explain the origins of Areithoos' epithet κορυνήτης (7.9). The Venetus A scholia include many such backstories. The one at 7.9 is attributed to Pherecydes.

οἵ τ' ἀμφ' Ἄρμ' ἐνέμοντο καὶ Εἰλέσιον καὶ Ἐρυθράς,
οἵ τ' Ἐλεῶν' εἶχον ἠδ' Ὕλην καὶ Πετεῶνα,
Ὠκαλέην Μεδεῶνά τ' ἐϋκτίμενον πτολίεθρον,
Κώπας Εὔτρησίν τε πολυτρήρωνά τε Θίσβην

Iliad 2.495–502

and Arkesilaos and Prothoenor and Klonios
who inhabited Hyria and rocky Aulis
and Skhoinos and Skolos and many-peaked Eteonos
and wondrous Graia and Mykalessos with its broad dancing places
and those who inhabited Harma and Eilesios and Erythrai
and those who held Eleon and Hyle and Peteon,
Okalea and Medeon the well-built citadel,
Kopai and Eutresis and Thisbe of the many doves

Was there a real place named Mykalessos and did it actually have broad dancing places? Why is Medeon a "well-built citadel" but Okalea is not described at all? Did Thisbe really have many doves, and if so how do we know? How did such places and epithets make it into the epic tradition to begin with? Again, it would be beyond the scope of this chapter to definitively answer these questions (and again I point to the very thorough work of Visser 1997 with additional bibliography *ad loc.*). But by exploring further the epithets used of Mykalessos and Thisbe in this passage, I believe we can once again gain an appreciation for why the *Iliad* must be understood as a multiform tradition that evolved dynamically over time. We will see once again that the Catalogue of Ships constantly draws upon a vast storehouse of epic material, centuries in the making, with the result that each entry becomes almost like an archaeological excavation, through which we must carefully sift to uncover other long-lost epics. In what follows I build on previous work in which I have discussed the poetics of various other kinds of noun-epithet combinations, and here as always I am much indebted to the work of Milman Parry, whose first doctoral thesis was entitled *L'Épithète traditionelle dans Homère; Essaie sur un problème de style homérique* (= The Traditional Epithet in Homer).[21]

Lang's work suggests that the walk-on characters in the *Iliad* are in fact local heroes whose deeds in the Trojan War and/or other epic narratives would have been sung in particular places. At some point what had previously been local songs came to be performed more widely and by other, nonlocal singers, or at the very least, their heroes came to be incorporated into a wider narrative

---

[21] See Dué and Ebbott 2010 *ad* 10.3 and 10.283 for definitions and the history of scholarship on epithets.

tradition that eventually resulted in our *Iliad*. By making it into the *Iliad*, these local heroes became part of a Panhellenic poetic tradition at some distance removed from the local songs in which they originated. If this conceptualization is correct, we have to understand that different singers and different audiences may have known more or less specific information about these heroes and the towns from which they hailed, depending on their familiarity with the local traditions that formed these characters' backstories. And yet, as a notional totality at least, the full biography of these more local heroes was at some point known to the epic tradition as a whole.

Likewise, this notional totality that I am invoking possessed a broad knowledge of the geography of Greece, although it is clear that much as the dialect of the Homeric epics evolved to incorporate Aeolic and Ionic and even Attic elements, so too did new places come into the system, sometimes (no doubt) at the expense of other places, which had fallen out of circulation. Just as in the case of a character like Briseis, a place like Mykalessos or Thisbe may had syntagmatic associations, that is, details that were true and specific to the actual towns, as well as paradigmatic associations (characteristics that they share with other epic places, details that may or may not have had anything to do with their "real" geographical features). Each place may have had at one time a set of particular epithets and formulas used of it by bards familiar with the locale. Some or all of that formulaic language may have at one point become a part of the larger, more Panhellenic epic tradition, but not all of what came into the system stayed in the system. As the tradition and its formulaic diction evolved, so too did the poets' and audiences' conception of those places evolve.

It is this evolution that explains at least in part why the political geography of the Catalogue of Ships cannot be tied to one particular era. Some towns mentioned in the Catalogue (e.g., Eutresis in 2.502) were uninhabited after the end of the Bronze Age,[22] which might suggest a Bronze Age date for the Catalogue, but others were not particularly important in the Bronze Age and flourished only in later times.[23] Athens, so important a city from Archaic times onwards, was a relatively minor fortified citadel in the Bronze Age, which might explain why it barely features in our *Iliad* and might be another indication of a Bronze Age date for the Catalogue. And yet the geographical evidence preserved in the Bronze Age Linear B tablets often does not match up with that of the Homeric texts.[24]

---

[22] Eutresis was reoccupied beginning in the sixth century BCE; see Simpson and Lazenby 1970:27.

[23] Sparta seems to have displaced the Bronze Age Therapne completely; see Dickinson 2011.

[24] An example would be Pylos, whose territory as revealed by the Linear B tablets does not match what is described in the Catalogue (Dickinson 2011).

The work of E. S. Sherratt discussed in chapter 1 suggests that we should not be looking for a single political reality reflected in the Catalogue of Ships, and that it would be fruitless to attempt to separate Bronze Age geographical details from later ones. Elements from more than one reality entered the system of formulaic diction and were seamlessly integrated over time. At the same time, as this process was ongoing, the reality of any particular location (its particular natural features, precise geographical location, etc.) faded in importance, and instead its poetic/epic identity superseded it. A place like Mykalessos was understood within the tradition to have broad dancing places, and it may well have had them at one time, but poets of later eras need not have known whether or not this was this was the case. Within the poetic tradition, Mykalessos had broad dancing places.

Mykalessos was not the only place to have broad dancing places, however; Sparta and other cities as well are described this way in the *Odyssey* (Elis 4.635; Iolkos 11.265; Sparta 13.414 and 15.1; Hypereia [in the vicinity of the Cyclopes] 6.4).[25] Archaeological remains are not sufficient to tell us whether these places actually had broad dancing places. A place that certainly did have them was Knossos on Minoan Crete, which, as we have seen, is intriguingly remembered on the shield of Achilles as having a dancing place made by Daidalos for Ariadne (*Iliad* 18.590–592):

> ἐν δὲ χορὸν ποίκιλλε περικλυτὸς ἀμφιγυήεις,
> τῷ ἴκελον οἷόν ποτ' ἐνὶ Κνωσῷ εὐρείῃ
> Δαίδαλος ἤσκησεν καλλιπλοκάμῳ Ἀριάδνῃ.

> And on it a dancing place was wrought by the very famous god who
>   was lame in both legs,
> like the one which once in broad Knossos
> Daidalos made for Ariadne of the beautifully braided hair.

Here the dancing place is not said to be broad; instead Knossos itself is described as broad (εὐρείῃ).

I see two possibilities here. One is that Mykalessos really did have a spacious dancing place, more so than other places, and this detail about the town has been preserved in epic diction. Another is that the memory of great cities of the Bronze Age past such as Knossos (whose preserved frescoes and seals from the Mycenaean period depict what appears to be choral dancing) resulted in the creation within the poetic diction of a generic and ornamental epithet analogous to "good at the war shout" (βοὴν ἀγαθὸς), which Mary Ebbott and I have

---

[25] For the use of the epithet in lyric poetry see Visser 1997:125n40.

discussed extensively in connection with *Iliad* 10.283 (Dué and Ebbott 2010 *ad loc.*). As we write there:

> But let us notice first that Parry does not say here that this epithet has no meaning at all; he says only that it does not specify one hero in a way that it specifies no other hero. In other words, the heroes designated βοὴν ἀγαθός are, indeed, good at the battle shout. The fact that more than one hero is so designated suggests that such a skill would have been considered a good and useful one for a warrior, just as the formula itself is good and useful for the singer who is composing in performance.

Just as being good at the war shout was considered a good quality for the epic hero to have, so too it seems that having broad dancing places was a quality associated with ancient cities.[26]

Geoffrey Kirk, in the section of his commentary on the *Iliad* that introduces the Catalogue of Ships, argues that all of the epithets used to describe cities in the Catalogue "save about eight can be divided into one or other of four general categories of meaning" (Kirk 1985:175).[27] The categories are as follows: well-built town; rocky, steep, high; fertile, broad, by sea/river; lovely, holy, rich. I have some disagreements with Kirk's classification (for example, he groups πολυτρήρωνά ["of the many doves," on which see below] with adjectives meaning rocky or steep and he does not include εὐρύχορον in his groupings at all), but I can see his point. Most cities in the Catalogue are described in ways that might be considered generic and ornamental, that is to say, not particular to any real city of any particular era. They have characteristics that would be good and useful for any city. Mykalessos may have at one time been renowned for its dancing places, but later audiences more likely understood the epithet along the lines of "having broad dancing places, in the way that all good cities do" or possibly "having broad dancing places, in the way that all cities of the heroic past did." Whatever syntagmatic meaning the epithet once had has given way to a more paradigmatic one.

Thisbe on the other hand is an example of a place with a particular natural feature that seems to have been preserved within the tradition, not unlike the way that the very ancient vestiges of the Arcado-Cypriote dialect have been preserved within formulaic diction. Modern travelers[28] have observed that the

---

[26] For more on Bronze Age connections to the dancing place for Ariadne see Lonsdale 1995.

[27] See also Visser 1997:112–146. εὐρύχορος is discussed at 124–125, and πολυτρήρων at 139–140.

[28] Including James Frazer in his edition of Pausanias (vol. 5, p. 162) and Michael Wood in his book and documentary *In Search of the Trojan War*.

place believed to be ancient Thisbe (as evidenced by inscriptions) is indeed inhabited by many doves, as its epithet πολυτρήρωνά suggests.[29] Could this be an example of an epithet with syntagmatic meaning—meaning specific to the real Thisbe—that has persisted within the system? If so it is not the only such place: Messe (in the region of Sparta) is likewise designated πολυτρήρωνά at *Iliad* 2.582 in the same metrical position. Messe too has been observed by modern travelers to be a home to birds: "The identification of Messe with the site at Tigani receives some support from the constant din created by the 'pigeons and seafowl' in the cliffs of Thyrides to the south, which calls to mind the Homeric epithet πολυτρήρων" (Simpson and Lazenby 1970:77).

I have been suggesting that places—like heroes and, at a more basic level, formulas—had to enter the system of Homeric diction at some point, and that the formulaic diction associated with those places changed as the system evolved. Some formulas persisted and may have retained something of their original meaning for centuries, until the epics crystallized into the form in which we now have them, while most other formulas evolved to become more generic, in that they were associated with cities in general. Mykalessos and Thisbe are just two examples of places whose traditional epithets underwent this evolution. Singers from those regions or the towns themselves may have indeed known them to have particular characteristics, but later singers and later audiences from other places most likely only knew them by their poetic identities, which may or may not have maintained characteristics particular to them. The fact that only a handful of places are described as εὐρύχορον and πολυτρήρωνά in our surviving evidence suggests that the formulas were created and used because they were indeed true of those places, but we must be aware of the limitations of our evidence. As Mary Ebbott and I note with reference to βοὴν ἀγαθός, if the *Iliad* did not survive and we had only the *Odyssey*, we might think that only Menelaos was ever so described. If more epic poetry survived, and especially if more catalogue poetry survived, we might find many such cities described as having dancing places and being full of doves. Even so, as I have tried to argue here and elsewhere, the fact that multiple cities are described as εὐρύχορον and πολυτρήρωνά does not make these traditional descriptions devoid of meaning, it just gives them meaning of a different kind, a kind that is quite typical of oral poetry.[30]

---

[29] See also Strabo 9.411, who observed them near the city's port.

[30] For more on the identification of Mykalessos and Thisbe and other named towns with actual historical places see Simpson and Lazenby (1970), although not all identifications of places mentioned in the Catalogue are universally accepted. On Mykalessos and Thisbe see also Visser 1997:302–311 and 316–324.

The questions I have explored here are just a few out of many. I offer these arguments because I think they help us to conceptualize the Catalogue of Ships as a dynamic document within a multiform tradition. Such a document would naturally have raised many questions for later, literate editors and scholars in antiquity, just as it has for modern ones. We can understand how the difficulties encountered by these editors, who were working within a different paradigm from the one in which the *Iliad* was actually created, led to the omission of the Catalogue altogether from some editions. The result might be a more logical and concise poem—qualities that seem to have been prized by Alexandrian critics, as we saw in chapter 2 and as we will see again in my concluding chapter. Even though we don't know the Catalogue to have been athetized by Zenodotus or Aristarchus or anyone else, we can easily imagine them doing so, and, as I say, this preference for concision and logic might explain the Catalogue's omission and special treatment in various manuscripts.

What is less clear is whether the Catalogue was ever omitted in earlier stages of the transmission, that is to say, in performance. The loss or omission of the Catalogue of Ships from a full performance of the *Iliad* would be a tremendous loss indeed. The Catalogue offers countless points of entry into a thousand years or more of epic tales. As Sammons shows us, the Catalogue allows us to understand the *Iliad* against the backdrop of the tradition from which it has emerged. How we understand the *Iliad*'s relationship to that tradition may be a matter of debate, but that there is a vital and dynamic relationship is not in doubt.

At the same time, we might do well to try to imagine a performance of the Catalogue that is indeed separate from the *Iliad* we now know. Richard Martin has inferred from scattered references in the scholia and on the basis of comparative evidence from other oral traditions that "portions of hexameter verse that we moderns may consider organic in a poem were once treated by some ancient scholars as detachable," the reason being that they could be performed independently, as showpieces.[31] How might an audience's experiences of such separate performances impact their understanding of the Catalogue when it was performed as part of the *Iliad*? A multitextual approach to the *Iliad* once again allows us to have it both ways. We can imagine an Iliad without the Catalogue of Ships, perhaps very much the lesser for it, the Iliad known to the owner of that third-century papyrus and the readers of the Townley and the Genavensis in the Middle Ages. We can imagine an expert performer of Catalogue poetry, amazing his audience with his ability to call before their eyes a tremendous array of heroes and their stories. And finally we can imagine the delight with

---

[31] See Martin 2005:171–172, citing Revermann 1998, with reference to the shield of Achilles, discussed in chapter 3 as well as further below. See also Slings 2000:70.

which a visitor to Athens' Panathenaic festival clapped or shouted with recognition upon hearing the contingent from his hometown mentioned in a performance of such a monumental epic poem as the *Iliad*. Sure, Achilles was the son of a goddess and many would call him the best of the Achaeans, but he was no Peneleos or Leitos...

"A better *mētis*"

At the beginning of book 10 in the Townley manuscript of the *Iliad*, the first scholion reads:

> φασὶ τὴν ῥαψῳδίαν ὑφ' Ὁμήρου ἰδίᾳ τετάχθαι καὶ μὴ εἶναι μέρος τῆς Ἰλιάδος, ὑπὸ δὲ Πεισιστράτου τετάχθαι εἰς τὴν ποίησιν

> They say that this epic composition was arranged separately by Homer and not to be part of the *Iliad*, but it was arranged into that poem by Peisistratos.

Once again we are confronted with the possibility of a considerably shorter, and perhaps more logical *Iliad*. *Iliad* 10, also commonly referred to as the Doloneia,[32] has long been felt to be different from the rest of the *Iliad* somehow, and many modern editors reject it as un-Homeric. The book narrates—using unusual diction that sometimes feels more Odyssean than Iliadic—a night expedition undertaken by Odysseus and Diomedes, in which the two heroes capture and kill the Trojan spy Dolon and then go on to kill the newly arrived Trojan ally Rhesos and his companions and steal Rhesos' famed horses. Even though ambushes, cattle raids, and other forms of alternative warfare abound in the epic tradition, modern discomfort with the actions narrated in *Iliad* 10 have caused the book's place in the *Iliad* to be questioned again and again. That the book at times exhibits unusual diction and oddities of language, special items of clothing, and other unusual features, has cemented the feeling among many critics that the Doloneia does not belong in our *Iliad*.

Analyst scholars in the nineteenth century in particular seized upon the scholion quoted above from the Townley as proof of *Iliad* 10's inauthenticity. Walter Leaf was one such scholar, who sought in his commentary on the *Iliad* to separate the earlier and later strata of the poem, and thereby explain aspects of the work that seemed to him incongruous or inelegant. Although Leaf understood the various songs of the *Iliad* to be orally composed and transmitted (Leaf

---

[32] In the scholia and elsewhere it is referred to as the νυκτεγερσία (see e.g. the A scholia *ad* 10.1). In Aelian 13.14 it is called the Doloneia (Δολώνειάν).

1900:xvi), his commentary connects the songs to individual authors, some of whom he judges to be more skilled than others. *Iliad* 10 receives much of Leaf's harshest criticism. Arguing that *Iliad* 10 (like *Iliad* 9) "can never have existed independent of the Μῆνις [the song of Achilles' wrath]" (Leaf 1900:423), he summarizes the place of the book in the epic tradition this way: "Everything points, in fact, to as late a date as this [the second half of the seventh century BCE] for the composition of the book. It must, however, have been composed before the *Iliad* had reached its present form, for it cannot have been meant to follow on I [*Iliad* 9]. It is rather another case of a parallel rival to that book, coupled with it only in the final literary redaction" (Leaf 1900:424). Leaf's audience would have been well aware of the near-universal condemnation of the book in his day, and of the perceived structural problems that Leaf alludes to here. *Iliad* 9 takes up too much of the night, it had been argued, to allow for another episode. The reference to Achilles at 10.106–107, Leaf suggests, also seems out of place immediately after the failed embassy. Rhesos and the capture of his horses are not mentioned anywhere else in the epic, much as the embassy to Achilles goes unmentioned in places where it seems logical (to us) to do so.

In his brief introduction to *Iliad* 10, Leaf gives, in addition to these structural objections, three primary reasons for believing the book to be a late composition. He says that it has a "mannered style" that is at odds with the "harmony and symmetrical repose of the Epic style," and he finds the length of preparations that begin the book out of proportion with the length of the narration of the night mission itself (Leaf 1900:423–424). He next offers linguistic evidence, consisting of unusual word forms and other forms that come from later stages of the Greek language. And, finally, he cites "pseudo-archaisms," words that he argues are deliberately used by the poet to create the illusion of antiquity. Such objections have been largely countered by the work of later scholars (Dué and Ebbott:8–12 and *passim*). But although much of his introduction is devoted to these three points, they may not have been what influenced Leaf's thinking the most. Leaf's introduction to the book in fact begins with a quotation of the Townley scholion, which seems to reveal that already in antiquity *Iliad* 10 was thought at least by some to be a separate composition. He adds: "These noteworthy words ... correspond too closely with the probabilities of the case to allow us to treat them as a mere empty guess." For Leaf, the scholion confirms a generally understood feeling about the book—one that does not need extensive argumentation.

The condemnation of the book since the days of Leaf is so widespread that even a relatively recent book devoted to the theme of ambush in the *Odyssey* (Edwards 1985), written from an avowedly Parry-Lord perspective, does not discuss *Iliad* 10, which contains our most extensive example of an ambush in surviving Greek epic.[33] Ignoring *Iliad* 10 is a strategy employed by many scholars, who no doubt feel they must ignore it so as not to incur the charge of making arguments about Homer based on an "interpolated," "un-Homeric," or otherwise problematic text. Even while admitting that most conventional arguments against the book have proven flawed, Hainsworth's (1993) commentary asserts that points that seem of little weight unto themselves add up to only one conclusion—namely, that *Iliad* 10 does not belong in our *Iliad*. West brackets the entire book in his 1998–2000 edition, and a recent translation of the *Iliad* by Stephen Mitchell omits it altogether.[34]

Modern scholars cite the Townley scholion as evidence that *Iliad* 10 is not genuine in some way, but in so doing they seem to ignore that the scholion does posit "Homer" as the composer, which suggests that book 10 is indeed traditional. In fact, the comment is evidence neither that *Iliad* 10 is "un-Homeric" nor that it is by a later author who fit his composition to the *Iliad*, as some would have it. Mary Ebbott and I have published a set of essays and a commentary on *Iliad* 10 that takes a different approach to the questions raised by the book, one that allows for the book's inclusion in our *Iliad* as we now know it, but also acknowledges the possibility that *Iliad* 10 was not always included in every performance (Dué and Ebbott 2010).

---

[33] Two major exceptions are Shewan 1911 and Danek 1988. (See now Elmer 2018.) Danek offers a spirited defense of *Iliad* 10 as an orally composed, traditional piece of poetry. But rather than emphasize its shared features with Homeric poetry, Danek emphasizes the book's unusual features. Much like Shewan before him, Danek argues that the Doloneia is good poetry composed by a good poet, but for Danek that poet is not Homer. He is instead a poet working in the same tradition, somewhat later than the composer of the *Iliad*. This poet strives for a personal style that is lively. He makes clever use of convention, deliberately alludes to the *Iliad*, tries to introduce colloquial words, attempts to make scenes more visually stimulating, and intentionally varies formulaic language. The fieldwork of Parry and Lord, however, is at odds with Danek's hypothesis. Danek assumes that his poet of the Doloneia could both be traditional and seek to create a personal style. But poets in a traditional process like that which Parry and Lord describe do not seek to innovate. Parry asserted that such a poet "would not think of trying to express ideas outside the traditional field of thought of the poetry" and "make[s] his verses easily by means of a diction which time has proved to be the best" (Parry 1932:7–8 [= Parry 1971:330]). Other more positive assessments of *Iliad* 10 include Petegorsky 1982:175–254, Thornton 1984:164–169, and Stanley 1993:118–128. But Stanley's concluding remarks about the book reveal an essentially negative view of the actions of Odysseus and Diomedes in *Iliad* 10: "Their achievement, now and later, is based not on heroic honor but on clever exploitation; and its rewards are merely a surplus of things, not tokens of glory" (1993:128). Mary Ebbott and I make precisely the opposite argument in Dué and Ebbott 2010, namely, that *mētis* and *biē* are complementary paths to achieving glory and distinction (*kleos* and *kudos*) in Homeric epic and that both *mētis* and *biē* are prized as being characteristic of the "best" of the Achaeans.

[34] The translator Stephen Mitchell is not the same Stephen Mitchell who is a curator of the Milman Parry Collection of Oral Literature and who coauthored (with Gregory Nagy) the introduction to the second edition (2000) of Albert Lord's *The Singer of Tales*.

Mary Ebbott and I understand *Iliad* 10 to have been composed and performed within a long oral tradition of such poetry, and we argue that book 10 is an example of a very ancient theme, the *lokhos* (ambush and related alternative warfare). As I noted already in chapter 1, for us, the theme of *lokhos*, with its traditional structure and diction, long predates our received text of the *Iliad*. *Iliad* 10, we argue, gives us our best look at an alternative type of warfare poetics, namely the poetics of ambush. Using comparative evidence as well as what we know of the Epic Cycle and the epic tradition as a whole, we assert that such warfare was not construed as unheroic and should not be viewed as un-Homeric in some way (however "Homer" is conceived), but is in fact simply a traditional theme (as defined by Albert Lord), the *lokhos*, with its own traditional language, subthemes, conventions, and poetics (Dué and Ebbott 2010:31–87). The *polemos* (what we frequently refer to as "conventional battle") too is a theme, and the two are not entirely antithetical to one another. The best heroes star in both kinds of warfare. Some overlap of diction is therefore inevitable, but *polemos* and *lokhos* each represent a distinct narrative tradition that is recognizably different from the other.

In the history of Homeric scholarship *Iliad* 10 has often been asserted to be "Odyssean," and that assessment has been used to maintain a variety of theories about the book (including that it is a "late" composition). In the model that we propose, *Iliad* 10 need only be viewed as related to the *Odyssey* in that it shares the theme of ambush and has Odysseus as a central character. In other words, *Iliad* 10 and the *Odyssey* seem similar in terms of language because they partake of the same theme.[35] Other examples of the theme in the wider epic tradition, to the extent that we can reconstruct it, include the ambushes of Tydeus and Bellerophon (these stories are referred to at *Iliad* 4.376–400 and 6.187–190). In *Iliad* 13.276–287 Idomeneus praises Meriones' abilities as an ambush fighter and describes the qualities of the good versus the bad ambush warrior, calling the *lokhos* the place "where the merit of men most shines through" (λόχον, ἔνθα μάλιστ' ἀρετὴ διαείδεται ἀνδρῶν 10.277). On the shield of Achilles (*Iliad* 18.509–540), a group of men from the city at war form an ambush party (see λόχῳ in 513 and λοχῆσαι in 520), which is led by Athena and Ares. The use of the word ἐννύχιος at *Iliad* 21.37 strongly suggests that Lykaon was ambushed by Achilles, as does the description by Andromache of Achilles' killing of her brothers (*Iliad* 6.421–424). In *Iliad* 11 (101–106) we are told the story of Antiphos and Isos, two sons of Priam, whom Achilles ambushed while they watched their sheep on Mount Ida and then sold for ransom. In *Iliad* 20 both Aeneas and Achilles refer to a time when Achilles

---

[35] On this point see also Petegorsky 1982:176.

ambushed Aeneas while he was working alone as a shepherd on Mount Ida.[36] These episodes should not surprise us, given the prominence of the ambush of Troilos by Achilles in other Archaic sources, including early vase paintings (see Plate 7b) and the *Cypria*. In *Iliad* 1, Achilles castigates Agamemnon for not going into ambush with the "best of the Achaeans." In the *Odyssey*, the episode of the wooden horse and the capture of Troy is referred to three times as an ambush (*Odyssey* 4.277, 8.515, 11.525). Several ambushes are featured in Odysseus' Cretan lies. Menelaos ambushes Proteus, the suitors set an unsuccessful ambush for Telemakhos, and both the killing of the Cyclops and the slaughter of the suitors are structured as ambushes. This last episode has been explored in great detail by Anthony Edwards, whose 1985 work *Achilles in the Odyssey* devotes a lengthy chapter to the ambush theme. Episodes from the Epic Cycle include not only the ambush of Troilos by Achilles and possibly the death of Achilles himself at the hands of Paris and Apollo but also the ambushes of Palamedes and Helenos in episodes that featured Odysseus and Diomedes. In Hesiodic epic, the castration of Ouranos by Kronos is called an ambush (λόχῳ, *Theogony* 174).

These numerous examples show us that the ambush of Dolon (and later, Rhesos) that takes place in *Iliad* 10 is in no way an unusual plot line. A poet composing this story would have made use of the same traditional diction and narrative patterns that are used for these other ambushes, and we demonstrate this for our *Iliad* 10 throughout our commentary. In this sense we respectfully disagree with the analyses of Leaf and of Fenik (1964), who ultimately concludes that a later, inferior (oral) poet, whom he calls "the K[appa] poet," has only semi-successfully adapted earlier mythological material to this place in the *Iliad*. Georg Danek took a similar stance in an important 1988 monograph on book 10, differing from Fenik, however, in that he stresses the poet's skill as an oral poet and his individual style. By approaching ambush as a theme in strict accordance with the way Albert Lord used that term, we can view *Iliad* 10 not as an idiosyncratic work that does not belong in our *Iliad*, but rather as our only extended example in that epic poem of what was once a common, traditional theme. An episode like the Doloneia then might well be very old, with its own set of very old, traditional formulas.

Why might an ancient poet have wanted to include an ambush episode like the Doloneia in the *Iliad*? Dan Petegorsky has argued that instead of misapplying conceptions about authorship, relationships between "texts," or the idea of "lateness" with respect to the Doloneia, we should focus on the Doloneia's thematic importance within the *Iliad*.[37] His examination of the presence and function of

---

[36] See 20.89–96 and 188–193 and cf. *Odyssey* 15.386–387. For more on this episode and Achilles as an ambusher see below, p. 143.

[37] Petegorsky 1982:175–254.

the Doloneia in the *Iliad*, he asserts, shows "how important the episode is in contributing to the thematic coherence of the poem as a whole" (Petegorsky 1982:177). The Doloneia, Petegorsky persuasively argues, far from being "separate" or divorced from the rest of the *Iliad*, serves the epic's overall momentum as it builds towards Achilles' return as the only way to overcome Hektor. His discussion is complex and compelling, especially as concerns the role of *mētis* in the *Iliad*, but I will attempt to summarize the thrust of the argument here. In the previous episode on this night, the embassy to Achilles, Achilles has refused to return to battle to face the threat Hektor poses and, noting the wall that the Achaeans have built, has advised them that the wall will not hold Hektor back (*Iliad* 9.346–355). Later, Achilles says that the Achaean leaders will need to come up with a "better *mētis*" (μῆτιν ἀμείνω *Iliad* 9.421–426). This challenge, Petegorsky argues, evokes a theme of *mētis*, or, looking at it thematically, his challenge "demands that they make use of essentially Odyssean skills in an Iliadic context" (Petegorsky 1982:177–178). Unlike all the other plans that the Achaeans attempt in Achilles' absence, however, this one does succeed—but not in turning back Hektor. Instead, its success actually highlights that the only way to succeed against Hektor is through Achilles' strength, which is the programmatic message of the *Iliad*, with its focus on Achilles.

The Doloneia does, however, remind us that Troy itself will eventually be taken by *mētis*. In effect, the Doloneia exposes the limited role of *mētis* within the *Iliad* through thematic contrast. Nestor's words about Achilles and Hektor at *Iliad* 10.103–107, his offer of *kleos* for the spying mission that is tied to a *nostos* (*Iliad* 10.211–213), and even the references to the superiority of the horses of Achilles at *Iliad* 10.401–404 and at *Iliad* 10.555–557 all serve to emphasize the necessity of Achilles' strength for effecting the death of Hektor and, consequently, the taking of Troy.[38]

To sum up, Petegorsky argues that Achilles' challenge to the Achaeans in *Iliad* 9—to seek a better *mētis* to save the ships—evokes a particular kind of episode, an Odyssean one, in which Odysseus is the star, *mētis* prevails, and *nostos* is achieved. Recalling the arguments Mary Ebbott and I have made that intersect with Petegorsky's examination of these thematic elements, we would rephrase the thematic evocation he reveals—namely, that Achilles' challenge evokes an ambush theme. We can build on Petegorsky's arguments by saying

---

[38] Petegorsky (1982:209–211) refutes Fenik's assertion that the Doloneia cannot portray the night mission as an assassination attempt against Hektor, showing that it is not the attempt that the *Iliad* excludes, but rather the success of such an attempt, since Achilles must be the killer of Hektor. Fenik (1964:20) also makes the (in our view, baseless) argument that an assassination attempt would be an unacceptable portrayal of Odysseus and Diomedes (whereas a "negative" portrayal of Odysseus and Diomedes is consistent in the *Rhesos*). Fenik here seems to ascribe his own understanding of ambush as "negative" to an epic tradition that includes many such episodes.

that the plan and ambush in *Iliad* 10 show how *mētis* succeeds when the force used in the *polemos* does not. Or, with the ambush of Rhesos understood in its larger tradition, we can extend Petegorsky's reasoning and say that the ambush reveals how *mētis* overcomes an enemy who cannot otherwise be beaten in the *polemos*. In the Iliadic tradition, Hektor can only be overcome in the *polemos*— and by Achilles only. So, although Rhesos is explicitly only an indirect threat and is a greater threat implicitly, his ambush nevertheless reveals the important role of *mētis* and ambush in the overall epic tradition about Troy and the general suppression of that importance in the *Iliad*. That general suppression may also account for the dearth of direct references to the events of the Doloneia in the subsequent books of the *Iliad*.

Parry and Lord's fieldwork and the resulting thesis that the *Iliad* was composed within a multiform and dynamic oral-traditional system likewise encourage us to take a fundamentally different starting point in attempting to answer the questions surrounding the Doloneia. Rather than begin with the question of authorship or authenticity, a Parry-Lord approach would seek to understand how *Iliad* 10 relates to the larger system of oral composition in performance in which the *Iliad* was composed. For example, because of certain duplications in the plots of books 9 and 10 of the *Iliad*, as well as the time elapsed during the course of the night on which these events take place, we have seen that it has been argued that *Iliad* 10 is a clumsy forgery (by someone other than "Homer") meant to replace *Iliad* 9. (Note, however, that *Iliad* 9 was also suspected throughout the nineteenth century of not being composed by "Homer.")

Instead of relying on such an unsatisfactory avoidance of the issues noted by scholars, a Parry-Lord approach might be as follows. First, we can make an analogy with the South Slavic tradition, where Parry and Lord documented the fact that the most accomplished singers could expand their songs indefinitely by adding episodes paratactically, as the mood of the audience or occasion required. The events of the night in question highlight the effects of Achilles' wrath and withdrawal, which constitute the central theme of the poem. It is in keeping with the poetics of an oral tradition to add additional episodes to this particular night. Second, *Iliad* 10 is the only surviving example of an extended narrative about a night raid in Homeric poetry, even though we know there were many such episodes in the larger epic tradition. The night raid/ambush is a traditional theme, with its own traditional language, subthemes, conventions, and poetics, but nonetheless part of the same system of oral poetry to which the entire *Iliad* belongs.

Finally, as Albert Lord himself suggested (Lord 1960:194), just because the theme of ambush is a very old one, this does not mean that the Doloneia would have been included in every performance of the *Iliad*. *Iliad* 10 may be a legitimate multiform of *Iliad* 9, both books orally composed within the same traditional poetic system and therefore both equally "Homeric." Much as I suggested above in connection with the Catalogue of Ships, it is possible to imagine there being performed in antiquity a shorter Iliad that did not include the Doloneia, or one that included the Doloneia but not the embassy to Achilles. It is also possible to imagine the Doloneia as a song performed on its own. The scholion with which I began this discussion is compatible with all of these scenarios. The system was flexible and designed to meet the needs of the performer, who responded to the mood of the audience and the occasion as he composed. The fact that *Iliad* 9 or 10 or the Catalogue of Ships could be omitted in performance or performed as an independent song makes them no less authentic; rather, they are evidence for the flexibility of a poem that only came to life in performance.

"And on it he wrought the earth, and heaven, and the sea"

We have now seen two examples of a phenomenon whereby large sections of our *Iliad* might be perceived as "separate" or at least capable of being performed independently. I have attempted to show that their detachability does not make these passages any less Homeric (however we define that term); rather, their inclusion or not is one of the many choices a composer would make in the course of composition in performance. This flexibility seems to have led, as in the case of the Catalogue of Ships, to a multiform textual transmission. Many papyri and manuscripts contain the Catalogue, but some do not, and others format it in a special way. The passage that describes the decoration of the shield of Achilles made by Hephaistos in *Iliad* 18 is a third example of this phenomenon. Martin Revermann, noting that this passage is referred to as the Ὁπλοποιία in the scholia and in Athenaeus, has argued that the shield could be performed separately (Revermann 1998:37).

The scholia tell us explicitly that the description of the making of the shield was athetized by Zenodotus:

> ὅτι Ζηνόδοτος ἠθέτηκεν ἀπὸ τούτου τοῦ στίχου τὰ λοιπά, ἀρκεσθεὶς τῇ κεφαλαιώδει προεκθέσει. Ὅμηρος δὲ οὐκ ἂν προετραγῴδησεν τὰ κατὰ τὰς φύσας, εἰ μὴ καὶ τὴν τῆς ποικιλίας κατασκευὴν ἔμελλε διατίθεσθαι. (A scholia at 18.483)

> [There is a sign] because Zenodotus athetized the rest after this verse, satisfied with the summary preface. But Homer would not have narrated in tragic style the things in the bellows, if he was not intending to incorporate the preparation of the decoration.

As we saw in chapter 2, Zenodotus seems to have in many if not most places preferred a considerably shorter *Iliad* than the one we know.[39] We are fortunate that it was evidently Alexandrian practice to comment on a received text but not to alter that text beyond adding annotations such as critical signs. The commentaries keyed to such signs were published in separate scrolls.[40] If Zenodotus had made an edition that excised all athetized verses from the text, and subsequent scholars commented only on that edition, we would know much less Homeric poetry than we do now. The editors of the Homer Multitext have a very different approach to the text than that of Zenodotus, but the result is similar. We don't throw anything away, and thereby preserve the evidence for others to discover.

The shield of Achilles is one of the most celebrated and discussed passages in the *Iliad*, one that reverberates throughout the poetic tradition and through the centuries, and I would not even attempt to summarize the wealth of scholarship, ancient and modern, associated with its extended *ekphrasis*.[41] I once participated as a teaching assistant in a course taught by Gregory Nagy, in which the entire *Iliad* was read through the lens of the shield of Achilles, that is, through the meaning made possible by connecting the images on the shield with the larger narrative and the larger poetic tradition. Indeed, my participation in that course has greatly influenced my own subsequent research and teaching on the poetics of the *Iliad*. Many of the ideas that were discussed in the course were published by Nagy in his article "The Shield of Achilles: Ends of the *Iliad* and Beginnings of the Polis" (1997a). That article builds on an analysis by Leonard Muellner (Muellner 1976:100–106) of the trial scene in the "city at peace," depicted on the shield in verses 18.490–508, in which two men argue about compensation for a wrongful death while judges arbitrate and their fellow citizens watch. Since both Nagy and Muellner are associate editors of the Homer Multitext, it seems appropriate to highlight some key ideas from the article here, in order to situate the shield within the arguments being made in this book.

Nagy argues (following Lessing) that the shield passage should not be read solely in its linear position within the *Iliad* as we now know it. It is not frozen rigidly in place, with a fixed and static significance, like the decoration on a real, humanly made shield, but it is a dynamic, living, work-in-progress (1997a:204):

---

[39] Zenodotus' athetesis in no way jeopardized the passage's place in the textual transmission, and the wealth of scholia suggest that, like the Catalogue of Ships, it was an intensely studied passage in antiquity.

[40] See above, chapter 1, note 54.

[41] In-depth treatments include Atchity 1978, Taplin 1980, Edwards 1997:269–286, Rabel 1989, Nagy 1990a:250–255 and 2015d (part 4), Stanley 1993, and Becker 1995, but of course these are only the tip of the iceberg.

From the standpoint of the *Iliad* as a linear progression, there is a sense of closure as the main narrative comes to an end in Book 24. From the standpoint of the Shield passage, however, the *Iliad* is open-ended. In other words, the vehicle re-opens the tenor. In order to make this argument, I must first confront a paradox: the world as represented on the Shield seems to be closed and unchanging, as opposed to the openness of the *Iliad* to changes that happen to the figures in the story while the story is in progress. The question is, however, what happens when the story draws to a close? Now the figures inside the *Iliad* become frozen into their actions by the finality of what has been narrated. This freezing is completed once all is said and done, at the precise moment when the whole story has been told. This moment, which is purely notional from the standpoint of Iliadic composition, gets captured by the frozen motion picture of the Shield. Time has now stopped still, and the open-endedness of contemplating the artistic creation can begin.

The open-endedness that Nagy describes means that it is possible to make connections forwards and backwards to events that precede and follow the creation of the shield in the larger epic tradition. The entire *Iliad*, from book 1 all the way through the ransom and funeral of Hektor in book 24, can be more fully appreciated with reference to the images on the shield. This is the kind of meaning made possible by an oral traditional system, in which the audience is as familiar with the shield when listening to a performer performing book 1 or book 9 or book 16 as they are when they come at last to book 18 or when they come to the end of the poem.

Nagy, building on the analysis of Muellner, zeroes in on the litigation scene at 18.490–508 as a case in point for the open-endedness of the shield. Arguing that ultimately, Achilles himself can be understood to be the plaintiff (i.e., the one attempting to pay compensation for a wrongful death), the defendant (the one refusing to accept any compensation), and even the man who is dead, Nagy highlights a multiform attested in 18.499. I will quote the passage (using the translation of Nagy) here before continuing:

> λαοὶ δ᾽ εἰν ἀγορῇ ἔσαν ἀθρόοι· ἔνθα δὲ νεῖκος
> ὠρώρει, δύο δ᾽ ἄνδρες ἐνείκεον εἵνεκα ποινῆς
> ἀνδρὸς ἀποφθιμένου· ὃ μὲν εὔχετο πάντ᾽ ἀποδοῦναι
> δήμῳ πιφαύσκων, ὃ δ᾽ ἀναίνετο μηδὲν ἑλέσθαι

> *Iliad* 18.497–500

> The people were gathered together in the assembly place, and there
>> a dispute
> had arisen, and two men were disputing about the blood-price
> for a man who had died [*apo-phthi-*]. The one made a claim to pay
>> back in full,
> declaring publicly to the district, but the other was refusing to
>> accept anything.

Zenodotus athetized the entire description of the shield, but he did not omit it from his edition of the poem. And so while the Venetus A reads ἀποφθιμένου in 18.499 ("a man who had died"), a scholion in the Venetus A is able to tell us that Zenodotus knew the reading ἀποκταμένου ("a man who was killed"):

παρὰ Ζηνοδότῳ "ἀποκταμένου" καὶ ἐν ταῖς πλείσταις· καὶ ἔστιν οὐκ ἀπίθανος ἡ γραφή

In Zenodotus [the reading is] "ἀποκταμένου" and also in most [editions]. And the reading is not unlikely.

I will now quote the key paragraphs, for the purposes of this book, of Nagy's article (1997a:204–205):

> Our case in point is the scene of the litigants in the City at Peace…. In order to pursue this point, I focus on an instance of textual variation at *Iliad* 18.499 between *apophthimenou* 'a man who died' and *apoktamenou* 'a man who was killed'. The second variant, as we learn from the scholia, was noted by Zenodotus. If indeed the Shield passage, as a vehicle, can refer to the main narrative of the *Iliad* as the tenor, then the referent of this variant *apoktamenou* can be Patroklos, as suggested by *Iliad* 24 where Achilles accepts the *apoina* or compensation from Hektor's father Priam for the death of Patroklos. If Patroklos is the referent, this variant can also bring an ulterior meaning into the Ajax speech in *Iliad* 9: Achilles is justified in refusing compensation or *apoina* in the Embassy Scene of *Iliad* 9 because, in the long run, the compensation in question concerns the death of Patroklos, not the loss of Briseis. In the long run, Agamemnon has a share in causing the death of Patroklos and is therefore justified in offering compensation for it.
>   In the longer run, however, it was Achilles himself who caused the death of Patroklos, since he could not in good conscience accept the compensation of Agamemnon for Briseis—and since Patroklos consequently took his place in battle. In the longer run, then, Achilles can

be a defendant as well as a plaintiff in a litigation over the death of Patroklos. In the longest run, though, Achilles can even be the victim himself, since the *Iliad* makes his own death a direct consequence of the death of Patroklos. No wonder the plaintiff of the Shield scene will not accept compensation: potentially, he is also the defendant and even the victim! In this light, it becomes hard for the narrative to say that anyone is liable for killing Achilles. It becomes easier now to think of the hero not as *apoktamenou* 'a man who was killed' but as *apophthimenou* 'a man who died'.

Unlike an Alexandrian editor, Nagy is not advocating that we choose one reading over the other. Instead we can appreciate both readings as generated and having meaning within the system of Homeric poetry. The case of *apoktamenou* and *apophthimenou* is just one example of multiformity within the textual tradition of the shield, a choice to be made by the performer. Revermann, whose thesis about the detachability of the shield I cited above, argues that such separate performances made the shield even more subject to the kinds of expansion and compression that are natural to oral poetry.[42] But, as I have suggested already in chapter 3, this kind of multiformity should not be viewed as problematic or something to explain away. Rather it is an opportunity for those who are willing to see the Homeric text as being open-ended. If we are unbound by the limitations of a literate mindset that insists on freezing the text in a fixed state, we can not only appreciate the array of Iliads that were known to audiences in antiquity but also better understand the poetics of the *Iliad* that has come down to us.

Fortunately, no one in antiquity besides Zenodotus seems to have questioned the place of the shield of Achilles in our *Iliad*—or at least, if they did, it has not affected its secure place in the manuscripts. But I hope this very brief discussion of the poetics of the litigation scene on the shield make clear what is at stake when we try to apply literate and scholarly aesthetics to a poem that was composed and received within a tradition that assigned meaning very differently from those of the Hellenistic and later eras. Again, we are fortunate that the Alexandrian editors used athetesis marks and did not in most cases remove verses judged to be "not by Homer" from their editions. The loss of this passage would have changed the course of Western literature. But the shield is also incredibly vibrant within its own tradition. Whether the Shield of

---

[42] Revermann terms the kind of variation to which he refers "rhapsodic intervention" and explicitly rejects attested multiforms for the passage on the shield addressed by his article. His assumptions and methodology differ considerably from my own, but I find his thesis helpful to think with about the transmission of the shield.

Achilles was ever a song in its own right, or was always meant to be part of the *Iliad*, it is a passage that immensely deepens our understanding of the larger themes of the *Iliad*, particularly as they intersect with the brief but intense life cycle of its central hero, Achilles. Nagy's and Muellner's arguments about the ramifications of the litigation scene provide just one snapshot view of the layers of meaning that have been worked into the shield description over the long history of its composition. Its many other scenes of war and peace have far more ramifications still. In this way the shield becomes a grand example of what we stand to lose, when we screen out attested multiforms. Some attested multiforms, as we have seen in chapter 2, are as minute as a single letter. Others involve entire books and sweeping segments of text. All have the power to contribute to a far deeper understanding of the epic tradition within which the *Iliad* was composed.

"He stood before the gates, insatiably eager to do battle with Achilles"

We have been examining different choices a performer might make in performance—whether to include the Doloneia or not, or the shield of Achilles or not—as well as the natural multiformity that any one of those episodes might exhibit. The poetics of expansion and compression happen primarily on a horizontal axis: episodes are included or not, particular verses are included or not, objects are described in detail or not, a character's backstory is told explicitly or left unsung. For my final example in this chapter I would like to consider a different kind of multiformity, one that operates on a vertical axis, and one that gets at the heart of my opening questions in the introduction to this book. How might the story of the *Iliad* be told differently? Are there attested variations that actually change the story?

The short answer is no. The inherent conservatism of a tradition that claims to channel the eyewitness account of the Muses (*Iliad* 2.484–487) means that we should not expect shocking differences of plot, even after a thousand years of composition in performance, especially in the carefully regulated Panathenaic tradition. But the long answer is far more nuanced. The *Iliad* itself seems preoccupied in places with this very question. I opened this book with the passage in *Iliad* 20 in which Zeus fears that now that Achilles has returned to battle Troy will be sacked too soon, "beyond fate." And as I noted there, book 20 is fixated on the possibility that various events and encounters will happen at the wrong time. It as if the *Iliad* is signaling its awareness of other ways of telling the tale, but at the same time making it clear that it would be incorrect—that is, untraditional—to do so.

At the start of book 15, Zeus wakes from his seduction-induced slumber only to realize that Hera has tricked him and that the plot of the narrative is spinning out of his control. Hektor is down, the Trojans are being routed, and the Greeks are winning. His reaction is one of violent anger, and he quickly reestablishes with Hera how the story will go:[43]

ἔρχεο νῦν μετὰ φῦλα θεῶν, καὶ δεῦρο κάλεσσον
Ἶρίν τ' ἐλθέμεναι καὶ Ἀπόλλωνα κλυτότοξον,
ὄφρ' ἢ μὲν μετὰ λαὸν Ἀχαιῶν χαλκοχιτώνων
ἔλθῃ, καὶ εἴπῃσι Ποσειδάωνι ἄνακτι
παυσάμενον πολέμοιο τὰ ἃ πρὸς δώμαθ' ἱκέσθαι,
Ἕκτορα δ' ὀτρύνῃσι μάχην ἐς Φοῖβος Ἀπόλλων,
αὖτις δ' ἐμπνεύσῃσι μένος, λελάθῃ δ' ὀδυνάων
αἵ νῦν μιν τείρουσι κατὰ φρένας, αὐτὰρ Ἀχαιοὺς
αὖτις ἀποστρέψῃσιν ἀνάλκιδα φύζαν ἐνόρσας,
φεύγοντες δ' ἐν νηυσὶ πολυκλήϊσι πέσωσι
Πηλεΐδεω Ἀχιλῆος· ὃ δ' ἀνστήσει ὃν ἑταῖρον
Πάτροκλον· τὸν δὲ κτενεῖ ἔγχεϊ φαίδιμος Ἕκτωρ
Ἰλίου προπάροιθε πολέας ὀλέσαντ' αἰζηοὺς
τοὺς ἄλλους, μετὰ δ' υἱὸν ἐμὸν Σαρπηδόνα δῖον.
τοῦ δὲ χολωσάμενος κτενεῖ Ἕκτορα δῖος Ἀχιλλεύς.
ἐκ τοῦ δ' ἄν τοι ἔπειτα παλίωξιν παρὰ νηῶν
αἰὲν ἐγὼ τεύχοιμι διαμπερὲς εἰς ὅ κ' Ἀχαιοὶ
Ἴλιον αἰπὺ ἕλοιεν Ἀθηναίης διὰ βουλάς.

Iliad 15.54–71

Go now among the ranks of the gods and summon
to come here Iris and Apollo famed for his bow,
in order that Iris among the warriors of the bronze-wearing
    Achaeans
may go, and tell lord Poseidon
to cease from battle and go home,
and in order that Apollo may urge Hektor to battle,
and breathe rage [*menos*] into him again, and he may forget his
    pains,
which now wear out his senses, and then the Achaeans
he may turn back, stirring up the headlong flight that is lacking in
    battle resolve,
and they, fleeing, will fall among the ships with many benches

---

43 See also Slatkin 1991:111 and above, p. 3, note 3.

> of Achilles the son of Peleus. And he will cause his companion to rise up,
> Patroklos. And him radiant Hektor will kill with his spear
> before Troy after he [Patroklos] has killed many other flourishing young men,
> and among them my son, brilliant Sarpedon.
> Furious about this, brilliant Achilles will kill Hektor.
> And from this point forward I will continuously make
> a pursuit [of the Trojans] from the ships until the Achaeans
> take steep Troy through the counsels of Athena.

Here we have the remainder of the *Iliad* (and beyond), more than nine books' worth of material, compressed into only eighteen verses, not unlike the compressed story of Achilles in the Catalogue of Ships, or Proklos' summaries of the poems of the Epic Cycle. Zeus' anger suggests that it was in theory possible for the story of Troy to turn out another way, if he hadn't woken up and regained control of the narrative. As I see it, such concerns about getting the story right point to a flourishing world of song in which there were rival versions of tradition (as paradoxical as that sounds). My work on the character of Briseis, for example, leads me to believe that rival traditions about her life history were in circulation at some early stage in the crystallization of the *Iliad*.

Is it possible to reconstruct any of these rivals for our *Iliad*? Unfortunately, our evidence for the system I have been attempting to describe is very limited. As we have seen, the vast majority of the evidence that we can assemble primarily falls within periods 4 and 5 of Nagy's evolutionary model, discussed in chapter 1, by which point the text had largely crystallized into the form in which we now know it. Our knowledge of local, non-Panathenaic versions of the *Iliad* is far more limited still. Sherratt's arguments about "generative" periods and periods of "maintenance" (also discussed in chapter 1) are helpful for theorizing about far earlier and far more fluid phases of the Homeric tradition, but it would be difficult to assert with any confidence what those earlier Iliads (or, earlier songs about Troy) were like. Presumably the heroes wore boar's tusk helmets and used long thrusting spears and carried tower shields; just possibly the deaths of Achilles, Patroklos, and Hektor were closely interconnected just as in our *Iliad*. Perhaps, as I have speculated at various points in this book, earlier Iliads were not so tightly focused around the anger of Achilles in the tenth year of the war, and could incorporate chronologically earlier or later episodes in a more linear fashion, if the singer chose to do so.

Perhaps, as suggested by the Theran frescoes, and as is implied by Achilles' boasts about sacking twenty-three cities on land and sea (*Iliad* 19.328–329), in earlier Iliads Achaean heroes went on raids of various sorts and regularly engaged in ambush.[44] A speech of the Second Sophistic writer Dio Chrysostom states explicitly (although, admittedly, as part an extended clever critique of Homer) that Achilles did indeed fill his time this way:

τὸν δὲ λοιπὸν χρόνον τὰ μὲν ἐποίουν κακῶς, τὰ δ᾽ ἔπασχον, καὶ μάχαι μὲν οὐ πολλαὶ ἐγένοντο ἐκ παρατάξεως· οὐ γὰρ ἐθάρρουν προσιέναι πρὸς τὴν πόλιν διὰ τὸ πλῆθος καὶ τὴν ἀνδρείαν τῶν ἔνδοθεν· ἀκροβολισμοὶ δὲ καὶ κλωπεῖαι τῶν Ἑλλήνων· καὶ Τρωίλος τε οὕτως ἀποθνήσκει παῖς ὢν ἔτι καὶ Μήστωρ καὶ ἄλλοι πλείους. ἦν γὰρ ὁ Ἀχιλλεὺς ἐνεδρεῦσαι δεινότατος καὶ νυκτὸς ἐπιθέσθαι. ὅθεν Αἰνείαν τε οὕτως ἐπελθὼν ὀλίγου ἀπέκτεινεν ἐν τῇ Ἴδῃ καὶ πολλοὺς ἄλλους κατὰ τὴν χώραν, καὶ τῶν φρουρίων ᾕρει τὰ κακῶς φυλαττόμενα.

Dio Chrysostom 11.77–78

In the years that followed, the Greeks both did and suffered damage. However, not many pitched battles were fought, since they did not dare to approach the city because of the number and courage of the inhabitants. Skirmishes and forays there were on the part of the Greeks, and it was thus that Troïlus, still a boy, perished, and Mestor and many others; for Achilles was very skillful in laying ambushes and making night attacks. In this way he almost caught and slew Aeneas upon Mount Ida and many others throughout the country, and he captured any forts that were poorly guarded.[45]

It would be easy to dismiss Dio as a late author playing a literary game with the *Iliad*, much as Dares and Dictys of Crete and Philostratus' *Heroikos* are not typically seen as reliable guides to early epic tradition. And perhaps, in an abundance of caution, we really should not try to use Dio as a clue to what the *Iliad* was like fifteen hundred years before his time.

And yet, I am tempted to. I have found in the course of my research several places where the variations on the *Iliad* offered by Second Sophistic writers are supported by far earlier witnesses.[46] Again I return to Briseis, with whom I began

---

[44] Leaf in fact attempts to reconstruct such a tradition, which he calls "The Tale of the Great Foray." See Dué 2002:61–62. See alao Lambrou 2018.
[45] The translation is that of Cohoon (1932).
[46] Dictys of Crete survives only in a Latin translation of the fourth century CE, although internal evidence and a papyrus fragment of the Greek text date Dictys considerably earlier, to between 66 and roughly 200 CE. To what extent we may use the Latin text of Dictys to reconstruct earlier traditions is a difficult but potentially productive question. In my 2002 book (ch. 3) I show that although Dictys' fictional retelling of the Trojan War makes substantial departures from the

this chapter, who we are told (by the Venetus A scholia) had the name Hippodameia in early Greek poetry. The same scholion that gives us the name Hippodameia tells us that Chryseis (i.e., "daughter of Chryses") had the name Astynome. So too in Dictys of Crete (2.17) are Briseis and Chryseis named Hippodameia and Astynome. In Dictys, Briseis is captured in Achilles' sack of Pedasos, which contradicts the numerous references in the *Iliad* to her having been captured in Lyrnessos, but the Townley scholia at *Iliad* 16.57 state that in the *Cypria*, she was in fact captured in Pedasos (τὴν Πήδασον οἱ τῶν Κυπρίων ποιηταί, αὐτὸς δὲ Λυρνησ‹σ›όν).

It could be argued that Dictys and Dio are making use of Cyclic epic traditions here, particularly the *Cypria*, and that in no way should these accounts be seen as reflective of the Iliadic tradition. And again I will concede that they may not be. But I would point out that Achilles' ambush exploits (highlighted by Dio) are alluded to repeatedly throughout the *Iliad*. As we have seen, Achilles castigates Agamemnon for not going into ambush with the "best of the Achaeans" in the opening episode of the poem. An ambush is featured on the shield of Achilles, and formulaic language indicates that Achilles ambushed Andromache's brothers, Aeneas, Antiphos, Isos, and Lykaon. These are in addition to Achilles' ambush of Troilos, which is featured prominently in other non-Homeric Archaic sources.

In fact, Achilles seems to be exceedingly good at ambush. Virtually every other example of ambush in the epic tradition that Mary Ebbott and I located features two ambushers, or two leaders of a much larger ambush (Dué and Ebbott 2010:70–71).[47] But Achilles in every case ambushes solo. I am even tempted to interpret Achilles' traditional epithet "swift-footed" (ποδάρκης, πόδας ὠκύς, and ποδώκης) as referring to his ambush skills.[48] Ambush requires speed because the ambusher typically lies in wait, surprises his victim, and then chases him as he flees. When Achilles taunts Aeneas in book 20 about the time he ambushed him on Mount Ida, he explicitly refers to chasing after him with his swift feet:

> ἦ οὐ μέμνῃ ὅτε πέρ σε βοῶν ἄπο μοῦνον ἐόντα
> σεῦα κατ' Ἰδαίων ὀρέων ταχέεσσι πόδεσσι
> καρπαλίμως; τότε δ' οὔ τι μετατροπαλίζεο φεύγων.

> *Iliad* 20.188–190

Homeric account, he is sometimes in agreement with very old sources against the *Iliad*. For a survey of the relationship between the text of the *Iliad* and that of Dictys see Venini 1981.

47 Cf: *Iliad* 10.224–225: σύν τε δύ' ἐρχομένω καί τε πρὸ ὃ τοῦ ἐνόησεν / ὅππως κέρδος ἔῃ "When two men go together, one perceives even before the other / what is the best strategy").

48 On these three epithets for Achilles and their connections to ambush see also Dué and Ebbott 2010 ad 10.316, which I expand upon here. Dunkle (1997) notes that Achilles' speed is not what brings down Hektor in *Iliad* 22.

> Don't you remember when you, being alone from your cattle,
> I chased down from the peaks of Ida with swift feet,
> speedily? At that time you did not look back as you fled.

The chase takes Achilles all the way to Lyrnessos, which he then proceeds to sack (taking Briseis as his prize), while Aeneas makes his escape. Aeneas, earlier in book 20, recounts this exact same episode when Apollo (disguised as Lykaon) urges him to fight Achilles. Aeneas too refers to Achilles' swift feet when invoking this prior encounter (οὐ μὲν γὰρ νῦν πρῶτα ποδώκεος ἄντ' Ἀχιλῆος / στήσομαι 89–90).

Achilles is called ποδώκης twenty-two times in the *Iliad* and twice in the *Odyssey*. That that word is associated with the theme of ambush is supported by the fact that in *Iliad* 10.316 Dolon is likewise described as ποδώκης. Dolon is of course overtaken and eventually killed by Odysseus and Diomedes in that book, and so evidently he is not swift enough.[49] But it seems that both the victim of ambush and the successful ambusher can be thought of as swift. In one of his Cretan lies, Odysseus claims to have ambushed and killed Orsilokhos, a son of Idomeneus, in Crete, and he says that Orsilokhos (whose very name contains the word *lokhos*) is swift-footed (πόδας ὠκύν), faster than all other seafaring men in wide Crete (*Odyssey* 13.259–270).

There is some evidence that the death of Achilles himself at the hands of Paris and Apollo, foreshadowed throughout the *Iliad*, might have been narrated as an ambush in at least one epic tradition. Surviving evidence (including what we know of the now-lost *Aithiopis*) indicates that in Archaic myth Achilles died after receiving an arrow wound to the ankle (Burgess 1995:225), and the Skaian Gate is pointed to as the location in several sources.[50] But in some (primarily late) accounts of Achilles' death, Paris ambushes him in the sanctuary of Thymbraion when he comes, unarmed, to arrange his marriage to Polyxena.[51] These late sources may reflect an alternative epic tradition about Achilles' death by ambush at the hands of Paris and Apollo. Intriguingly, Thymbrē (the location of the sanctuary of Thymbraion) is mentioned only in book 10 (at line 430) in our *Iliad*. It is associated with ambush in the larger epic tradition around the Trojan War in that it is the site of Achilles' ambush of Troilos (according to the scholia in the Townley manuscript on *Iliad* 24.257; see also Apollodorus *Epitome* 3.32). If these late sources do ultimately go back to an Archaic epic

---

[49] It is worth noting, however, as Mary Ebbott points out to me, that Dolon is overcome not purely by speed, but a combination of *mētis* and speed. The same is true for Orsilokhos and indeed Achilles, in the variations in which he is killed by ambush (discussed below).

[50] The ancient evidence is collected in Burgess 2009:38–39; see also Burgess 1995.

[51] See Dictys of Crete 3.2ff., Dares 27, Hyginus 110, and Philostratus, *Heroikos* 51.1, with Burgess 1995.

tradition, it would be another example of a swift-footed ambusher falling victim to ambush.

This brings me at last to a curious scholion in the Venetus A manuscript at line 22.188:

σημειῶδες ὅτι μόνος Ὅμηρός φησι μονομαχῆσαι τὸν Ἕκτορα, οἱ δὲ λοιποὶ πάντες ἐνεδρευθῆναι ὑπὸ Ἀχιλλέως.

It is significant that only Homer says that Achilles fought Hektor in man-to-man combat. All the rest say that Hektor was ambushed by Achilles.

Unlike the scholion about Briseis' name, we are not told anything about who οἱ λοιποί are. "Homer" is not compared or contrasted with other "*arkhaioi*" or "*neōteroi*" in this comment, as we find elsewhere in the scholia. A search of the full corpus of Greek in the *Thesaurus Linguae Graecae* database turns up no other place where "only Homer" says or does anything. A survey of uses of the phrase οἱ δὲ λοιποὶ πάντες turns up no meaningful pattern for deducing who οἱ λοιποί might be in this context. But the very fact that Homer is frequently contrasted with other poets (including those of the Epic Cycle) in the Venetus A scholia means we should at least consider the possibility that οἱ λοιποί are other epic poets. In the Panhellenic Iliadic tradition, Achilles kills Hektor in man-to-man combat. But there was another way to tell the story in the larger epic tradition: Achilles could have used his solo ambusher skills to take down Hektor.

This alternative tradition is not necessarily a later, inferior one. It is simply not the canonical one. By the standards of the *Iliad* we know, it would almost certainly be deemed ὑπὲρ μόρον. But although our sources for Achilles' ambush exploits are varied and in some cases quite late, they may well point to the existence of far earlier phases of the poetic tradition about Achilles and his activities over the course of the Trojan War. For the scholars working in the library of Alexandria, whose work is excerpted in the Venetus A, Homer was clearly the poet *par excellence*, and they were not particularly interested in this earlier or noncanonical material that had not made it into the Panhellenic *Iliad*, unless it somehow provided support for their conception of Homer and the correct Homeric text. Modern editors likewise are typically dismissive of deviation from the medievally transmitted *Iliad* and *Odyssey*, whether that be in the form of plus verses, weakly attested variations within the text, or alternative mythological and poetic traditions not featured in "Homer."

But those of us working on the Homer Multitext, informed as we are by the research and fieldwork of Milman Parry and Albert Lord on oral poetry, *are* interested in this material. We do want to know about the raw data, so to speak, of epic tradition, out of which the *Iliad*, the *Odyssey*, and the poems of the Epic Cycle took shape, with which ancient poets and audiences were familiar. If we know, for example, that an epic poem about the Trojan War could have narrated the death of Hektor as an ambush, it then becomes meaningful that our *Iliad* does not do it that way. As we have seen with reference to the Doloneia, our *Iliad* is not primarily composed within the poetics of ambush, but rather within the poetics of what we might call the *polemos* (or conventional battle). *Iliad* 10 can best be understood by way of its thematic contrast with the rest of the poem. The choice by the poets of the *Iliad* tradition to depict Achilles as primarily a *promakhos anēr*, in contrast to Odysseus, who is primarily the hero of *mētis* within his poem, surely explains why the version of Hektor's death that we know won out over that of "all the rest," who told it differently.

Finally, this scholion about "Homer," in contrast with "all the rest," forces us to confront what we mean by Homer. For the editors of the Homer Multitext, "Homer" is shorthand for a poetic tradition that encompasses the *Iliad* and the *Odyssey* in all of their historical iterations, as well these poems as notional, multi-form entities that interacted with and drew upon a vast expanse of traditional material. I do not wish to reopen here old debates (addressed in Dué 2002, Dué and Ebbott 2010, and elsewhere) about whether a poem like the *Iliad* requires a new kind of criticism, one that does not hinge on reconstructing the choices and intent of a single poet. Clearly, it does, and I'll have more to say about this in my concluding chapter.[52] Instead I prefer to end this long chapter on a positive note by saying that the tools for doing a new kind of criticism have come into existence, and the data needed for testing any number of hypotheses about the *Iliad* are becoming available for those wishing to take a multitextual approach to Homeric epic.[53]

---

[52] For extended demonstrations of how the poetics of Homeric poetry work differently and must be approached differently, see Muellner 2006 and forthcoming and Dué and Ebbott 2010.

[53] See, e.g., Roughan, Blackwell, and Smith 2016; Wauke, Schufreider, and Smith (forthcoming); and Churik, Smith, and Blackwell (forthcoming).

Conclusion

"In Appearance Like a God"
Textual Criticism and the Quest for the One True Homer

Aristarchus athetized at least seven passages of three verses or more in *Iliad* 20 alone. Each athetesis gives us insight into an editor who was struggling to account for a mythological and poetic tradition that was multiform and at times contradictory. Some passages cause issues with narrative continuity, some passages Aristarchus felt would be better placed elsewhere, and others he felt to be not in keeping with his conception of Homer. For example, at *Iliad* 20.178–186, the Venetus A reads as follows, and verses 180–186 are marked with the athetesis mark, the *obelos* (folio 263v):

> Αἰνεία τί σὺ τόσσον ὁμίλου πολλὸν ἐπελθὼν
> ἔστης; ἦ σέ γε θυμὸς ἐμοὶ μαχέσασθαι ἀνώγει
> ἐλπόμενον Τρώεσσιν ἀνάξειν ἱπποδάμοισι
> τιμῆς τῆς Πριάμου; ἀτὰρ εἴ κεν ἔμ' ἐξεναρίξῃς,
> οὔ τοι τοὔνεκά γε Πρίαμος γέρας ἐν χερὶ θήσει·
> εἰσὶν γάρ οἱ παῖδες, ὃ δ' ἔμπεδος οὐδ' ἀεσίφρων.
> ἦ νύ τί τοι Τρῶες τέμενος τάμον ἔξοχον ἄλλων
> καλὸν φυταλιῆς καὶ ἀρούρης, ὄφρα νέμηαι
> αἴ κεν ἐμὲ κτείνῃς; χαλεπῶς δέ σ' ἔολπα τὸ ῥέξειν.

> Aeneas, why do you stand there, having come so far out from the
>   crowd?
> Does your *thumos* compel you to fight with me,
> hoping to rule among the horse-taming Trojans
> over the honor of Priam? But if you slay me,

> not for the sake of this will Priam place a prize of honor in your
>   hand.
> For he has sons, and he is steadfast and not witless.
> Or have the Trojans now apportioned out some plot of land
>   surpassing all others for you,
> a beautiful plot with orchards and ploughland, in order that you may
>   inhabit it
> if you kill me? But I expect that you will accomplish this with
>   difficulty.

In this passage the best of the Achaeans confronts the future hero of the *Aeneid* with the kind of boasting that is typical of the Homeric battlefield. Flyting is "an essential part of the hero's strategic repertoire" (Martin 1989:72), as has been well documented in a number of modern studies of this competitive genre of speech within the *Iliad*.[1] But in the left margin of the Venetus A we find the following comment explaining all the *oboloi*:

> ἐλπόμενον Τρώεσσι· ἀθετοῦνται στίχοι ἑπτά, ὅτι εὐτελεῖς εἰσι τῇ κατασκευῇ καὶ τοῖς νοήμασι, καὶ οἱ λόγοι οὐ πρέποντες τῷ τοῦ Ἀχιλλέως προσώπῳ.

> Seven verses are athetized, because they are shabby in their ornamentation and thought, and the words are not fitting for the character of Achilles.

Aristarchus, of course, believed in a real Homer, a divinely inspired authorial figure whose poetic abilities and aesthetics were by default whatever Aristarchus and other scholars of his day deemed to be the ideal. Whatever appeared to be inept or inelegant or unworthy of a character could not possibly have been composed by Homer. Aristarchus' cuts (in the form of athetesis) were not as drastic as those of his predecessor Zenodotus, but if he had created an edition in which athetized verses were in fact removed, his Homer too would have been a lot slimmer than the one we know.

What Aristarchus wanted to take away, I want to take back. Building on the work of earlier scholars who have demonstrated why we should expect the *Iliad* to be multiform (especially Lord 1960 and Nagy 1996a), I have attempted in this book to provide a picture of the kinds of multiformity that survive in the textual tradition, and to show how that multiformity can affect our understanding of the poem and the broader poetic system in which it was composed. It is not my

---

[1]   On the poetics of flyting see Martin 1989:68–75, Mackie 1996:55–56, Camerotto 2007, and Lentini 2013:§4. On this passage in particular see Lentini 2013.

assertion that every attested verse of the *Iliad* belonged to every performance of the poem—quite the opposite. But our usual methods of textual criticism do not work for the *Iliad*.[2] When confronted with multiformity, we cannot, as scholars have for millennia now, fall back on the criterion of "not worthy of Homer," in order to make scholarship easier or more comfortable. In this concluding chapter I give a few final examples of the ways in which conventional textual criticism, both ancient and modern, fails us when it comes to a poem like that *Iliad* that was composed in performance over the course of many centuries. Ultimately, I return to my initial assertion that a paradigm shift—in the form of a multitext edition (together with a multitextual approach to the Homeric poems in general)—is required, even if that means conceiving of the work of interpretation in entirely new ways.

***

Let us consider a scholion in the Venetus A on *Iliad* 3.100. At this point in the narrative, Hektor has proposed on behalf of his brother Alexander a duel between the two men who claim Helen, Alexander and Menelaos. In his reply, Menelaos agrees that he should fight Alexander alone because the original dispute was between the two of them. The marginal note in the Venetus A here records a multiform of this reply.

The main text of the Venetus A, as well as the texts of the Venetus B and the two Escorial manuscripts and most modern editions, reads:

> εἴνεκ' ἐμῆς ἔριδος καὶ Ἀλεξάνδρου ἔνεκ' ἀρχῆς
> because of my conflict and because of the way it started with
> Alexander

The scholion, however, preserves Zenodotus' alternative reading of ἄτης in place of ἀρχῆς, which then means "because of Alexander's error" (though the word *atē* is obviously hard to translate and encompasses much more than a simple mistake). The note itself reads:

> ὅτι Ζηνόδοτος γράφει ἔνεκ' ἄτης. ἔσται δὲ ἀπολογούμενος Μενέλαος ὅτι ἄτη περιέπεσεν ὁ Ἀλέξανδρος. διὰ μέντοι τοῦ ἔνεκ' ἀρχῆς. ἐνδείκνυται ὅτι προκατῆρξεν:~

> [It is marked] because Zenodotus writes "because of [his] error." This would be Menelaos saying in his defense that Alexander [was the one who] had fallen into error. With "because of his beginning," however, it reveals that he began the hostilities.

---

[2] On this topic see also Dué and Ebbott 2009, 2010:153–166, and 2017.

Even in this one brief note in the margins of the Venetus A, we catch a glimpse of the multiformity of the *Iliad*. The differing readings give us evidence that multiple versions of the *Iliad* were available to the Alexandrian scholars. Why should we not consider Zenodotus' reading a true multiform or, we might also say, a performance variation, a potential end to a line in a performance when the *Iliad* was an oral poem? One piece of evidence in support of doing so is that the phrase Ἀλεξάνδρου ἕνεκ' ἄτης appears in this same position, after the weak caesura and completing the line, in at least two other lines:

> *Iliad* 6.356, in which Helen says to Hektor that Hektor has had to take the brunt of the suffering caused by herself and Alexander's error, and

> *Iliad* 24.28, where the narrator most famously alludes to the Judgment of Paris.

Here is verse 24.28 in context:

> τὸν δ' ἐλεαίρεσκον μάκαρες θεοὶ εἰσορόωντες,
> κλέψαι δ' ὀτρύνεσκον ἐΰσκοπον ἀργεϊφόντην.
> ἔνθ' ἄλλοις μὲν πᾶσιν ἑήνδανεν, οὐδέ ποθ' Ἥρῃ
> οὐδὲ Ποσειδάων' οὐδὲ γλαυκώπιδι κούρῃ,
> ἀλλ' ἔχον ὥς σφιν πρῶτον ἀπήχθετο Ἴλιος ἱρὴ
> καὶ Πρίαμος καὶ λαὸς Ἀλεξάνδρου ἕνεκ' ἄτης,
> ὃς νείκεσσε θεὰς ὅτε οἱ μέσσαυλον ἵκοντο,
> τὴν δ' ᾔνησ' ἥ οἱ πόρε μαχλοσύνην ἀλεγεινήν.

Iliad 24.23–30

> The blessed gods kept feeling pity as they looked upon him,
> and they kept urging the watchful Argeiphontes to steal [the body].
> Then it was pleasing to all the others, but not ever to Hera
> nor to Poseidon nor to the grey-eyed maiden—
> rather they persisted in hating holy Ilion as before
> and Priam and the people because of the *atē* of Alexander,
> who insulted the goddesses when they arrived at his inner
> courtyard,
> and found best the one who offered him grief-causing lust.

At the *Iliad* 24 line, an intermarginal scholion in the Venetus A records ἕνεκ' ἀρχῆς as an alternate reading. The line at *Iliad* 6.356 likewise reads ἀρχῆς in several papyri and some manuscripts as either the main reading or an alternate one. So in each of these three lines, we have evidence for both multiforms, and that evidence tells us something about how oral composition in performance works, when a singer either by training or under the circumstances of performance might choose one or the other phrase in any of these places. Either Alexander started the whole Trojan War (with his choice of Aphrodite in the Judgment, and by implication Helen) or, in taking a woman, he fell victim, like Agamemnon (*Iliad* 19.91), to *atē*.

This evidence should lead us to pause before making any pronouncements about how often the Judgment of Paris is alluded to in the *Iliad*. Commentators often say that there is only one reference to it in the whole epic—in book 24[3]— but if Menelaos could use the same phrase in book 3 that we see expanded on in 24 to indicate the Judgment and encapsulate that traditional theme via the word *atē*, our understanding and our interpretation of that frequency would have to change.[4] It cannot be denied then that the multiforms in the scholia have much to teach us about the composition of the poetry. In turn, they provide substantial food for thought about how we then interpret the poetry that has been transmitted. The benefit to be gained from this particular scholion, and the many others like it, is not that it dramatically alters the sense of that one particular line, but that it makes a significant difference in our understanding of the system of Homeric epic as a whole.

***

I want to move from this example to make a larger point about editorial practice when it comes to an oral poem like the *Iliad*. How do we deal with the multiformity of the *Iliad* when we approach the text as an editor? The choices we make affect how students and scholars of the *Iliad* will understand the poem.

Martin West's 1998–2000 Teubner edition of the *Iliad* is the most recent printed scholarly edition that I know of. West prints ἀρχῆς at 3.100. Here is what he does with the *Iliad* 24 reference to the Judgment of Paris that we just looked at:

> τὸν δ' ἐλεαίρεσκον μάκαρες θεοὶ εἰσορόωντες,
> κλέψαι δ' ὀτρύνεσκον ἐΰσκοπον ἀργεϊφόντην.
> ἔνθ' ἄλλοις μὲν πᾶσιν ἑήνδανεν, οὐδέ ποθ' Ἥρῃ
> οὐδὲ Ποσειδάων' οὐδὲ γλαυκώπιδι κούρῃ,
> ἀλλ' ἔχον ὥς σφιν πρῶτον ἀπήχθετο Ἴλιος ἱρὴ
> καὶ Πρίαμος καὶ λαὸς Ἀλεξάνδρου ἕνεκ' ἄτης,

---

[3] For a most recent example, Mackie begins his discussion of *Iliad* 24 and the Judgment of Paris by stating, "Despite the importance of the Judgement of Paris in the story of the Trojan War, the *Iliad* has only one explicit reference to it" (Mackie 2013:1). See also below on West 2011.

[4] The phrase Ἀλεξάνδρου ἕνεκ' ἄτης in *Iliad* 6.356 is followed by Helen's prediction that they will be a subject of song for future generations, suggesting that "Alexander's error" here too has a thematic connection to the Judgment and the epic tradition as a whole.

[ὃς νείκεσσε θεὰς ὅτε οἱ μέσσαυλον ἵκοντο,
τὴν δ᾽ ᾔνησ᾽ ἥ οἱ πόρε μαχλοσύνην ἀλεγεινήν.]

Iliad 24.23–30

The blessed gods kept feeling pity as they looked upon him,
and they kept urging the watchful Argeiphontes to steal [the body].
Then it was pleasing to all the others, but not ever to Hera
nor to Poseidon nor to the grey-eyed maiden—
rather they persisted in hating holy Ilion as before
and Priam and the people because of the *atē* of Alexander,
[who insulted the goddesses when they arrived at his inner
      courtyard,
and found best the one who offered him grief-causing lust.]

West prints ἄτης here, because that is the reading of most manuscripts, although, as we have seen, ἀρχῆς is also attested. The limitations of a print edition in dealing with the multiformity of an oral tradition are evident here. West brackets the next two lines, however, as being apparent interpolations ("*interpolata videntur*"). He does not altogether remove them, but he makes clear that he does not consider them Homeric. Why? His *apparatus criticus* simply states *ath. quidam*, "Some have athetized."[5] In other words, all manuscripts have them, but the verses were not universally approved of in antiquity.

We find this note about the athetesis in the Venetus A scholia:

παρ᾽ Ἀριστοφάνει καί τισι τῶν πολιτικῶν "ἥ οἱ κεχαρισμένα δῶρ᾽
ὀνόμηνε"... ἀθετεῖ γὰρ Ἀρίσταρχος διὰ τὴν <μαχλοσύνην> τὸν στίχον. **A**

In Aristophanes and in some of the city editions [the reading is] "who promised him pleasing gifts" ... For Aristarchus athetizes the verse because of the word μαχλοσύνην.

This note actually informs our understanding of two different possible reasons for athetesis. On the one hand, some ancient editions contained a different text than what we find in the Venetus A.[6] On the other, Aristarchus evidently did not think Homer would have referred to Alexander's lust. But not only do all manuscripts and papyri have these verses, but a variation on these verses, i.e.

---

5   For a fuller explanation see West's *Studies in the Text and Transmission of the Iliad* (2001), 197–198 and below. In West 2011:33 he calls the passage "very probably interpolated" (see also West 2011:140 and 412).

6   For the phrase κεχαρισμένα δῶρ᾽ in the edition attributed to Aristophanes and the city editions cf. *Iliad* 20.298–299, *Odyssey* 16.184–185.

a multiform, is also attested in the scholia! Bracketing them may make the text less messy, but it also actively removes from consideration (at the very least psychologically by way of the bracketing) valuable evidence for the poetic system and the mythological background of the *Iliad*.

In his 2011 commentary on the *Iliad*, West writes: "It seems unlikely that P would introduce his only reference to the Judgment of Paris at this late stage or that he would have contemptuously dismissed the δῶρ' ἐρατὰ χρυσῆς Ἀφροδίτης (Γ 64) as μαχλοσύνη." (West 2011:412). Such a statement reflects West's conception of a literate "Homer" (whom he designates simply as P) who composes much as a modern poet would. I and my collaborators on the Homer Multitext find such a conception untenable in light of the fieldwork of Parry and Lord, decades of subsequent scholarship, and modern anthropological study of oral traditions. Making a textual choice on the basis of "what Homer would have done" is no less flawed now than it was in Aristarchus' time. In any case, as we have seen, 24.29–30 may very well not be the only reference in the *Iliad* to the Judgment of Paris, if we take all multiforms into account and keep in mind the hypertext-like, referential possibilities of formulaic diction.[7]

***

Another passage that West brackets, despite universal manuscript support, is 19.326–337, a reference to Neoptolemos in Achilles' lament for Patroklos. Here are the verses in context:

> οὐ μὲν γάρ τι κακώτερον ἄλλο πάθοιμι,
> οὐδ' εἴ κεν τοῦ πατρὸς ἀποφθιμένοιο πυθοίμην,
> ὅς που νῦν Φθίηφι τέρεν κατὰ δάκρυον εἴβει
> χήτεϊ τοιοῦδ' υἷος: ὃ δ' ἀλλοδαπῷ ἐνὶ δήμῳ
> εἵνεκα ῥιγεδανῆς Ἑλένης Τρωσὶν πολεμίζω:
> [ἠὲ τὸν ὃς Σκύρῳ μοι ἔνι τρέφεται φίλος υἱός,
> εἴ που ἔτι ζώει γε <u>Νεοπτόλεμος θεοειδής.</u>
> πρὶν μὲν γάρ μοι θυμὸς ἐνὶ στήθεσσιν ἐώλπει
> οἶον ἐμὲ φθίσεσθαι ἀπ' Ἄργεος ἱπποβότοιο
> αὐτοῦ ἐνὶ Τροίῃ, σὲ δέ τε Φθίην δὲ νέεσθαι,
> ὡς ἄν μοι τὸν παῖδα θοῇ ἐνὶ νηΐ μελαίνῃ
> Σκυρόθεν ἐξαγάγοις καί οἱ δείξειας ἕκαστα
> κτῆσιν ἐμὴν δμῶάς τε καὶ ὑψερεφὲς μέγα δῶμα.
> ἤδη γὰρ Πηλῆά γ' ὀΐομαι ἢ κατὰ πάμπαν
> τεθνάμεν, ἤ που τυτθὸν ἔτι ζώοντ' ἀκάχησθαι

---

[7] On traditional referentiality and Homeric "hypertextuality" see Tsagalis 2010a and above, p. 111.

γήραΐ τε στυγερῷ καὶ ἐμὴν ποτιδέγμενον αἰεὶ
λυγρὴν ἀγγελίην, ὅτ᾽ ἀποφθιμένοιο πύθηται.]

Iliad 19.321–337

For I could not suffer another thing worse,
not even if I were to learn that my father had died,
who surely now in Pythia sheds a tender tear
for want of such a son. Meanwhile I am in a foreign land
fighting with the Trojans for the sake of Helen at whose name one
    shudders.
[Or if I learned that he who is being raised as my own son in Skyros
    (had died),
—if somewhere <u>Neoptolemos who is in appearance like a god</u> still
    lives at least.
For before now the heart in my chest hoped
that I alone would perish far from horse-pasturing Argos
here in Troy, and that you would return to Phthia,
in order that my child in the swift black ship you might lead
from Skyros and show him everything,
my property and slaves and great high-roofed house.
For by now I suppose that Peleus at least is altogether
dead, or perhaps still alive he is grieved
by hateful old age and always waiting for
sorrowful tidings of me, when he shall learn that I have died.]

West seems to generally object to the passage because it includes material he deems Cyclic, that is, that it belongs to the Epic Cycle: "This and the other passage that alludes to Neoptolemos, Ω 466 f., must be regarded as rhapsodic interpolations designed to take account of a figure who featured in the *Little Iliad*, *Iliou Persis*, and *Nostoi*, and was known to POd (λ 492 ff.). In Il. we have a consistent picture of Ach. as a doomed young man whose divine mother and distant, aged father are his only family" (West 2011 *ad loc.*). But the fact is, as West admits, there are several references to Neoptolemos in the *Iliad* and the *Odyssey*.[8] At 24.465–467 Hermes tells Priam to beseech Achilles by his father, mother, and son (though he does not in fact mention Neoptolemos by name). West brackets this passage also. In *Odyssey* 11, Achilles asks Odysseus about Neoptolemos. West sees the *Iliad* passages as being incompatible with

---

[8] I was only able to consult West's 2017 edition of the *Odyssey* in the final stages of preparing this manuscript for publication. I note that he allows references to Neoptolemus in the *Odyssey*, on the assumption that that work was composed by a different poet.

the "consistent picture" that is created if they are left out, but that consistent picture only works if the ancient audience somehow remained unaware of all the other coexisting song traditions that did feature Neoptolemos. While I can agree that Neoptolemos did not play a large role within the poetics of the Iliadic epic tradition, the *Iliad* did not exist in a mythological or poetic vacuum, such that he could never be invoked.

In antiquity, both Aristarchus and Aristophanes seem to have athetized verse 19.327 (not the whole passage, as West does, but just that line) because Skyros is not so far from Troy that Achilles would not have heard news of him and because they deemed *theoeides* to be inappropriate. The following note is found on folio 258r of the Venetus A:

καὶ Ἀριστοφάνης προηθέτει τὸν στίχον, ὥς φησι Καλλίστρατος[.] τό τε γὰρ ἐπὶ παιδὸς κομιδῇ λέγεσθαι διστακτικῶς <εἴ που ἔτι ζώει> καὶ ταῦτα μηδὲ πόρρω τῆς Σκύρου κειμένης ὕποπτον τό τε <θεοειδής> ἀκαίρως προσέρριπται· τεκμήριον δὲ τῆς διασκευῆς τὸ καὶ ἑτέρως φέρεσθαι τὸν στίχον· "εἴ που ἔτι ζώει γε Πυρῆς ἐμός, ὃν κατέλειπον":~

Also Aristophanes previously athetized the verse, as Kallistratos says. For the fact that he speaks at all doubtfully about his son ("εἴ που ἔτι ζώει"), and these things with Skyros lying not far away, is suspect, and θεοειδής is thrown in inaptly. And the existence of a different version of the verse is evidence of the recension [i.e. that the text has been edited]: "If my Pyrrhos still lives at least, whom I left behind."

Let me first note that once again athetesis is employed partly in response to the existence of more than one version of the text. Once again West has bracketed a passage that has not only universal manuscript support but additional support in the fact that more than one version of it existed in antiquity. For him, as for the Alexandrian editors, the existence of multiple versions of the passage makes it suspect. A Parry-Lord approach to the history of the text expects multiformity, and so can admit both as authentically generated verses.

But there is more to say about the logic of the scholion from a Parry-Lord perspective. Why is θεοειδής used ἀκαίρως? I'm really not sure why Aristophanes and/or Aristarchus felt this to be the case. Richard Martin has written two articles that show that this word, which is also used of Telemakhos the first time we ever see him in the *Odyssey*, evokes a traditional theme in Homeric poetry, that of the beautiful young man who must grow up and prove himself. Martin argues that the word encompasses the entirety of the story arc, from the moment when the young man is still very much untested and lacking in maturity to the time when he does in fact develop a character that matches his looks. I quote Martin here:

> My point is that the use of the formula *theoeides* marks out Homer's handling of this traditional theme, which we can call "the hero grows up." When an audience keyed into the traditional formulaic system first hears Telemachus described as "having the appearance of a god," it receives a package of thematic messages, as it were, a box of potential narrative directions. This character, the son of Odysseus, could turn out to be like Paris, *Alexandros theoeides*, all *Schein* and no *Sein*, an indolent golden boy who relies on looks to get by. Or he could be like Euryalus [in the *Odyssey*]—arrogant but essentially educable. (1993:232–233)

I don't want to reargue Martin's arguments, but I would suggest that a thorough analysis grounded in the way formulaic language operates is the right approach here, and could lead us to a greater understanding of the full impact of calling Neoptolemos θεοειδής. It might lead us to a fuller appreciation of the heart-break in Achilles' words—unlike Odysseus, he will not see his son grown up and matured. Might we find here in the *Iliad*, as so often in the *Odyssey*, an implicit contrast between the fates of the two central heroes of Homeric epic? Perhaps that is a stretch, but certainly we would need to marshal all available evidence to find out.

It is precisely this desire to preserve the full range of evidence for formulaic diction that causes me to find West's bracketing of yet another relevant passage very troubling. These verses come from Helen's lament for Hektor in *Iliad* 24:

> Ἕκτορ ἐμῷ θυμῷ δαέρων πολὺ φίλτατε πάντων,
> [ἦ μέν μοι πόσις ἐστὶν Ἀλέξανδρος θεοειδής,
> ὅς μ' ἄγαγε Τροίηνδ': ὡς πρὶν ὤφελλον ὀλέσθαι.]

Iliad 24.763–764[9]

> Hektor, dearest by far to my *thumos* of all my brothers-in-law,
> indeed my husband is Alexander with the looks of a god,
> who led me to Troy. How I ought to have died before then.

In his *apparatus* West writes simply *seclusi*—"I have excluded." In West's *Studies in the Text and Transmission of the Iliad*, he makes arguments against the verses based on logic and rhetorical flow and because it is obvious that Alexander is

---

[9] Note that the reading ὤφελλ' ἀπολέσθαι was also known in antiquity, and the manuscript Escorial Ω.1.12 has ὤφελ' ἀπολέσθαι.

her husband: "No one needs to be reminded why Hector is Helen's δαήρ" (West 2001:282).

Here again I find a lack of sensitivity to formulaic language on the part of West, and especially a lack of sensitivity to the traditional language of lament. In women's laments for the dead in the Greek tradition, as I have explored elsewhere in my work (Dué 2002 and 2006a, building on Alexiou 1974), it is common for women to narrate their own life history and to contrast it with their present circumstances. Longing for death is also a traditional feature of laments. A close examination of these verses within the poetics of lament could easily show that they are perfectly formulaic and traditional.[10] Why would we want to exclude them from our understanding of the *Iliad*?

Achilles' lament for Patroklos, including the verses about Neoptolemos, is typical as well. Many laments contain a narrative of both the past and the future—Briseis' lament for Patroklos earlier in book 19 does this, as Pucci (1993) has shown. Peleus and Neoptolemos are Achilles' past and future. Understanding Achilles' words within the context of women's songs of lament for the dead opens up a host of poetic possibilities. By likening Achilles' grief to that of Briseis and the soon-to-be captive women of Troy, the *Iliad* depicts Achilles not only as having the greatest κλέος of all, but also profound ἄχος (and the two, in fact, go hand in hand). Achilles himself makes the connection in *Iliad* 18.121–125: "But now may I win good *kleos*, and may I cause some one of the deep-girdled Trojan and Dardanian women to wipe the tears from their delicate cheeks with both hands and lament unceasingly. And they may know that too long I have held back from battle." Andromache's song of sorrow is thus Achilles' song of glory. But Achilles' song is also a lament for Patroklos—and for himself:

> πάντες δ' ὑλοτόμοι φιτροὺς φέρον...
> κὰδ δ' ἄρ' ἐπ' ἀκτῆς βάλλον ἐπισχερώ, ἔνθ' ἄρ' Ἀχιλλεὺς
> φράσσατο Πατρόκλῳ μέγα ἠρίον ἠδὲ οἷ αὐτῷ.

> *Iliad* 23.123–126

All who had been cutting wood bore logs...
they threw them down in a line upon the seashore at the place where Achilles
would make a mighty funeral mound for Patroklos and for himself.

---

10 Cf. 3.173–175 (Helen to Priam), 3.428–429 (Helen to Alexander), 6.344–348 (Helen to Hektor), and 19.59–60 (Achilles of Briseis) as well as Hecuba at 22.431–2 and Andromache at 22.481. For just such an analysis of Helen's speech throughout the *Iliad* within the poetics of lament see Ebbott 1999.

In chapter 1 I suggested that the *Iliad* that survives for us exhibits a tension between two competing traditional themes: Achilles' μῆνις and his ἄχος. Where West sees interpolated "Cyclic" material that is extraneous to the *Iliad*, I find evidence for the wider poetic traditions from which our *Iliad* emerged and with which it interacted.

Our two approaches are not entirely incompatible: in some respects these are merely two different ways of labeling and conceptualizing the same phenomenon. The distinction lies in what we do with the text that survives. While West, like Aristarchus, separates out the portions of the poem he believes are attributable to a master poet and distinguishes (via bracketing and in some cases omission) others as not Homeric, the editors of the Homer Multitext have made the decision to treat each historical instantiation of the *Iliad* as just that: a whole unto itself, worthy of study for its own sake as well as for what it teaches us about the larger Homeric tradition.

This fundamental editorial decision—that is, to represent each historical instantiation of the *Iliad* as a whole worthy of study (in comparison with other historical instantiations)—has been the subject of criticism in Massimo Magnani's recent (2018) analysis of the strengths and weaknesses of the Homer Multitext. Magnani is careful to point out that the unusual choices we have made as editors are grounded in the *Iliad*'s special status as a poem composed in performance, and he notes that we rely on Albert Lord's formulation that for poetry composed in performance, there is no "original" that can be reconstructed. But he laments the absence of a single text to read (the establishment of which he calls "the final objective of every philological operation") as well as the absence of a traditional *apparatus criticus*. Given that we have chosen to study the multiformity that survives in the Homeric tradition as natural and expected reflexes of oral composition in performance, Magnani feels that we have failed to adequately make distinctions between what he calls "aedic" and "rhapsodic variations." Magnani concludes, "There will certainly be a moment when the critical editor will be supported or even replaced by the AI, but the task of choosing the best possible text in a methodologically correct manner cannot but remain the essential purpose of the philological activity for most of the manuscript traditions handed down by a plurality of manuscripts" (2018:100).

I will have more to say below about the question of distinguishing between "aedic" and "rhapsodic" variations—we do indeed actively seek to blur such distinctions. But as for the absence of an *apparatus criticus*, Mary Ebbott and I have argued elsewhere about the problems inherent in a typical *apparatus* (see, e.g., Dué and Ebbott 2009, 2010:153–159, and 2017, and above, p. 13). Only the most specialized consulters of an *apparatus criticus* can decode what the *apparatus* is attempting to convey, and even they will be often at a loss. As I have explored in Chapter 4, there are types of information that an *apparatus* simply can't convey, especially when meaning is conveyed visually within a manuscript, as is so often the case in the Venetus A. (A glance at even a single folio will confirm this assertion.) But Magnani's point is well taken. How can a user of the Homer Multitext make comparisons between readings without an *apparatus criticus*? In fact, during this phase of the project we have chosen not to worry excessively about how precisely our data will be used to make such comparisons. Our energy thus far has been focused on first and foremost simply creating the archival data that we hope others will use in dynamic and unforeseen ways. Even after twenty years of work we have only fully edited and published one manuscript of the *Iliad* and select papyri; there are lifetimes of work still to do. The Homer Multitext will only begin to be realized when all of the oldest manuscripts with scholia have been completely edited and published, and all of the extent papyri, and all of the works that quote the Homeric epics.

That said, now that we do have a complete data set, tools are coming into existence that will soon make the need for an *apparatus criticus* obsolete. Many different types of searching, text analysis, and topic modeling are already in common use by humanists, and those employing such methods now have the complete Venetus A manuscript of the *Iliad* to work with. There is no need to build software or online tools specific to the Homer Multitext, though we have in fact made some tools available on our project website and will continue to do so. But because our data has been created and encoded in generic, archival, and open source formats, we can trust that as the tools of our discipline evolve, our data will be compatible with them.

On a more conceptual level, the editors of the Homer Multitext have concluded that making the evidence of the historical sources available to every individual reader, thereby allowing them the tools and access to make editorial judgments for themselves, outweighs the practical advantages of an *apparatus criticus*, as useful as it may have been for scholars of earlier eras. The fact is, print editions will continue to exist in physical libraries for those desiring to do the kind of philology that Magnani describes. The editors of the Homer Multitext have never desired to replicate or facilitate nineteenth- or twentieth-century philology. Rather, we feel that it is time, and now possible, to ask new questions.

***

My aim in this concluding chapter is not to single out for censure the late Martin West, whom I have greatly admired since my earliest days as a student of Greek poetry and from whose scholarship I have learned much of what I know about textual criticism. Rather my aim has been to show how a multitextual approach solves problems for Homeric criticism and opens up possibilities for the next generation of Homeric scholarship that conventional textual criticism cannot.

The seeds of this book were planted many years ago. Many of my initial studies of Homeric poetry arose out of a dissatisfaction with the concept of "invention" in Homeric studies (Dué 2002:83–89, 2006b). "Invention" is a term frequently used by critics who try to find the authorial genius behind the *Iliad* or the *Odyssey*.[11] If the *Iliad* and the *Odyssey* were composed in a traditional, oral medium, we ask ourselves, what then is Homer's contribution? I felt back then and still feel today that we are severely limited by modern concepts of authorship in our approach to the Homeric poems. We just are not comfortable with a Homer who doesn't consciously strive to "invent" anything, a Homer whose contribution is his skillful composition in performance using traditional techniques and formulaic language, a Homer who is not particularly different from any of the other skilled performers who came before or after him, a Homer who is one of many.

The concept of the inventing Homer is double edged. When we encounter a passage that seems poetically sophisticated, we often assign it to Homer: "Oh that part about Achilles' grief for Patroklos, that's good stuff, Homer invented him" (the implication being that an oral tradition could not produce something that good).[12] Likewise when something is really bad: "Well the whole thing about Niobe having to eat but being a stone, frankly, it is awkward. It must be awkward because Homer somehow 'broke free' of the oral tradition, invented the story, and couldn't quite fit it in right." The paradox with a traditional system such as the South Slavic one that Parry and Lord studied—and, I believe, the system in which the *Iliad* and the *Odyssey* were composed—is that innovation occurs, without a doubt, but the singers composing within that system do not strive to innovate. They claim to reproduce the same song word for word every time, yet they never do.[13] It is only outsiders to the tradition who can come and observe innovation happening. For those on the inside, the tradition remains constant. This is something that our culture does not easily relate to. Imagine Shakespeare not wanting to be innovative, or Monet, or Frank Lloyd Wright. The people we admire, the people we call geniuses, are innovators. And so it is not

---

[11] For Homeric scholarship that makes use of the term "invention" see, e.g., Fenik 1978, West 1999, and Graziosi 2002 (Graziosi's study turns this approach on its head and instead explores how the ancient Greeks invented the figure of Homer in a multitude of ways, in various places, and at various points in time—hence her title *Inventing Homer*).

[12] On Patroklos as an allegedly invented character see Dué 2002:83.

[13] See also chapter 1, p. 21. Cf. Parry's interviews with South Slavic singers quoted in Lord 1960:26–28, as well as Lord 1960:44–45: "We must hasten to assert that in speaking of 'creating' phrases in performance we do not intend to convey the idea that the singer *seeks originality* or fineness of expression.... To say that the *opportunity* for originality and for finding the 'poetically' fine phrase exists does not mean that the *desire* for originality also exists" (emphasis in the original).

surprising that ever since the eighteenth century scholars have been inventing (and continually reinventing) a Homer who is just such an original genius.[14]

What we need to fully grasp the poetics and textual transmission of an oral traditional poem is a paradigm shift in Homeric scholarship. The concept of the paradigm shift was first articulated by Thomas Kuhn in his 1962 book, entitled *The Structure of Scientific Revolutions.* As my colleague John Lienhard at the University of Houston noted in an episode of his radio program, *The Engines of Our Ingenuity*, Kuhn demonstrated that "science develops, not by accretion, but by replacement—by paradigm replacement."[15] In other words, we cannot make a scientific breakthrough unless we can somehow step out of our own paradigm and conceive of an entirely new one. Lienhard goes on to assert in the episode that many have attempted to point out flaws in Kuhn's bold assertions, but no one has been able to undermine their fundamental validity. In fact, "as Kuhn's detractors have gone at him, and stripped him of his original hyperbole, they've left him much stronger." He speculates: "Perhaps the villain in all this is our need to pin everything on one creator genius—Einstein, Edison, Bell. That erases all the labor needed to complete any really good idea." Lienhard compares the attacks on Kuhn's work to the criticism levied against Charles Darwin and the theory of evolution: "I'm astonished by people who try to refute natural selection by going back to Darwin himself. Never mind that we've spent a century and a half weaving the connecting tissue of evolution by natural selection. You'd think Darwin had written the last word on the subject, not the first."

As I listened to that episode the first time I heard it, I could not help but think of the paradigm shift in Homeric studies initiated by the fieldwork of Milman Parry and Albert Lord in the former Yugoslavia. Parry's 1928 doctoral dissertation on the traditional epithet in Homer is a brilliant demonstration of the economy and traditionality of Homeric diction, but, as I noted in chapter 1, even Parry himself did not grasp the implications of this work initially:

> My first studies were on the style of the Homeric poems and led me to understand that so highly formulaic a style could be only traditional. I failed, however, at the time to understand as fully as I should have that a style such as that of Homer must not only be traditional but also must be oral. It was largely due to the remarks of my teacher (M.) Antoine

---

[14] For a historical overview of the intellectual context in which notions of originality and genius came to dominate Homeric criticism see Simonsuuri 1979 as well as Dué 2006b and McLane and Slatkin 2011. Graziosi has explored ancient inventions of Homer, but, as she herself suggests, her work should impel us to look at the way that we continue to invent Homer in modern scholarship (2002:6).

[15] The episode (no. 1835) is entitled "Revisiting Stirrups" and can be accessed here: http://www.uh.edu/engines/epi1835.htm.

Meillet that I came to see, dimly at first, that a true understanding of the Homeric poems could only come with a full understanding of the nature of oral poetry. It happened that a week or so before I defended my theses for the doctorate at the Sorbonne, Professor Mathias Murko of the University of Prague delivered in Paris the series of conferences which later appeared as his book *La poésie populaire épique en Yougoslavie au début du XXe siècle.* I had seen the poster for these lectures but at the time I saw in them no great meaning for myself. However, Professor Murko, doubtless due to some remark of (M.) Meillet, was present at my *soutenance* and at that time M. Meillet as a member of my jury pointed out with his usual ease and clarity this failing in my two books. It was the writings of Professor Murko more than those of any other which in the following years led me to the study of oral poetry in itself and to the heroic poems of the South Slavs. (A. Parry 1971:439)

It was only when Parry went to Yugoslavia to observe the still-flourishing South Slavic oral epic song tradition that he came to understand that Homeric poetry was not only traditional but oral—that is, composed anew every time in performance, by means of a sophisticated system of traditional phraseology and diction. For Parry, witnessing the workings of a living oral epic song tradition was a paradigm shift. Suddenly, by analogy with the South Slavic tradition, the workings of the Homeric system of composition became clear to him.

Parry planned a series of publications based on his observations and subsequent analysis of Homeric poetry that were never completed. His surviving writings have been incredibly influential, but he died in 1935 at the age of 33, long before he had a chance to realize the many implications of his fieldwork. Albert Lord's *The Singer of Tales* was published in 1960, just two years before Kuhn's *The Structure of Scientific Revolutions.* In retrospect it is quite clear that when Parry and Lord went searching for an analogy for the composition of the Homeric epics, they were at the same time searching for Homer—that is to say Homer the man, the author, and the poetic genius (Dué 2006b). Although the work of both men made possible the paradigm shift that I am advocating for in this concluding chapter, both Parry and Lord in varying degrees operated under the authorial model of understanding the composition of the Homeric epics that prevailed in their own day. We can see this older paradigm reflected especially in some of Albert Lord's earliest writing. Lord went to Yugoslavia for the first time at the age of 22, from June 1934 until September 1935. Parry described his activities as follows:

My assistant, Mr. Albert Lord, is shortly leaving for a month in Greece. His help has been altogether indispensable to me, and I may say that I have done twice as much work since I had his very able assistance. He has relieved me altogether of the very long labeling and cataloguing of the manuscripts and discs, has helped me with the keeping of accounts and the presentations of reports, has typed some 300 pages of my commentary on the collected texts, and most particularly he has ably run the recording apparatus while we are working in the field, this for the first time leaving me free to be with the singer before the microphone, and to oversee and take part in the putting of questions to the singers.... I myself feel the greatest gratitude to him for the help which he has given me and the expedition is under the greatest obligation to him. (From M. Parry, "Report on Work in Yugoslavia, October 20, 1934–March 24, 1935," Milman Parry Collection of Oral Literature, p. 12)

Albert Lord took photographs throughout the trip and kept a record of his experiences with a view to submitting them to a popular magazine such as *National Geographic*. The essay that he wrote, dated March 1937, was entitled "Across Montenegro: Searching for Gúsle Songs" but was never in fact published.[16] We can see already in this early essay a fascination with two singers in particular that would shape much of Lord's subsequent professional scholarship on the creative process of oral traditional poetry and the analogy between the South Slavic and the Homeric song traditions. The first was known as Ćor Huso ("Blind Huso"), a singer of a previous generation who was credited by many of the singers Parry interviewed as being the teacher of their teacher, and the source for all the best songs. Lord recounts one of these interviews (conducted by Nikola Vujnović) as he describes their initial attempts to find singers in Kolashin:

In Kolashin we got to work. During the last century this was the home of one of the greatest singers. The name of old One-eye Huso Husovitch was a magic one in those days, and still is among the Turks (Moslems) in the region further east where the old masters of Kolashin now dwell. We sought eagerly for every trace of his tradition. What was he like? How did he sing? How did he make his living? How did he die? And so on. We had heard of him first from Sálih Uglian [sic] in Novi Pazar. From Huso Salih had learned his favorite song about the taking of Bagdad and its queen by Djérdjelez Aliya, hero of the Turkish border. In Salih's own words, caught by our microphone, we have a bit of the tradition of the blind singer's way of life.

Nikola: From whom did you learn your first Bosnian songs?

---

[16] I am grateful to Stephen Mitchell, curator of the Milman Parry Collection of Oral Literature, for providing me with a copy of this essay.

Salih: I learned Bosnian songs from One-eye Huso Husovitch from Kolashin.

N: Who was he? How did he live? What sort of work did he do?

S: He had no trade, only his horse and his arms, and he wandered about the world. He had only one eye. His clothes and his arms were of the finest. And so he wandered from town to town and sang to people to the gusle.

N: And that's all he did?

S: He went from kingdom to kingdom and learned and sang.

N: From kingdom to kingdom?

S: He was at Vienna, at Franz's court.

N: Why did he go there?

S: He happened to go there, and they told him about him, and went and got him, and he sang to him to the gusle, and King Joseph gave him a hundred sheep, and a hundred Napoleons as a present.

N: How long did he sing to him to the gusle?

S: A month.

N: So there was Dutchman who liked the gusle that much?

S: You know he wanted to hear such an unusual thing. He had never heard anything like it.

N: All right. And afterwards, when he came back, what did he do with those sheep? Did he work after that, or did he go on singing to the gusle?

S: He gave all the sheep to his relatives, and put the money in his purse, and wandered about the world.

N: Was he a good singer?

S: There could not have been a better.

(Trans. Milman Parry)

Lord later wrote that for Parry Huso came to symbolize "the Yugoslav traditional singer in much the same way in which Homer was the Greek singer of tales par excellence." He continues: "Some of the best poems collected were from singers who had heard Ćor Huso and had learned from him" (Lord 1948b:40). Yet Parry and Lord do not seem to have questioned the existence of Huso, even though, as John Foley has demonstrated, he is clearly legendary or "at most...a historical character to whom layers of legend have accrued" (Foley 1998:161). So taken was Parry with the analogy between Homer and Huso that before his death he planned a series of articles entitled "Homer and Huso," which Lord completed based on Parry's abstracts and notes.[17]

The second singer highlighted in the essay is the one whose picture would grace the cover of *The Singer of Tales*, that is to say, Avdo Međedović. *The Singer of Tales*, which publishes the results of Parry and Lord's investigation of the South Slavic song tradition and applies them to the Homeric *Iliad* and *Odyssey*, was Lord's fulfillment of Parry's own plan to write a book of that title.[18] The singer referred to in the title is of course generic, because much of what was groundbreaking about Parry and Lord's work was their demonstration of the system in which traditional oral poetry is composed, wherein many generations of singers participate. But Lord's essay makes clear (as does, to a lesser extent, *The Singer of Tales*) that there is also a particular singer behind the title that Parry and later Lord used to denote their work. That singer is simultaneously Avdo and Homer himself.

Just as Ćor Huso embodied for Parry the Yugoslav traditional singer, Avdo was for Lord on a practical level a living, breathing example of a supremely talented oral poet to whom Homer could be compared. Lord's *Singer of Tales* is remarkable for its straightforward exposition of the practical workings of the traditional system in which poets like Avdo composed their songs; it is no surprise therefore that he found a great deal of power in the concrete example that Avdo provided. Avdo dictated songs, was recorded on disk, and was even captured on a very early form of video called "kinescope." Their initial encounter was in the 1930s, and Lord found him and recorded him again in the 1950s. He was in many ways the test case for Lord's theories about the South Slavic (and by extension the Homeric) poetic system.

The photograph of Avdo featured on the cover of *The Singer of Tales* was one that Lord had taken on his first trip to Yugoslavia and was to accompany his unpublished essay. The caption reads: "Avdo Medjedovitch, peasant farmer, is the finest singer the expedition encountered. His poems reached as many as fifteen thousand lines. A veritable Yugoslav Homer!" Here is Lord's fuller description of Avdo in the essay:

> Lying on the bench not far from us was a Turk smoking a cigarette in an antique silver "cigárluk" (cigarette holder). He was a tall, lean and impressive person. At a break in our conversation he joined in. He knew of singers. The best, he said, was a certain Avdo Medjédovitch, a peasant farmer who lived an hour way. How old is he? Sixty, sixty-five.

---

[17] Lord 1936, 1938, 1948a; see also Lord 1948b and 1970.
[18] Parry was able to complete only twelve pages of this book before his death. They are published in Lord 1948b.

Does he know how to read or write? Nézna, bráte! (No, brother!) And so we went for him.... Finally Avdo came, and he sang for us old Salih's favorite of the taking of Bagdad in the days of Sultan Selim. We listened with increasing interest to this short homely farmer, whose throat was disfigured by a large goiter. He sat cross-legged on the bench, sawing the gusle, swaying in rhythm with the music. He sang very fast, sometimes deserting the melody, and while the bow went lightly back and forth over the string, he recited the verses at top speed. A crowd gathered. A card game, played by some of the modern young men of the town, noisily kept on, but was finally broken up. The next few days were a revelation. Avdo's songs were longer and finer than any we had heard before. He could prolong one for days, and some of them reached fifteen or sixteen thousand lines. Other singers came, but none could equal Avdo, our Yugoslav Homer.

In these excerpts I think we can see how important Avdo was for Lord's earliest conception of Homer as an oral poet. Whereas Parry's never-completed articles comparing the South Slavic and Homeric traditions focused on the hazy figure of Ćor Huso, Lord, when invited to give a lecture on *La poesia epica e la sua formazione*, entitled his talk "Tradition and the Oral Poet: Homer, Huso, and Avdo Medjedović"(see Lord 1970). As early as his 1948 article, "Homer, Parry, and Huso," Lord links Avdo directly with Parry's Huso: "During the summer of 1935, while collecting at Bijelo Polje, Parry came across a singer named Avdo Međedović, one of those who had heard Ćor Huso in his youth, whose powers of invention and story-telling were far above the ordinary."

Lord's comments about Avdo, especially in these earliest descriptions of him, focus on his excellence as a composer (despite the weakness of his voice), his superiority to other poets, and the length of his songs. It is not insignificant that in his unpublished essay Lord misestimates the length of Avdo's song at fifteen–sixteen thousand verses, the approximate length of the *Iliad*, whereas in fact the longest song that Avdo recorded was 13,331 verses long. By 1948 Lord was careful to report the accurate total of Avdo's verses, but he made certain to point out how extraordinary the length of Avdo's songs were in comparison with his fellow singers, whose songs averaged only a few hundred lines. Clearly it was Lord's first impression that Avdo provided the answer to the still hotly debated Homeric Question.

It would be easy to criticize Lord's youthful essay, and few people would find it necessary to do so. And even if we jump forward, decades later, it seems obvious that Lord initially conceived of the paradigm of a dictating oral poet Homer because he was imagining him in Avdo's image. The technology used to record Avdo was cutting edge at that time, and Lord would never have been so anachronistic as to suggest that Homer was recorded on audio disk, but to assume the technologies required for writing (pen, ink, loose or bound sheets of readily available "paper," skilled scribes, etc.) for "Homer's time" is an equally anachronistic projection. As much as Lord's work is responsible for setting in motion the paradigm shift in Homeric studies that has allowed many scholars to abandon the "Homer as original genius" genre of criticism, he himself had his blind spots on this crucial point. Lord could have his Homer and his oral tradition too. But it is also true that Lord never speculated about the historical circumstances under which the *Iliad* and the *Odyssey* might have been dictated. For Lord, the question of the text fixation of the Homeric poems was not essential; rather he was concerned with the dynamic process, that is to say their ongoing recomposition in performance.

Parry, unlike Lord, did not have the opportunity to rethink his earlier work, or to conduct further fieldwork, or to spend decades studying the the South Slavic tradition and the Homeric poems as Lord did. His early writings on the economy of Homeric diction are a brilliant first step towards an entirely new way of conceiving of the composition of the Homeric poems, but they are only the beginning. Like Kuhn or Darwin, Parry's work has been assailed by many as mistaken in this or that particular, or not sufficiently thorough to have worked out all aspects of the system it seeks to describe.

As Mary Ebbott and I discuss in our 2010 book, *Iliad 10 and the Poetics of Ambush*, much scholarship has been devoted to refining Parry's initial findings about the economy of Homeric diction and the nature of the Homeric formula. There is strong resistance among those who feel that Parry's work somehow minimizes the artistry of the poems or that the principles he outlined restrict the creativity of poets composing in this medium. Thus even those who accept Parry's findings often seek to amend significant aspects of his arguments. We feel that the scope of Parry's and Lord's insights has been ignored, misread or misrepresented, or dismissed too quickly. Some (though certainly not all) efforts to revise Parry and Lord are built on a misunderstanding of the principles they documented in their fieldwork and a lack of awareness of, or at least appreciation for, the kind of meaning made possible by an oral poetic tradition.

That is not to say that our approach and the interpretations offered in our book on *Iliad* 10 have not also greatly benefited from the work of scholars who have sought to better understand such essential concepts as the Homeric formula and the complex relationship between orality and literacy in ancient Greece. There is, however, a significant difference between scholarship that expands the central insights of Parry and Lord's work, even while modifying certain notions or definitions, and scholarship that sets out to "prove" Parry (more often than Lord) "wrong" in order to conclude, usually with no further justification, that Homer wrote, or somehow "broke free" of the oral tradition of these epics. These criticisms, like those cited by Lienhard against Kuhn and Darwin, seem to me to react to Parry as if he had "written the last word on the subject, not the first." As Lienhard concludes at the end of the episode:

> Kuhn, White, and Darwin are fine reminders that nothing is finished in its first incarnation. Did the Wright brothers get it wrong because they put the tail in front? Was Edison wrong to record sound on a wax cylinder instead of a CD? I suppose if we need only to be absolutely right we'll shy away from any of our important progenitors. But, if we want to see creative change in full flower, we have to go to the delicious flawed beginnings.

Building on Parry's beginnings and Lord's subsequent decades of scholarship, as well as the findings of those who have been inspired by Lord's work—such as John Foley, Richard Martin, Leonard Muellner, and Gregory Nagy (all of whom approach Homeric poetry as a system rather than a man)—Mary Ebbott and I propose that it is now possible to enact the paradigm shift in Homeric studies that Parry and Lord set in motion. The paradigm shift we envision is borne out in our many years of work as coeditors of the Homer Multitext, and indeed it has only been made fully possible by that work. In our 2010 book, rather than looking to the intention or skill of a particular composer in order to explain the poetry, we attempted to ground our readings in the meanings made possible by an oral tradition. In de-emphasizing authorship we did not deny the possibility that some form of authorship, in terms of the poet as a creative artist composing in performance, could exist in this oral tradition. But we asserted that when the search for Homer's genius is abandoned, many more illuminating possibilities present themselves.

The implications of such a shift are as true for the whole of Homeric poetry as they are for *Iliad* 10:

> What is at stake in taking this approach is a better understanding of the language, structure, evolution, and cultural meaning of the epics. Our arguments confront deeply entrenched ideas about the Doloneia. The condemnation of *Iliad* 10 is so extensive that even a relatively recent book devoted to the theme of ambush, written from an avowedly oralist perspective, does not discuss *Iliad* 10, our most extensive example of ambush in surviving Greek epic. Ignoring or only barely acknowledging *Iliad* 10 is a strategy employed by many scholars, who likely feel they must ignore it so as not to incur the charge of making arguments about Homer based on an "interpolated," "un-Homeric,"

or otherwise problematic text. Nevertheless, we feel that there is an entirely different way of treating this book. Rather than dismiss it as "un-Homeric" or pass over it in silence, we propose to show that *Iliad* 10 offers us unique insight into such important topics as the process of composition-in-performance, the traditional themes of Archaic Greek epic, the nature of the hero, and the creativity and artistry of the oral traditional language.

It strikes me as I revisit these words that I would now happily substitute "attested multiforms" wherever it currently says "Doloneia" or "*Iliad* 10" in that paragraph.

There is a maxim, often attributed to Aristarchus but in fact transmitted in Porphyry's *Homeric Questions*, that we should seek to understand Homer from Homer: Ὅμηρον ἐξ Ὁμήρου σαφηνίζειν. If we want to elucidate Homer using Homer, doesn't it help to have more Homer? It has been a central aim of this book to show that there is good reason to include more material within our definition of "Homer" than is usually provided in a typical printed edition or translation. If we fully embrace the fieldwork that Parry and Lord and those who have followed in their footsteps have conducted, and evaluate each instance of multiformity that is attested in our ancient sources for what it teaches us about composition in performance and the poetics of an oral tradition, we will no longer draw sharp distinctions between "Homer," or "the poet," or "P," and the "rhapsodes," who have so often been seen as mere reproducers of another's creative work.[19] Rather we will see all singers in this tradition, from the Bronze Age down through the Hellenistic period, as operating within a system that evolved and changed over time and eventually, under the influence of a variety of pressures (regulated performance, Panhellenism, increasing literacy, among others), crystallized.

I submit that we should also cease to draw sharp boundaries between material deemed to be pristine, Homeric, or "by Homer" and that of other Archaic epic traditions. I do not mean to suggest that each song tradition did not have, to a certain extent, its own poetics, traditional themes, characters, accompanying formulaic language, and structure, but I believe that in the early phases of these traditions at least, the boundaries were far more fluid than we typically admit. By approaching the *Iliad* this way, we lose "Homer," the individual genius, and we lose a fixed and monolithic entity that we can analyze as a self-contained unit. But we gain infinitely more Iliads to inform our appreciation of the one we know, and a greatly expanded poetic universe. We may lose "intertextuality,"

---

[19] On this point see González 2013 and forthcoming (c), as well as the discussion in Ready and Tsagalis (forthcoming):2–4, with additional bibliography *ad loc.*

but we gain "resonance" (Lord 1960:65; Graziosi and Haubold 2005), "traditional referentiality" (Foley 1999), "interformularity" (Bakker 2013:157–169), and "interaction" among speech and musical genres both past and present (Martin, forthcoming). These methodologies, all of which are grounded in an understanding of oral poetics and Homeric poetry as a system, open our eyes to the world of epic song in which each new performance was composed and received by its audience.

***

The creation of a Homer Multitext was first contemplated in the late 1990s in the midst of a different kind of paradigm shift within academia and the broader culture. The idea of a digital edition of the Homeric epics was without a doubt a response to the widespread adoption of the Internet as a means for scholarly communication, and previous editors of the Homeric epics simply could not have conceived of such an edition.

My collaborators and I were able to envision a multitext edition of the *Iliad* that was not constrained by the boundaries of the printed page, the cost of paper, the logistics of binding, the expense of color ink, or the need for specialized typesetting. Not only was it suddenly possible to imagine a freely accessible digital edition, but in those early days it was already possible for pioneers in this kind of work to imagine—as Ross Scaife, Christopher Blackwell, and Neel Smith did—a digital edition encoded for posterity, one that did not rely on proprietary software or soon-to-be obsolete tools or applications. A true scholarly edition, as they envisioned it, would not only provide free access to data, but would also openly license that data for scholarly use (and re-use) and verification by others. In bringing that vision to reality we have theorized and experimented and gone back to the drawing board many times. We are certainly in the midst of the "delicious flawed beginnings" of a new way of doing things. The digital tools and methods available to our students when they conduct research using our edition evolve from year to year, far beyond our early imaginings. But because our gaze has always been to the future, and is guided by an appreciation of the long past of Homeric scholarship, I am hopeful that we have built a foundation upon which many others will collaboratively construct a new paradigm.

Bibliography

Ahlberg-Cornell, G. 1992. *Myth and Epos in Early Greek Art: Representation and Interpretation.* Jonsered, Sweden.

Alexiou, M. 1974. *The Ritual Lament in Greek Tradition.* Cambridge. 2nd ed., Lanham, MD, 2002.

Allan, W. 2005. "Arms and the Man: Euphorbus, Hector, and the Death of Patroclus." *Classical Quarterly* 55:1–16.

Allen, T. W. 1899. "On the Composition of Some Greek Manuscripts: The Venetian Homer." *Journal of Philology* 26:161–181.

——. 1921. *The Homeric Catalogue of Ships.* Oxford.

——. 1924. *Homer: The Origins and Transmission.* Oxford.

——, ed. 1931. *Homer Ilias.* Oxford.

Antonaccio, C. Forthcoming. "The Material World of Homeric Epic." In Pache (forthcoming).

Apthorp, M. J. 1980. *The Manuscript Evidence for Interpolation in Homer.* Heidelberg.

Atchity, K. J. 1978. *Homer's Iliad: The Shield of Memory.* Carbondale.

Bachvarova, M. 2016. *From Hittite to Homer: The Anatolian Background of Ancient Greek Epic.* Cambridge.

Bakker, E. 2010. *A Companion to the Ancient Greek Language.* Malden.

——. 2013. *The Meaning of Meat and the Structure of the Odyssey.* Cambridge.

——. Forthcoming. "The Language of Homer." In Pache (forthcoming).

Barchiesi, A. 2001. *Speaking Volumes: Narrative and Intertext in Ovid and Other Latin Poets.* Trans. M. Fox and S. Marchesi. London.

Barnes, T. 2011. "Homeric ἀνδροτῆτα καὶ ἥβην." *Journal of Hellenic Studies* 131:1–13.

Bastianini, G., and A. Casanova, eds. 2012. *I papiri omerici. Atti del convegno internazionale di studi, Firenze 9–10 giugno 2011.* Florence.

Beck, D. 2005. *Homeric Conversation.* Hellenic Studies 14. Washington, DC.

——. Forthcoming. "Lament." In Pache (forthcoming).

Becker, A. 1995. *The Shield of Achilles and the Poetics of Ekphrasis.* Lanham, MD.

Berman, K. 1972. "Some Propertian Imitations in Ovid's *Amores.*" *Classical Philology* 67:170–177.

Bernabé, A., ed. 1987. *Poetae Epici Graeci: Testimonia et Fragmenta.* Vol. I. Leipzig.

Betancourt, P. 2007. *Introduction to Aegean Art.* Philadelphia.

Bierl, A. 2015. "New Trends in Homeric Scholarship." In Bierl and Latacz 2015: 177–203.

Bierl, A., and J. Latacz, eds. 2015. *Homer's Iliad: The Basel Commentary. Prolegomena.* Berlin.

Bing, P. 1988. *The Well-Read Muse: Present and Past in Callimachus and the Hellenistic Poets.* Göttingen.

Bird, G. 2009. "Critical Signs—Drawing Attention to 'Special' Lines of Homer's *Iliad* in the Manuscript Venetus A." In Dué 2009a:89–115.

——. 2010. *Multitextuality in the Homeric Iliad: The Witness of the Ptolemaic Papyri.* Hellenic Studies 43. Washington, DC.

Blackwell, C., and C. Dué. 2009. "Homer and History in the Venetus A." In Dué 2009a:1–18.

Boardman, J., and C. E. Vaphopoulou-Richardson, eds. 1986. *Chios.* Oxford.

Bolling, G. M. 1925. *The External Evidence for Interpolation in Homer.* Oxford.

Boreel, S., and H. Yi. 2017. "ὑπέρμορον or ὑπὲρ μόρον: A Centuries Old Question." Presented at the Center for Hellenic Studies, July 14, 2017.

Boyd, T. 1995. "A Poet on the Achaean Wall." *Oral Tradition* 10:181–206.

Brock, N. Van. 1959. "Substitution rituelle." *Revue Hittite et Asianique* 65:117–146.

Brockliss, W. Forthcoming. *Homeric Imagery and the Natural Environment.* Hellenic Studies 82. Washington, DC.

Brügger, C., M. Stoevesandt, and E. Visser, eds. 2003. *Homers Ilias. Gesamtkommentar,* Band II, 2. *Gesang,* Faszikel 2: *Kommentar.* Munich.

Bulloch, A. W., E. S. Gruen, A. A. Long, and A. Stewart, eds. 1993. *Images and Ideologies: Self-Definition in the Hellenistic World.* Berkeley.

Burgess, J. 1995. "Achilles' Heel: The Death of Achilles in Ancient Myth." *Classical Antiquity* 14:217–243.

——. 1997. "Beyond Neo-analysis: Problems with the Vengeance Theory." *American Journal of Philology* 118:1–19.

——. 2001. *The Tradition of the Trojan War in Homer and the Epic Cycle.* Baltimore.

——. 2005. "The Death of Achilles by Rhapsodes." In Rabel 2005:119–134.

——. 2009. *The Death and Afterlife of Achilles.* Baltimore.

Butler, H., and E. Barber, eds. 1933. *The Elegies of Propertius.* Oxford.

Butler, S., trans. 1898. *The Iliad of Homer.* London.

Camerotto, A. 2007. "Parole di sfida: Funzioni ed effetti nel duello eroico." *Lexis* 25: 163–175.

Camps, W., ed. 1965. *Propertius: Elegies Book IV.* Cambridge.

Carlisle, M. 1999. "Homeric Fictions: Pseudo-words in Homer." In Carlisle and Levaniouk 1999:55–91.

Carlisle, M., and O. Levaniouk, eds. 1999. *Nine Essays on Homer*. Lanham, MD.

Carter, J. B., and S. P. Morris, eds. 1995. *The Ages of Homer: A Tribute to Emily Townsend Vermeule*. Austin.

Casali, S. 2009. "Ovidian Intertextuality." In Knox 2009:341–354.

Cerulli, E., ed. 1970. *Atti del Convegno Internazionale sul Tema: La poesia epica e la sua formazione*. Rome.

Churik, N., N. Smith, and C. Blackwell. Forthcoming. "Testable Distant Reading in Scholia, Lexica and Paraphrases." In Cogitore and Pierrazo forthcoming.

Clark, M. 2002. "Fighting Words: How Heroes Argue." *Arethusa* 35:99–115.

Cogitore, I., and E. Pierrazo, eds. Forthcoming. *Digital Humanities and Antiquity / Humanités numériques et antiquité*. Grenoble.

Cohoon, J., ed. and trans. 1932. *Dio Chrysostom. Discourses 1-11*. Cambridge, MA.

Collins, D. 2004. *Master of the Game: Competition and Performance in Greek Poetry*. Hellenic Studies 7. Washington, DC.

Conte, G. 1986. *The Rhetoric of Imitation: Genre and Poetic Memory in Virgil and Other Latin Poets*. Ithaca.

Cook, E. 1995. *The Odyssey at Athens: Myths of Cultural Origin*. Ithaca.

——. Forthcoming. "Mythic Background." In Pache (forthcoming).

Danek, G. 1988. *Studien zur Dolonie*. Vienna.

——. 2002. "Traditional Referentiality and Homeric Intertextuality." In Montanari and Ascheri 2002:3–19.

Darwin, C. 1859. *On the Origin of Species*. London.

Davies, A., and W. Meid, eds. 1976. *Studies in Greek, Italic, and Indo-European Linguistics Offered to Leonard R. Palmer*. Innsbruck.

Davies, M., ed. 1988. *Epicorum Graecorum Fragmenta*. Göttingen.

——. 1989. *The Epic Cycle*. Bristol.

——. 2016. *The Aethiopis: Neo-Neoanalysis Reanalyzed*. Hellenic Studies 71. Washington, DC.

De Jong, I. 2004. *Narrators and Focalizers: The Presentation of the Story in the Iliad*. 2nd ed. London.

Dickinson, O. 2011. "Catalogue of Ships." In M. Finkelberg ed., *Greeks and Pre-Greeks: Aegean Prehistory and Greek Heroic Tradition* (Cambridge 2011) 150–155.

Dihle, A. 1970. *Homer-Probleme*. Opladen.

Di Luzio, A. 1969. "I papiri omerici d'epoca tolemaica e la costituzione del testo dell'epica arcaica." *Rivista di Cultura Classica e Medioevale* 11:3–152.

D'Ippolito, G. 1977. *Lettura di Omero: Il Canto V dell'"Odissea."* Palermo.

Dougherty, C. 2001. *The Raft of Odysseus: The Ethnographic Imagination of Homer's Odyssey*. Oxford.

Doumas, C. 1992. *The Wall Paintings of Thera*. Athens.

Dover, K. 1989. *Greek Homosexuality*. 2nd ed. Cambridge, MA.

Dué, C. 2000. "Poetry and the *Dēmos*: State Regulation of a Civic Possession." Stoa Consortium: http://www.stoa.org/projects/demos/home.

——. 2001a. "Achilles' Golden Amphora in Aeschines' *Against Timarchus* and the Afterlife of Oral Tradition." *Classical Philology* 96:33–47.

——. 2001b. "*Sunt Aliquid Manes*: Homer, Plato, and Alexandrian Allusion in Propertius 4.7." *Classical Journal* 96:401–413.

——. 2002. *Homeric Variations on a Lament by Briseis*. Lanham, MD.

——. 2006a. *The Captive Woman's Lament in Greek Tragedy*. Austin, TX.

——. 2006b. "The Invention of Ossian." *Classics@* 3: http://chs.harvard.edu/CHS/article/display/1334.

——. 2007. "Learning Lessons from the Trojan War: Briseis and the Theme of Force." *College Literature* 34:229–262.

——, ed. 2009a. *Recapturing a Homeric Legacy: Images and Insights from the Venetus A Manuscript of the Iliad*. Hellenic Studies 35. Washington, DC.

——. 2009b. "*Epea Pteroenta*: How We Came to Have Our *Iliad*." In Dué 2009a:19–30.

——. 2010. "Agamemnon's Densely-Packed Sorrow in *Iliad* 10: A Hypertextual Reading of a Homeric Simile." *Trends in Classics* 2:279–299.

——. 2011. "Paradigm Shifts." *Homer Multitext*: http://homermultitext.blogspot.com/2011/11/paradigm-shifts.html.

——. 2012. "Maneuvers in the Dark of Night: *Iliad* 10 in the Twenty-First Century." In Montanari, Rengakos, and Tsagalis 2012:165–173.

Dué, C., and M. Ebbott. 2009. "Digital Criticism: Editorial Standards for the Homer Multitext." *Digital Humanities Quarterly* 3.1: http://www.digitalhumanities.org/dhq/vol/003/1/000029/000029.html.

——. 2010. *Iliad 10 and the Poetics of Ambush: A Multitext Edition with Essays and Commentary*. Hellenic Studies 30. Washington, DC.

——. 2012. "Mothers-in-Arms: Soldiers' Emotional Bonds and Homeric Similes." *War, Literature, and the Arts* 24 (2012): http://wlajournal.com/wlaarchive/24_1-2/DueEbbott.pdf.

——. 2014. "An Introduction to the Homer Multitext Edition of the Venetus A Manuscript of the *Iliad*." The Homer Multitext: http://www.homermultitext.org/manuscripts-papyri/VenA-Introduction-2014.html.

——. 2017. "The Homer Multitext and the System of Homeric Epic." *Classics@* 14: https://chs.harvard.edu/CHS/article/display/6524.

Dunkle, R. 1997. "Swift-Footed Achilles." *Classical World* 90:227–234.

Durante, M. 1976. *Sulla preistoria della tradizione poetica greca 2: Risultanze della comparazione indoeuropea*. Rome.

Ebbott, M. 1999. "The Wrath of Helen: Self-Blame and Nemesis in the *Iliad*." In Carlisle and Levaniouk 1999:3–20.

———. 2009. "Text and Technologies: The *Iliad* and the Venetus A." In Dué 2009a:31–55.

———. Forthcoming. "Homeric Epic in Performance." In Pache (forthcoming).

Edmunds, L. 2000. *Intertextuality and the Reading of Roman Poetry*. Baltimore.

Edwards, A. 1985. *Achilles in the Odyssey*. Königstein.

Edwards, M. W. 1966. "Some Features of Homeric Craftsmanship." *Transactions of the American Philological Association* 97:115–179.

———. 1980. "Convention and Individuality in *Iliad* 1." *Harvard Studies in Classical Philology* 84:1–28.

———, ed. 1991. *The Iliad: A Commentary*, vol. 5: *Books 17–20*. Cambridge.

———. 1997. "Homeric Style and 'Oral Poetics.'" In Morris and Powell 1997:261–283.

———. 2005. "Homer's *Iliad*." In Foley 2005a:302–314.

Elmer, D. 2018. "The 'Narrow Road' and the Ethics of Language Use in the *Iliad* and the *Odyssey*." *Ramus* 44:155–183.

Erbse, H. 1960. *Beiträge zur Überlieferung der Iliasscholien*. Munich.

———, ed. 1969–1988. *Scholia Graeca in Homeri Iliadem (Scholia Vetera)*. 7 vols. Berlin.

Fantuzzi, M. 2012. *Achilles in Love: Intertextual Studies*. Oxford.

Farrell, J. 1991. *Vergil's Georgics and the Traditions of Ancient Epic: The Art of Allusion in Literary History*. New York.

Fenik, B. 1964. *Iliad X and the Rhesus: The Myth*. Collection Latomus 73. Brussels.

———. 1968. *Typical Battle Scenes in the Iliad: Studies in the Narrative Techniques of Homeric Battle Description*. Hermes Einzelschriften 21. Wiesbaden.

———. 1978. *Homer: Tradition and Invention*. Leiden.

Finkleberg, M. 2000. "The *Cypria*, the *Iliad*, and the Problem of Multiformity in Oral and Written Tradition." *Classical Philology* 95:1–11.

Finley, M. 1954. *The World of Odysseus*. New York.

Foley, J. 1991. *Immanent Art: From Structure to Meaning in Traditional Oral Epic*. Bloomington, IN.

———. 1995. *The Singer of Tales in Performance*. Bloomington, IN.

———. 1997. "Oral Tradition and Its Implications." In Powell and Morris 1997:146–173.

———. 1998. "Individual Poet and Epic Singer: The Legendary Singer." *Arethusa* 31:149–178.

———. 1999. *Homer's Traditional Art*. University Park, PA.

———. 2002. *How to Read an Oral Poem*. Urbana, IL.

———, ed. 2005a. *A Companion to Ancient Epic*. Oxford.

———. 2005b. "Analogues: Modern Oral Epics." In Foley 2005a:196–212.

Ford, A. 1999. "Reading Homer from the Rostrum: Poems and Laws in Aeschines' *Against Timarchus*." In Goldhill and Osborne 1999:231–256.

Frame, D. 1978. *The Myth of Return in Early Greek Epic*. New Haven.

———. 2009. *Hippota Nestor*. Hellenic Studies 37. Washington, DC.

Fränkel, H. 1962. *Dichtung und Philosophie des frühen Griechentums: Eine Geschichte der griechischen Epik, Lyrik und Prosa bis zur Mitte des fünften Jahrhunderts*. 2nd ed. Munich.

Frazer, J., ed. 1898. *Pausanias's Description of Greece*. London.

Ganzenmüller, C. 1911. "Aus Ovids Werkstatt." *Philologus* 70:274–437.

Geanakoplos, D. 1962. *Greek Scholars in Venice: Studies in the Dissemination of Greek Learning from Byzantium to Western Europe*. Cambridge, MA.

Gelzer, T. 1993. "Transformations." In Bulloch et al. 1993:130–151.

Giangrande, G. 1967. "'Arte Allusiva' and Alexandrian Poetry." *Classical Quarterly* 17:85–97.

———. 1970. "Hellenistic Poetry and Homer." *L'Antiquité Classique* 39:46–77.

Gold, B., ed. 2012. *A Companion to Roman Love Elegy*. Malden.

Goldhill, S., and R. Osborne, eds. 1999. *Performance Culture and Athenian Democracy*. Cambridge.

González, J. 2013. *The Epic Rhapsode and His Craft: Homeric Performance in a Diachronic Perspective*. Hellenic Studies 47. Washington, DC.

———. Forthcoming (a). "Hesiod and Homer." in Pache (forthcoming).

———. Forthcoming (b). "Homer and the Alphabet." In Pache (forthcoming).

———. Forthcoming (c). "Rhapsodes and the Homeridai." In Pache (forthcoming).

Graziosi, B. 2002. *Inventing Homer: The Early Reception of Epic*. Cambridge.

Graziosi, B., and J. Haubold. 2005. *Homer: The Resonance of Epic*. London.

Greetham, D. 1992. *An Introduction to Textual Scholarship*. New York.

———, ed. 1995. *Scholarly Editing: A Guide to Research*. New York.

Grenfell, B. and A. Hunt, eds. 1906. *The Hibeh Papyri* 1. Oxford.

Häag, R., ed. 1983. *The Greek Renaissance of the Eighth Century BC*. Stockholm.

Hainsworth, J. B. 1962. "The Homeric Formula and the Problem of its Transmission." *Bulletin of the Institute of Classical Studies* 9:57–68.

———. 1964. "Structure and Content in Epic Formulae: The Question of the Unique Expression." *Classical Quarterly* 14:155–164.

———. 1968. *The Flexibility of the Homeric Formula*. Oxford.

———. 1970. "The Criticism of an Oral Homer." *Journal of Hellenic Studies* 90:90–98.

———, ed. 1993. *The Iliad: A Commentary*, vol. 3: *Books 9–12*. Cambridge.

Hamilton, E., and H. Cairns, eds. 1961. *The Collected Dialogues of Plato*. Princeton.

Haslam, M. 1991. "Kleitias, Stesichoros, and the Jar of Dionysos." *Transactions of the American Philological Association* 121:35–45.

——. 1997. "Homeric Papyri and Transmission of the Text." In Powell and Morris 1997:55–100.

Haubold, J. 2002. "Greek Epic: A Near Eastern Genre?" *Proceedings of the Cambridge Philological Society* 48:1–19.

Hedreen, G. 1991. "The Cult of Achilles in the Euxine." *Hesperia* 60:313–330.

Henrichs, A. 1993. "Response." In Bulloch et al. 1993:171–195.

Higbie, C. 1997. "The Bones of a Hero, the Ashes of a Politician: Athens, Salamis, and the Usable Past." *Classical Antiquity* 16:279–308.

Hinds, S. 1998. *Allusion and Intertext: Dynamics of Appropriation in Roman Poetry.* Cambridge.

Horrocks, G. 1997. "Homer's Dialect." In Morris and Powell 1997:193–217.

——. 2010. *Greek: A History of the Language and Its Speakers.* 2nd ed. Malden.

Householder, F., and G. Nagy. 1972. *Greek: A Survey of Recent Work.* The Hague.

Howald, E. 1924. "Meleager und Achill." *Rheinisches Museum* 73:402–425.

Hubbard, M. 1974. *Propertius.* London.

Hunter, R., ed. 2005. *The Hesiodic Catalogue of Women: Constructions and Reconstructions.* Cambridge.

Hurwit, J. 1999. *The Athenian Acropolis: History, Mythology, and Archaeology from the Neolithic Era to the Present.* Cambridge.

Hutchinson, G., ed. 2006. *Propertius: Elegies Book IV.* Cambridge.

Iakovidis, S. 1983. *Late Helladic Citadels on Mainland Greece.* Leiden.

Immerwahr, S. 1990. *Aegean Painting in the Bronze Age.* University Park.

Jamison, S. 1991. *The Ravenous Hyenas and the Wounded Sun: Myth and Ritual in Ancient India.* Ithaca, NY.

——. 1994. "Draupadî on the Walls of Troy: *Iliad* 3 from an Indic Perspective." *Classical Antiquity* 13:5–16.

——. 1996. *Sacrificed Wife/Sacrificer's Wife: Women, Ritual, and Hospitality in Ancient India.* New York.

——. 1999. "Penelope and the Pigs: Indic Perspectives on the *Odyssey*." *Classical Antiquity* 18:227–272.

——. 2001. "The Rigvedic Svayamvara? Formulaic Evidence." In Karttunen and Koskikallio 2001:303–315.

Janko, R. 1982. *Homer, Hesiod, and the Hymns: Diachronic Development in Epic Diction.* Cambridge.

——, ed. 1992. *The Iliad: A Commentary.* Vol. 4. Cambridge.

——. 1994. Review of van Thiel 1991. *Gnomon* 76:289–295.

——. 1998. "The Homeric Poems as Oral Dictated Texts." *Classical Quarterly* 48:1–13.

——. 2016. "Going Beyond Multitexts: The Archetype of the Orphic Gold Leaves." *Classical Quarterly* 66:100–127.

Jansen, L., ed. 2014. *The Roman Paratext: Frame, Texts, Readers.* Cambridge.

Jensen, M. 1980. *The Homeric Question and the Oral Formulaic-Theory.* Copenhagen.

——. 2011. *Writing Homer: A Study Based on Results from Modern Fieldwork.* Copenhagen.

Jockers, M. 2013. *Macroanalysis: Digital Methods and Literary History.* Champaign.

Karttunen, K., and P. Koskikallio, eds. 2001. *Vidyārṇavavandanam: Essays in honour of Asko Parpola.* Studia Orientalia 94. Helsinki.

Katz, J. 2005. "The Indo-European Context." In Foley 2005a:20–30.

——. 2010. "Inherited Poetics." In Bakker 2010:357–369.

Kirk, G. S. (vols. I–II), B. Hainsworth (vol. III), R. Janko (vol. IV), M. W. Edwards (vol. V), and N. Richardson (vol. VI), eds. 1985–1993. *The Iliad: A Commentary.* Cambridge.

Knox, P., ed. 2009. *A Companion to Ovid.* Malden.

Kopff, E. 1981. "Virgil and the Cyclic Epics." *Aufstieg und Niedergang der römischen Welt* II 31.2:919–947.

——. 1983. "The Structure of the *Amazonia* (*Aethiopis*)." In Häag 1983:57–62.

Kossatz-Deissmann, A. 1981. "Achilleus." *Lexicon Iconographicum Mythologiae Classicae* i.1.27–200.

Kuhn, T. 1962. *The Structure of Scientific Revolutions.* Chicago.

Kullmann, W. 1956. *Das Wirken der Götter in der Ilias: Untersuchungen zur Frage der Entstehung des homerischen "Götterapparats."* Berlin.

Kullmann, W., and M. Reichel, eds. 1990. *Der Übergang von der Mündlichkeit zur Literatur bei den Griechen.* Tübingen.

Labarbe, J. 1949. *L' Homère de Platon.* Liège.

Lamberton, R., and J. Keaney, eds. 1992. *Homer's Ancient Readers.* Princeton.

Lambrou, I. 2018. "Homer and Achilles' Ambush of Troilus: Confronting the Elephant in the Room." *Greece and Rome* 65:75–85.

Lang, M. 1969. *The Palace of Nestor at Pylos in Western Messenia,* vol. 2: *The Frescoes.* Princeton.

——. 1995. "War Story into Wrath Story." In Carter and Morris 1995:149–162.

Langdon, S., ed. 1997. *New Light on a Dark Age: Exploring the Culture of Geometric Greece.* Columbia.

Lange, D. 1979. "Cynthia and Cornelia: Two Voices from the Grave." *Studies in Latin Literature and History* I. *Collection Latomus* 164:335–342.

Latacz, J. 1968. "ἄπτερος μῦθος—ἄπτερος φάτις: Ungeflügetle Worte?" *Glotta* 46:27–47.

——. 2004. *Troy and Homer: Towards a Solution of an Old Mystery.* Trans. K. Windle and R. Ireland. Oxford.

Lattimore, R., trans. 1951. *The Iliad of Homer.* Chicago.

Leaf, W., ed. 1900–1902. *The Iliad* I–II. London.

——. 1912. *Troy: A Study in Homeric Geography.* London.

Lehrs, Karl. 1833. *De Aristarchi studiis Homericis.* Ph.D. diss., University of Göttingen.

Lentini, G. 2013. "The Pragmatics of Verbal Abuse in Homer." *Classics@* 11: https://chs.harvard.edu/CHS/article/display/5137.

Lessing, G. 1962 [1766]. *Laocoön: An Essay on the Limits of Painting and Poetry.* trans. E. McCormick. Baltimore.

Létoublon, F. 1999. "*Epea Pteroenta* ('Winged Words')." *Oral Tradition* 14:321–335.

Leumann, M. 1950. *Homerische Wörter.* Basel.

Levaniouk, O. Forthcoming (a). "Homer and Indo-European Myth." In Pache (forthcoming).

——. Forthcoming (b). "Did Sappho and Homer Ever Meet?" In Ready and Tsagalis (forthcoming).

Lombardo, S., trans. 1997. *Iliad.* Indianapolis.

Lonsdale, S. 1995. "A Dancing Floor for Ariadne (*Iliad* 18.590–592): Aspects of Ritual Movement in Homer and Minoan Religion." In Carter and Morris 1995:273–284.

Lord, A. B. 1936. "Homer and Huso I: The Singer's Rests in Greek and South Slavic Heroic Song." *Transactions of the American Philological Association* 67:106–113.

——. 1938. "Homer and Huso II: Narrative Inconsistencies in Homer and Oral Poetry." *Transactions of the American Philological Association* 69:439–445.

——. 1948a. "Homer and Huso III: Enjambement in Greek and South Slavic Heroic Song." *Transactions of the American Philological Association* 79:113–124.

——. 1948b. "Homer, Parry, and Huso." *American Journal of Archaeology* 52:34–44.

——. 1953. "Homer's Originality: Oral Dictated Texts." *Transactions of the American Philological Association* 94:124–34.

——. 1960/2000. *The Singer of Tales.* Cambridge, MA. [2nd ed, 2000, ed. S. Mitchell and G. Nagy. Cambridge, MA.]

——. 1970. "Tradition and the Oral Poet: Homer, Huso, and Avdo Medjedovic." In Cerulli 1970:13–28.

——. 1991. *Epic Singers and Oral Tradition.* Ithaca.

——. 1995. *The Singer Resumes the Tale.* Ithaca.

Lowenstam, S. 1981. *The Death of Patroklos: A Study in Typology.* Königstein.

——. 2008. *As Witnessed by Images: The Trojan War Tradition in Greek and Etruscan Art.* Baltimore.

Ludwich, A. 1884–1885. *Aristarchs Homerische Textkritik nach den Fragmenten des Didymos.* Leipzig.

——. 1898. *Die Homervulgata als voralexandrinisch erwiesen.* Leipzig.

Mackie, C. 2013. "*Iliad* 24 and the Judgement of Paris." *Classical Quarterly* 63.1:1–16.

Mackie, H. 1996. *Talking Trojan: Speech and Community in the Iliad.* Lanham, MD.

Macleod, C., ed. 1982. *Iliad Book XXIV*. Cambridge.

Magnani, M. 2018. "The Other Side of the River: Digital Editions of Ancient Greek Texts Involving Papyrus Witnesses." In N. Reggiani, ed., *Digital Papyrology II: Case Studies on the Digital Edition of Ancient Greek Papyri* (Berlin 2018) 87–102.

Manning, S., C. Ramsey, W. Kutschera, T. Higham, B. Kromer, P. Steier, P, and E. Wild. 2006. "Chronology for the Aegean Late Bronze Age, 1700–1400 BC." *Science* (American Association for the Advancement of Science) 312 (5773): 565–569.

Marks, J. Forthcoming. "Epic Traditions." In Pache (forthcoming).

Martin, R. 1989. *The Language of Heroes: Speech and Performance in the Iliad*. Ithaca.

———. 1993. "Telemachus and the Last Hero Song." *Colby Quarterly* 29:222–240.

———. 2000. "Wrapping Homer Up: Cohesion, Discourse, and Deviation in the *Iliad*." In Sharrock and Morales 2000:43–65.

———. 2005. "Pulp Epic: The *Catalogue* and the *Shield*." In Hunter 2005:153–175.

———. Forthcoming. "Homer in a World of Song." In Pache (forthcoming).

Matthaios et al., eds. 2011. *Ancient Scholarship and Grammar: Archetypes, Concepts, and Contexts*. Berlin: De Gruyter.

Matthews, M. 1976. *The Expression ΥΠΕΡ MOIPAN in Homer*. Ph.D. dissertation, Harvard University.

Mayor, A. 2014. *The Amazons: Lives and Legends of Warrior Women across the Ancient World*. Princeton.

McLane, M., and L. Slatkin. 2011. "British Romantic Homer: Oral Tradition, 'Primitive Poetry,' and the Emergence of Comparative Poetics in Britain, 1760–1830." *ELH* 78:687–714.

McNamee, K. 1981. "Aristarchus and 'Everyman's' Homer." *Greek, Roman, and Byzantine Studies* 22:247–255.

———. 1992. *Sigla and Select Marginalia in Greek Literary Papyri*. Brussels.

———. 1995. "Missing Links in the Development of Scholia." *Greek, Roman, and Byzantine Studies* 36:399–414.

———. 2007. *Annotations in Greek and Latin Texts from Egypt. American Studies in Papyrology* 45. New Haven.

Meillet, A. 1923. *Origines indo-européennes des mètres grecs*. Paris.

Mellink, M., ed. 1986. *Troy and the Trojan War*. Bryn Mawr, PA.

Miller, J. 1993. "Ovidian Allusion and the Vocabulary of Memory." *Materiali e discussioni per l'analisi dei testi classici* 30:153–164.

Monsacré, H. 1984. *Les larmes d'Achille: le héros, la femme et la souffrance dans la poésie d'Homère*. Paris.

Montanari, F. 1998. "Zenodotus, Aristarchus and, the *Ekdosis* of Homer." In Most 1998:1–21.

———. 2002. "Alexandrian Homeric Philology: The Form of the *Ekdosis* and the *Variae Lectiones*." In Reichel and Rengakos 2002:119–140.

———. 2011. "Correcting a Copy Editing a Text Alexandrian Ekdosis and Papyri." In Montanari and Pagani 2011:1–15.

Montanari, F., and P. Ascheri, eds. 2002. *Omero tremila anni dopo*. Rome.

Montanari, F., S. Matthaios, and A. Rengakos, eds. 2015. *Brill's Companion to Ancient Greek Scholarship*. Leiden.

Montanari, F., and L. Pagani, eds. 2011. *From Scholars to Scholia: Chapters in the History of Ancient Greek Scholarship*. Trends in Classics 9. Berlin.

Montanari, F., A. Rengakos, and C. Tsagalis, eds. 2012. *Homeric Contexts: Neoanalysis and the Interpretation of Oral Poetry*. Trends in Classics 12. Berlin.

Moon, W., ed. 1983. *Ancient Greek Art and Iconography*. Madison.

Morgan, K. 1977. *Ovid's Art of Imitation: Propertius in the Amores*. Mnemosyne Suppl. 47. Leiden.

Morgan, L. 1988. *The Miniature Wall Paintings of Thera: A Study in Aegean Culture and Iconography*. Cambridge.

Morris, I. 1997. "Homer and the Iron Age." In Morris and Powell 1997:535–59.

Morris, I., and B. Powell, eds. 1997. *A New Companion to Homer*. Leiden.

Morris, S. 1989. "A Tale of Two Cities: The Miniature Frescoes from Thera and the Origins of Greek Poetry." *American Journal of Archaeology* 93:511–535.

———. 2000. "From Thera to Scheria: Aegean Art and Narrative." In Sherratt 2000:317–333.

Most, G.W., ed. 1998. *Editing Texts/Texte edieren*. Göttingen.

Muellner, L. 1976. *The Meaning of Homeric εὔχομαι Through Its Formulas*. Innsbruck.

———. 1996. *The Anger of Achilles: Mênis in Greek Epic*. Ithaca, NY.

———. 2006. "Discovery Procedures and Principles for Homeric Research." *Classics@* 3: https://chs.harvard.edu/CHS/article/display/1321.

———. 2012. "Grieving Achilles." In F. Montanari, A. Rengakos, and C. Tsagalis, eds., *Homeric Contexts: Neoanalysis and the Interpretation of Oral Poetry* (Berlin, 2012): 197–220.

———. Forthcoming. "Homeric Poetics." In Pache (forthcoming).

Nagler, M. 1974. *Spontaneity and Tradition: A Study in the Oral Art of Homer*. Berkeley.

Nagy, G. 1974. *Comparative Studies in Greek and Indic Meter*. Cambridge, MA.

———. 1976. "The Name of Achilles: Etymology and Epic." In Davies and Meid 1976:227–30.

———. 1979. *The Best of the Achaeans: Concepts of the Hero in Archaic Greek Poetry*. Baltimore. Rev. ed. with new introduction 1999.

———. 1990a. *Pindar's Homer: The Lyric Possession of an Epic Past*. Baltimore.

———. 1990b. *Greek Mythology and Poetics*. Ithaca, NY. Revised paperback edition 1992.

Nagy, G. 1996a. *Poetry as Performance*. Cambridge.

——. 1996b. *Homeric Questions*. Austin.

——. 1997a. "The Shield of Achilles: Ends of the *Iliad* and Beginnings of the Polis." In Langdon 1997:194–207.

——. 1997b. "Response: Nagy on Powell on Nagy: An inventory of debatable assumptions about a Homeric question." *Bryn Mawr Classical Review* 97.4.18: http://bmcr.brynmawr.edu/1997/97.04.18.html.

——. 2001. "Homeric Poetry and Problems of Multiformity: The 'Panathenaic Bottleneck.'" *Classical Philology* 96:109–119.

——. 2002. *Plato's Rhapsody and Homer's Music: The Poetics of the Panathenaic Festival in Classical Athens*. Hellenic Studies 1. Washington, DC.

——. 2004. *Homer's Text and Language*. Urbana, IL.

——. 2008a. *Greek: An Updating of a Survey of Recent Work*. Center for Hellenic Studies: https://chs.harvard.edu/CHS/article/display/5586.

——. 2008b. "Review of M. L. West, *Indo-European Poetry and Myth* (Oxford 2007)." *Indo-European Studies Bulletin* 13:60–65.

——. 2009. *Homer the Classic*. Hellenic Studies 36. Washington, DC.

——. 2010a. "Language and Meter." In Bakker 2010:370–387.

——. 2010b. "The Origins of Greek Poetic Language: Review of M. L. West, *Indo-European Poetry and Myth* (Oxford 2007)." *Classical Review* 60:333–338. A revised and expanded edition of this review is published by the Center for Hellenic Studies: http://chs.harvard.edu/CHS/article/display/4255.

——. 2013. *The Ancient Greek Hero in 24 Hours*. Cambridge, MA.

——. 2015a. "Looking through Rose-Colored Glasses while Sailing on a Sacred Journey." *Classical Inquiries* (9/3/2015): http://classical-inquiries.chs.harvard.edu/looking-through-rose-colored-glasses-while-sailing-on-a-sacred-journey-2/.

——. 2015b. "From Athens to Crete and Back." *Classical Inquiries* (9/7/2015): https://classical-inquiries.chs.harvard.edu/from-athens-to-crete-and-back/.

——. 2015c. "A Cretan Odyssey, Part 1." *Classical Inquiries* (9/17/2015): http://classical-inquiries.chs.harvard.edu/a-cretan-odyssey-part-1/.

——. 2015d. *Masterpieces of Metonymy: From Ancient Greek Times to Now*. Hellenic Studies 72. Washington, DC.

——. Forthcoming. "From Song to Text." In Pache (forthcoming).

Neumann, R. 1919. *Qua Ratione Ovidius in Amoribus Scribendis Properti Elegiis Usus Sit*. Göttingen.

Nünlist, René. 2009. *The Ancient Critic at Work: Terms and Concepts of Literary Criticism in Greek Scholia*. Cambridge.

O'Rourke, D. 2012. "Intertextuality in Roman Elegy." In Gold 2012:390–409.

—. 2014. "Paratext and Intertext in the Propertian Poetry-Book." In Jansen 2014:156–175.

Pache, C. 2014. "Theban Walls in Homeric Epic." *Trends in Classics* 6:278–296.

—, ed. Forthcoming. *Cambridge Homer Encyclopedia*. Cambridge.

Page, D. 1959. *History and the Homeric Iliad*. Berkeley.

Palmer, L. 1962. "The Language of Homer." In Wace and Stubbings 1962:75–178.

—. 1963. *The Interpretation of Mycenaean Greek Texts*. Oxford.

Papanghelis, T. 1987. *Propertius: A Hellenistic Poet on Love and Death*. Cambridge.

Parry, A., ed. 1971. *The Making of Homeric Verse: The Collected Papers of Milman Parry*. Oxford.

Parry, M. 1928. *L'épithète traditionelle dans Homère: essai sur un problème de style homérique*. Paris. [Trans. as "The Traditional Epithet in Homer" in A. Parry 1971:1–190.]

—. 1932. "Studies in the Epic Technique of Oral Versemaking. II. The Homeric Language as the Language of Oral Poetry." *Harvard Studies in Classical Philology* 43:1–50. [Repr. in A. Parry 1971:325–364.]

Parsons, P. 2012. "Homer: Papyri and Performance." In Bastianini and Casanova 2012:17–27.

Pasquali, G. 1952. *Storia della tradizione e critica del testo*. Florence.

Pelliccia, H. 1997. "As Many Homers as You Please." *New York Review*, vol. 44, no. 18, 44–48.

Perlman, S. 1964. "Quotations from Poetry in Attic Orators of the Fourth Century BCE." *American Journal of Philology* 85:155–172.

Pestalozzi, H. 1945. *Die Achilleis als Quelle der "Ilias."* Zurich.

Petegorsky, D. 1982. "Context and Evocation: Studies in Early Greek and Sanskrit Poetry." PhD diss., Berkeley.

Pfeiffer, R. 1968. *History of Classical Scholarship from the Beginnings to the End of the Hellenistic Age*. Oxford.

Porter, J. 2006. "Making and Unmaking: The Achaean Wall and the Limits of Fictionality in Homeric Criticism." *Classics@* 3: http://chs.harvard.edu/CHS/article/display/1307.

Powell, B. 1991. *Homer and the Origin of the Greek Alphabet*. Cambridge.

—. 1997a. "Homer and Writing." In Morris and Powell 1997:3–32.

—. 1997b. Review of Nagy 1996a. Bryn Mawr Classical Review 97.3.21: http://bmcr.brynmawr.edu/1997/97.03.21.html.

Pratt, L. 1993. *Lying and Poetry from Homer to Pindar: Falsehood and Deception in Archaic Greek Poetics*. Ann Arbor.

Price, K. 2008. "Electronic Scholarly Editions." In Schreibman and Siemens 2008:24.

Proctor, R. 1900. *The Printing of Greek in the Fifteenth Century*. Oxford.

Pucci, P. 1993. "Antiphonal Lament between Achilles and Briseis." *Colby Quarterly* 29:253–272. [Repr. in Pucci 1998:97–112.]

———. 1998. *The Song of the Sirens*. Lanham, MD.

Rabel, R. 1989. "The Shield of Achilles and the Death of Hector." *Eranos* 87:81–90.

———, ed. 2005. *Approaches to Homer: Ancient and Modern*. Swansea.

Rau, J. 2010. "Greek and Proto-Indo-European." In Bakker 2010:171–188.

Ready, J. 2015. "The Textualization of Homeric Epic by Means of Dictation." *Transactions of the American Philological Association* 145:1–75.

Ready, J., and C. Tsagalis, eds. Forthcoming. *Homer in Performance: Rhapsodes, Narrators, and Characters*. Austin.

Reichel, M., and A. Rengakos, eds. 2002. *EPEA PTEROENTA: Beiträge zur Homerforschung*. Stuttgart.

Rengakos, A. 1993. *Der Homertext und die hellenistischen Dichter*. *Hermes* Einzelschriften 64. Stuttgart.

Revermann, M. 1998. "The Text of *Iliad* 18.603–6 and the Presence of an *Aoidos* on the Shield of Achilles." *Classical Quarterly* 48:29–38.

Reynolds, L., and N. Wilson. 2014. *Scribes and Scholars: A Guide to the Transmission of Greek and Latin Literature*. 4th ed. Oxford.

Richardson, N., ed. 1993. *The Iliad: A Commentary*. Vol. 6. Cambridge.

Robbins, E. I. 1990. "Achilles to Thetis: *Iliad* 1.365–412." *Echos du Monde Classique* (= *Classical News and Views*) 9:1–15.

Robinson, P. 2009. "The Ends of Editing." *Digital Humanities Quarterly* 3.3: http://digitalhumanities.org/dhq/vol/3/3/000051/000051.html.

Roughan, C., C. Blackwell, and N. Smith. 2016. "Citation and Alignment: Scholarship Outside and Inside the Codex." *Manuscript Studies* 1:5–27.

Ruijgh, C. 1967. *Études sur la grammaire et le vocabulaire du grec mycénien*. Amsterdam.

Sammons, B. 2010. *The Art and Rhetoric of the Homeric Catalogue*. Oxford.

Sancisi-Weerdenburg, H., ed. 2000. *Peisistratos and the Tyranny: A Reappraisal of the Evidence*. Amsterdam.

Sandys, J. 1903–1908. *History of Classical Scholarship*. Cambridge, MA.

Schironi, F. 2018. *The Best of the Grammarians: Aristarchus on the Iliad*. Ann Arbor.

———. Forthcoming (a). "Early Editions." In Pache (forthcoming).

———. Forthcoming (b). "Homeric Scholia." In Pache (forthcoming).

Schmitt, R. 1967. *Dichtung und Dichtersprache in indogermanischer Zeit*. Wiesbaden.

———, ed. 1968. *Indogermanische Dichtersprache*. Darmstadt.

Schreibman, S., and R. Siemens, eds. 2008. *A Companion to Digital Literary Studies*. Oxford: http://www.digitalhumanities.org/companionDLS/.

Scodel, R. 1982. "The Achaean Wall and the Myth of Destruction." *Harvard Studies in Classical Philology* 86:33–50.

——. 2002. *Listening to Homer: Tradition, Narrative, and Audience.* Ann Arbor.

Seaford, R. 1994. *Reciprocity and Ritual: Homer and Tragedy in the Developing City-State.* Oxford.

Segal, Charles. 1992. "Bard and Audience in Homer." In Lamberton and Keaney 1992:3–29.

Shackleton Bailey, D. 1952. "Echoes of Propertius." *Mnemosyne* ser. 4, vol. 5:307–333.

Shapiro, H., M. Iozzo, and A. Lezzi-Hafter, eds. 2013. *The François Vase: New Perspectives.* Akanthus Proceedings 3. Kilchberg, Zurich.

Sharrock, A., and H. Morales, eds. 2000. *Intratextuality: Greek and Roman Textual Relations.* Oxford.

Shaw, M. 2000. "Sea Voyages: The Fleet Fresco from Thera, and the Punt Reliefs from Egypt." In Sherratt 2000:267–282.

Shear, I. 1998. "Bellerophon Tablets from the Mycenaean World? A Tale of Seven Bronze Hinges." *Journal of Hellenic Studies* 118:187–189.

Sherratt, E. 1990. "'Reading the Texts': Archaeology and the Homeric Question." *Antiquity* 64:807–824.

Sherratt, S., ed. 2000. *The Wall Paintings of Thera: Proceedings of the First International Symposium.* Athens.

Shewan, A. 1911. *The Lay of Dolon: Homer Iliad X.* London.

Shillingsburg, P. 1996. *Scholarly Editing in the Computer Age.* Ann Arbor.

Simonsuuri, K. 1979. *Homer's Original Genius: Eighteenth-Century Notions of the Early Greek Epic (1688-1798).* Cambridge.

Simpson, R. Hope, and J. Lazenby. 1970. *The Catalogue of the Ships in Homer's Iliad.* Oxford.

Sinos, D. 1980. *Achilles, Patroklos, and the Meaning of Philos.* Innsbruck.

Skomal, N., and E. Polomé, eds. 1987. *Proto-Indo-European: The Archeology of a Linguistic Problem. Studies in Honor of Marija Gimbutas.* Washington, DC.

Slatkin, L. 1991. *The Power of Thetis: Allusion and Interpretation in the Iliad.* Berkeley.

Slings, S. 2000. "Literature in Athens, 566–510 BC." In Sancisi-Weerdenburg 2000:57–77.

——, ed. 2003. *Platonis Rempublicam.* Oxford.

Snodgrass, A. 1998. *Homer and the Artists: Text and Picture in Early Greek Art.* Cambridge.

Stanley, K. 1993. *The Shield of Homer: Narrative Structure in the Iliad.* Princeton.

Stauber, J., ed. 1996. *Die Bucht von Adramytteion.* Vol. II. *Inschriften griechischer Städte aus Kleinasien* 51. Bonn.

Stewart, A. 1983. "Stesichoros and the François Vase." In Moon 1983:53–74.

Tanselle, G. 1995. "The Varieties of Scholarly Editing." In Greetham 1995:9–32.

Taplin, O. 1980. "The Shield of Achilles within the *Iliad.*" *Greece and Rome* 27:1–21.

Taplin, O. 1986. "Homer's Use of Achilles' Earlier Campaigns in the *Iliad*." In Boardman and Vaphopoulou-Richardson 1986:15–19.

Taylor, J. H. 1970. "*Amores* III.9: A Farewell to Elegy." *Latomus* 29:474–477.

Thiel, H. van, ed. 1991. *Homeri Odyssea*. Hildesheim.

——. 1992. "Zenodot, Aristarch und andere." *Zeitschrift für Papyrologie und Epigraphik* 90:1–32.

——. 1997. "Der Homertext in Alexandria." *Zeitschrift für Papyrologie und Epigraphik* 115:13–36.

——, ed. 2010. *Homer Ilias*. 2nd ed. Hildesheim.

——, ed. 2014a. *Scholia D in Iliadem. Proecdosis aucta et correctior 2014. Secundum codices manu scriptos.* Elektronische Schriftenreihe der Universitäts- und Stadtbibliothek Köln, 7. Universitäts- und Stadtbibliothek. Cologne.

——, ed. 2014b. *Aristarch, Aristophanes Byzantios, Demetrios Ixion, Zenodot. Fragmente zur Ilias gesammelt, neu herausgegeben und kommentiert.* Vols. I–IV. Berlin.

Thomas, C., and C. Conant. 2007. *The Trojan War*. Norman, OK.

Thomas, R. 1979. "On a Homeric Reference in Catullus." *American Journal of Philology* 100:475–476.

——. 1999. *Reading Virgil and His Texts: Studies in Intertextuality*. Ann Arbor.

Thornton, A. 1984. *Homer's Iliad: Its Composition and the Motif of Supplication.* Göttingen.

Tsagalis, C. 2004. *Epic Grief: Personal Laments in Homer's Iliad.* Berlin.

——, ed. 2010a. *Homeric Hypertextuality. Trends in Classics* 2.

——. 2010b. "The Dynamic Hypertext: Lists and Catalogues in the Homeric Epics." *Trends in Classics* 2:323–347.

Usher, M. 2000. "Variations: On the Text of Homer." In Watson 2000:81–107.

Van der Valk, M. 1963–1964. *Researches on the Text and Scholia of the Iliad.* Vols. 1–2. Leiden.

Venini, P. 1981. "Ditti Cretese e Omero." *Memorie dell'Istituto Lombardo* 37:161–198.

Vermeule, E. 1983. "The Hittites and the Aegean World. 3. Response to Hans Gütterbock." *American Journal of Archaeology* 87:141–143.

——. 1986. "'Priam's Castle Blazing': A Thousand Years of Trojan Memories." In Mellink 1986:77–92.

Visser, E. 1997. *Homers Katalog der Schiffe.* Stuttgart.

Volk, K. 2002. "*Kléos áphthiton* Revisited." *Classical Philology* 97:61–68.

Wace, A., and F. Stubbings, eds. 1962. *A Companion to Homer.* London.

Wackernagel, J. 1953. *Kleine Schriften.* I/II. Göttingen.

Wathelet, P. 1970. *Les traits éoliens dans la langue de l'épopée grecque.* Rome.

Watkins, C. 1987. "Linguistic and Archaeological Light on Some Homeric Formulas." In Skomal and Polomé 1987:286–298.

——. 1995. *How to Kill a Dragon: Aspects of Indo-European Poetics.* New York.

Watson, J., ed. 2000. *Speaking Volumes*. Leiden.

Wauke, M., C. Schufreider, and N. Smith. Forthcoming. "Recovering the History of Iliadic Scholia: Architecture and Initial Results from the Homer Multitext Project."

West, M. L. 1973a. "Greek Poetry, 2000–700 BC." *Classical Quarterly* 23:179–192.

——. 1973b. *Textual Criticism and Editorial Technique*. Stuttgart.

——. 1982. *Greek Metre*. Oxford.

——. 1988. "The Rise of the Greek Epic." *Journal of Hellenic Studies* 108:151–172.

——, ed. 1998–2000. *Homeri Ilias: Recensuit et Testimonia Congessit*. Stuttgart.

——. 1990. "Archaische Heldendichtung: Singen und Schreiben." In Kullmann and Reichel 1990: 33–50.

——. 1999. "The Invention of Homer." *Classical Quarterly* 49:364–382.

——. 2001. *Studies in the Text and Transmission of the Iliad*. Munich.

——, ed. and trans. 2003. *Greek Epic Fragments from the Seventh to the Fifth Centuries BC*. Cambridge, MA.

——. 2007. *Indo-European Poetry and Myth*. Oxford.

——. 2010a. "Rhapsodes at Festivals." *Zeitschrift für Papyrologie und Epigraphik* 173:1–13.

——. 2010b. "Rhapsodes at Festivals: Addenda." *Zeitschrift für Papyrologie und Epigraphik* 174:32.

——. 2011. *The Making of the Iliad: Disquisition and Analytical Commentary*. Oxford.

——. 2014. *The Making of the Odyssey*. Oxford.

——, ed. 2017. *Odyssea: Recensuit et Testimonia Congessit*. Stuttgart.

West, S. 1967. *The Ptolemaic Papyri of Homer*. Papyrologica Coloniensa 3. Köln.

Whitley, J. Forthcoming. "Homeric History: Placing the Epics in Time." In Pache (forthcoming).

Whitman, C. 1958. *Homer and the Heroic Tradition*. Cambridge, MA.

Wilson, D. 2005. "Demodokos' *Iliad* and Homer's." In Rabel 2005:1–20.

Wolf, F. 1795. *Prolegomena ad Homerum, sive De Operum Homericorum Prisca et Genuina Forma Variisque Mutationibus et Probabili Ratione Emendandi*. Halle.

——, ed. 1804–1807. Ὁμήρου ἔπη: *Homeri et Homeridarum Opera et Reliquiae*. 4 vols. Leipzig.

Wood, M. 1998. *In Search of the Trojan War*. 2nd ed. Berkeley.

Zarker, J. 1965–1966. "King Eëtion and Thebe as Symbols in the *Iliad*." *Classical Journal* 61:110–114.

Zetzel, J. 1978. "A Homeric Reminiscence in Catullus." *American Journal of Philology* 99:332–333.

Zingerle, A. 1869–1871/1967. *Ovidius und sein Verhältnis zu den Vorgängern und gleichzeitigen römischen Dichtern*. Innsbruck. Repr. Hildesheim.

Subject Index

Index Locorum

Homeric Passages

Other Ancient Texts

Aelian
  Varia Historia 13.14, 113
Aeschines
  Against Timarchus 132–136, 66n34;
    136, 66n34; 146, 66; 149, 66–78;
    151, 66n34
Aeschylus
  Phrygians fr. 267, 110n10
  Suppliants 800–801, 55–56
Anecdota Graeca 1.6, 44n50
Apollodorus
  Epitome 3.32, 145
Apollodorus 1.9.16, 121
Athenaeus
  Deipnosophistae 180d, 96; 181a–181b,
    96; 181b, 94; 181d, 97
  Epitome 1.12, 56

Carmina Epigraphica 132.1, 65n30;
    1190.3, 65n30; 2170, 65n30
Catullus 64.152–153, 56n3
Cicero
  De oratore 3.137, 44n50

Dares 27, 145n51
Dictys of Crete 2.17, 144; 3.2ff., 145n51
Dio Chrysostom 11.77–78, 143
Douris
  FGrHist 76 F 41, 27n17

Ephorus
  FGrHist 70 F 223, 27n17
Eratosthenes
  FGrHist 241 F 1d, 27n17
Euripides
  Orestes 1176, 17n1

Herodotus 2.118, 33n29; 2.145, 27n17;
    7.171, 27n17

Hesiod
  Shield of Herakles 207–215, 99–100
  Theogony 174, 132
Hipparchus 228–229, 44n49
Hyginus 110, 145n51

Ibycus
  PMG S151.47–48, 26

Juvenal 2.149, 65n30

Ovid
  Amores I 12.3, 65n29; III 1–2, 65; III
    9, 64; III 25–30, 65; III 31, 65
  Metamorphoses VI 542, 65n29

Philostratus
  Heroikos 51.1, 145n51
Pindar
  Isthmian 8, 15–16
Plato
  Apology 28c–d, 80n67
  Ion 535e, 21n8
  Republic 23.103, 81–82; 386 D, 62, 81
Plutarch
  Life of Lycurgus 4.4, 44n50
Propertius II 34.53, 65n29; III 24–25,
    66n31; IV 7, 60–66; IV 7.1, 60; IV
    7.3, 61; IV 7.7–8, 61; I; 7.1; 14, 61;
    IV 7.94, 61; IV 7.95–96, 61

Rig-Veda 1.9.7, 26; 1.40.4, 26; 8.103.5,
    26; 9.66.7, 26

Solon fr. 19, 37n33
Strabo 9.411, 126

Thucydides 1.8–11, 27n17; 1.11.1,
    33n29